✳

THE BAXTERS OF MAINE

Downeast Visionaries

THE BAXTERS

Tilbury House, Publishers   Gardiner, Mai

OF MAINE

Downeast
Visionaries

NEIL ROLDE

Tilbury House, Publishers
132 Water Street
Gardiner, ME 04345

First Edition: October, 1997

10 9 8 7 6 5 4 3 2 1

Cataloging-in-Publication Data
Rolde, Neil, 1931-
The Baxters of Maine : downeast visionaries / Neil Rolde.
    p. cm
    Includes bibliograpical references (p.) and index, ISBN 0-
    88448-190-5 (alk. paper), -- ISBN 0-88448-191-3 (pbk. :
    alk. paper)
    1. Baxter, James Phinney, 1831-1921. 2. Baxter, Percival
    Proctor, 1876-1969. 3. Politicians--Maine--Biography. 4.
    Maine--Politics and government--1865-1950. 5. Maine--
    Politics and government--1951-
    I. Title
    F25.B32R65 1997
    97444. 104'092'2--dc2
    [B]   97-29670
                                                           CIP

Design: Edith Allard, Crummett Mountain Design, Somerville,
    Maine
Jacket Photos: "Katahdin Reflected" by Scott Perry; Baxter photos
    courtesy of the Baxter Collection, Maine State Library
Editing and Production: Jennifer Elliott, Rebecca Schundler,
    Barbara Diamond
Layout: Nina Medina, Basil Hill Graphics, Somerville, Maine
Scans and Film: Integrated Composition Systems, Spokane,
    Washington
Jacket/Cover Printing: The John P. Pow Company, South Boston
Book Printing and Binding: Maple-Vail, Binghampton, New York

❋

Contents

To those Maine people *who, in the spirit of James Phinney Baxter and Percival Baxter, give of themselves and their resources to make our state, wonderful as it can be, even better.*

＊

Foreword

I first met the Governor Percival P. Baxter in the early spring of 1960, when I was a young ranger at Abol Campground. I was attending a three-day spring training session at the old Great Northern Paper hotel in Millinocket when Park Supervisor Helon Taylor informed us that Governor Baxter would be making his spring inspection trip to the park prior to Memorial Day weekend. When the governor arrived, I felt humbled by his presence but tried to be professional as I shook his hand and trembled in my boots. It was the first time I ever met a governor, and this was the most generous ever to Maine's people.

Governor Baxter was very gracious and spent considerable time with us on that warm and sunny day. It was the first time I heard him ask, "Are the people enjoying their Park?," a question he would ask each time he visited the park or when I visited him. From 1960 through 1967, when Governor Baxter visited his gift to the people of Maine—generally in the spring and fall—I had frequent opportunities to observe the pride he felt in the park and the staff that served it. In the winter of 1962, I made my first visit to his office in Portland, and he talked about his early trips to the park, his horseback rides to the Depot Camps at Basin Pond, and his visits to Russell Pond. By this time I was the seasonal ranger at Russell Pond, and I was extremely interested in every word this gentleman had to say, both about that particular area and the overall development of his "puzzle," as he frequently referred to building the park, one piece at a time.

Over thirty-two years, from 1931-1962, his persistence, negotiation skills, and longevity allowed him to bring his dream to reality. When I was first employed with the park, it was 193,254 acres in size. With Governor Baxter's last addition of more than 7,000 acres in 1962, I saw him complete his life's dream of bringing it to 201,018 acres.

In 1968, shortly after being appointed to my first supervisory position at the park, Governor Baxter wrote me on several occasions. All of his letters were supportive and put emphasis on the need to maintain the trust. Over the years these letters have continued to provide an inspiring message, and I frequently turn to them during difficult times.

When Governor Baxter was asked by a reporter why he had given so generously to Maine's people, he responded, "The people of Maine were gracious enough to allow me to serve as their legislator, senator, president of the senate, and ultimately chief executive. My gifts are merely a thank you to those of their generation and the generations to follow for allowing me that honor. I seek nothing in return except to do something lasting for the people of *Maine*."

Neil Rolde's *The Baxters of Maine* is an enduring story about a family committed to serving the people of its community, its state, its country, and its future generations. Neil's research, knowledge, and skills, combined with a keen sense of humor, make this a book that readers will thoroughly enjoy, from its first pages to its concluding remarks.

Although I have spent thirty-eight years learning as much about Governor Baxter and James Phinney Baxter as I could, I had not scratched the surface until I read the manuscript for this book. Its incredible detail gives the reader an increased appreciation for what the Baxter family did for its fellow citizens and fills those of us with associations to the Baxter legacies with a heartfelt pride.

—Irvin C. (Buzz) Caverly, Jr.
Director, Baxter State Park

✳

Introduction

IN A NINETEENTH-CENTURY OIL paint-
ing now a possession of the State of Maine, two well-dressed,
small children stare out from a dark forest clearing. Appropri-
ately entitled "Babes in the Woods," the work was a gift in
1996 of Maine philanthropist extraordinaire, the late Elizabeth Noyce, to the Maine State Museum. Had it not been for
the identity of the six-year-old boy pictured with his younger
sister, the portrait may well have been deemed unexceptional
because of its sentimentalized style and old-fashioned dramat-
ics, and this despite its place in Maine art history as the product of Lovell native Eastman Johnson, once known as the
"American Rembrandt" for his genre scenes and likenesses of
notable contemporaries.

The little boy in question was Percival Proctor Baxter,
quite possibly Maine's most memorable governor and certainly among the best loved of the state's citizens. To Maine
people, his name brings instant recognition of the fact that
with his own money he singlehandedly bought up more than
200,000 acres of Maine land, including its highest mountain,
Katahdin, and donated all of it as a magnificent park to the
state, to be kept forever wild and open to the public.

Percy Baxter was a complex and interesting man. He
lived into his nineties, never married, and came closest to having a family life when the little girl pictured with him, his sister Madeleine, widowed at a young age, came with her two
boys to keep house for him at the governor's mansion during
his two terms as chief executive, 1921-22; 1922-24. After his

stint in elective office ended, Percy lived the life of a tight-fisted Portland business executive, managing the properties he had inherited from his father, but at the same time being extraordinarily generous through his donations of money and property to the people of Maine.

He not only inherited the wealth of his father, James Phinney Baxter, who was mayor of Portland six times, but also his father's upright sense of public duty, philanthropic munificence, historic perspective, love of nature, and intellectual curiosity. When not at his office or home in downtown Portland, Percy was liable to be traveling anywhere in the world, particularly on the ocean cruises he loved to take. His twice-widowed father sometimes went with him in the early years of these trips, which often included assessing the political conditions in other countries.

The lives of the two Baxters cover a wide panorama of Maine history—from pre-Civil War into the upper third of the twentieth century. While the story of Percy and his unmatched gift of Baxter State Park may seem dominant, the father's and son's biographies are inextricably intertwined. These were public men who carefully guarded their private personas, and with their Yankee forebears' sparseness of emotion, left only tantalizing glimpses of their inner selves.

In 1882, when James Phinney Baxter took the two youngest of his eight children to Nantucket Island to have their portrait painted by Eastman Johnson, he was still more than a decade away from his entry into politics. He was a highly successful businessman, self-made, self-taught as a writer and amateur historian, and, no doubt, being a proper Victorian, somewhat embarrassed when his children began to misbehave during their first days at the studio.

That portrait represents the initial public view of a personage whose imprint on Maine is indelible. Betty Noyce said

THE "BABES IN THE WOODS" PORTRAIT, PAINTED BY
EASTMAN JOHNSON WHEN PERCIVAL BAXTER WAS SIX
AND HIS SISTER MADELEINE THREE.

of the picture that she imagined young Percy saying to
Madeleine as they stared out at the trees around them, "What
might you do with all these woods?"

Maine knows what he did. At a time when a public conservation ethic was still the mere spark lit by Theodore
Roosevelt, Percy Baxter was far ahead of his time in wanting

to save the most valued icon of Maine's natural beauty, Mount Katahdin and its surroundings. He did that and much, much more. And, as his story unfolds, it will be seen that he was no plaster saint but a person of incredible contradictions: tough, miserly, generous, compassionate, openly honest yet often secretive, anxious to please yet exasperating, charming, grumpy, brave, political, and more.

Percival Proctor Baxter inspires many adjectives. Unforgettable is probably the most apt.

—Neil Rolde
York, Maine

Acknowledgments

MANY PEOPLE HAVE HELPED ME in the preparation of this book. I owe special thanks to Dr. Houghton White and his wife Mary of Brunswick for the pictures and letters they let me use. "Hodie" White is the grandson of Rupert Baxter and great-grandson of James Phinney Baxter. Other members of the Baxter family—Rupert White, David Holmes, and John Baxter—have generously contributed material. Ben Keating of the Maine State Library has also been of special help in arranging for the use of photographs from the Baxter Collection. My thanks, also, to Gary Nichols, Maine State Librarian; Earle Shettleworth, director of the Maine Historic Preservation Commission; Buzz Caverly, Baxter Park Director, who not only wrote the foreword to this book but took time to give me a tour of the park; Tom Gaffney and the other librarians at the Portland Library; the many helpful librarians at the Baxter Memorial Library in Gorham; Dennis Thoet, director of the Friends of the Maine State Museum; and James McLoughlin of Harpswell.

✳

The Baxters of Maine

Downeast Visionaries

1

Legacies

POLITICIANS NOT ONLY DIE, most of them also fade away. The Baxters of Maine, James Phinney and Percival, father and son, are among the notable exceptions to the latter part of this rule. Decades after their deaths, they keep cropping up in headlines and public discourse like haunting, even pesky, ghosts on the stage of current events.

Consider a news story in the *Portland Press-Herald* on January 16, 1992, more than seventy years after the will of James Phinney Baxter was probated. In what could be considered the opening shot in a protracted legal battle between two New England cities, the article was titled in bold print: "PORTLAND WANTS BOSTON TO FORFEIT $1 MILLION." The subhead further spelled out the bone of contention: "City Says It Should Get Unused Money Bequeathed By The Baxters To Build A 'Pantheon' To Settlers." And the lead paragraph added the over-dramatic hyperbole editors so love: "Portland and Boston are on the brink of war."

When James Phinney Baxter died in 1921, among his other bequests he left $50,000 in a special trust to the city of Boston. Of that, there can be no dispute, nor of its purpose: the Massachusetts capital was to use this money and the interest derived from it to build a "pantheon," a temple on the order of England's Westminister Abbey, to honor the early Yankee pioneers, i.e., the Pilgrims and Puritans, who had established New England. Baxter's ancestors were among these seventeenth-century immigrants whom he wished to commemorate.

Before the money was handed over to Boston's Irish Catholic Mayor James Michael Curley, however, a few sharp Yankee stipulations were added. If, after the fund reached $1 million, Boston failed to erect this memorial building, the entire unspent grant would revert to Portland. There, it would be used for the establishment or maintenance of "public, humane, charitable, educational, or benevolent institutions or parks within the City of Portland." A number of such potential beneficiaries had already been created by James Phinney Baxter when he was mayor, such as the Portland Public Library and the greenbelt-surrounded thoroughfare around Back Cove that the city eventually named Baxter Boulevard.

When Percival Proctor Baxter died in 1969, his will left the "pantheon" another $200,000.

In 1985, as the combined funding was closing in on $1 million, Mayor Raymond Flynn of Boston put on a stalling act. He declared that the two funds were separate and he would take no action until James Phinney Baxter's original $50,000 had reached the agreed amount. But even under those terms, the elder Baxter's legacy easily topped $1 million by 1992.

So the long reach of history then created a public policy dispute worthy of contemporary press coverage, requiring attention and action by officials in two states, set to go to court. Both James Phinney Baxter and Percival Baxter, always embattled during their careers, would have found this blowup totally natural. Baxter family members joined the fray, as well. They backed Boston's claim on the grounds that James Phinney and Percival both wanted the "pantheon" built in the Massachusetts city.

On August 8, 1996, Maine Superior Court Justice Leigh I. Saufley rendered her opinion that the $2.2 million accumulated in the fund should stay with Boston. If Boston failed to use the money within five years, the sum could still revert to Portland.

Close to a year later, in May 1997, negotiations between the two cities seemed to be nearing final settlement. The preliminary agreement was that Portland would receive a lump sum payment of $400,000 and give up its claims, while Boston could use the remainder of the funds not to build a "pantheon" (clearly impossible at today's prices) but "for unspecified public projects and programs to promote understanding of immigrants who settled in New England." Boston also agreed to pay $125,000 of the $165,000 in legal fees this suit had cost.

Portland's share was to be used for improvements to the park around the Back Cove section of the city bordering Baxter Boulevard, which James Phinney literally created. One of the Portland councilors, speaking of the proposed out-of-court settlement, said, "If he were alive today, he would say this is where the money should go."

Creating the memorial desired by the Baxters would have been difficult if not impossible politically as well as finan-

4

cially. In an age of "political correctness," over-hallowing the WASP Yankee settlers of New England creates some resistance and calls for the sort of sensitivity the "Plimouth Plantation" museum has had to show in its treatment of Native Americans vis-à-vis the Pilgrims. *The Boston Globe*, indeed, came forth with a tongue-in-cheek presentation of what a $2 million plus "pantheon" might look like: a 100-foot-tall ice sculpture of the famous but intolerant clergyman of Salem Witchcraft Trial fame, Cotton Mather, mounted on Dorchester Heights, demanding that everyone go away; or a pantheon of everything banned in Boston or a "sonic *Mayflower*" at City Hall Plaza with sails made out of sports banners and voices of noteworthy citizens from the near and distant past.

Commenting on its own silliness, the Boston newspaper said: "It would appear that romancing the settlin' days of yesteryear just isn't what it used to be in the day of James Phinney."

That the controversy continues is typical of the grip from the past that the Baxters still manage to clamp on the future.

Another example. One would not think that a bronze statue occupying a place of honor in the Maine State Capitol could cause controversy, but with Percival Baxter, one never knows.

On March 31, 1991, the readers of the *Maine Sunday Telegram* awoke to a startling headline:

"BAXTER BACKERS FIGHT DECISION TO REMOVE BUST."

At issue was a bust of Percy that had been commissioned by order of the legislature in 1958 as a tribute to his magnanimous gift of Baxter State Park.

But suddenly the then-president of the state senate, Charles Pray of Millinocket, wanted it removed from the Hall of Flags, the rotunda-like space on the second floor of the statehouse where portraits of Maine's most distinguished public servants hang and battle flags dating back to the Civil War are displayed in tall glass cases.

Charles Pray, an Air Force veteran, tried to justify his unexpected demand by saying that he didn't think the bust belonged in the Hall of Flags, which, he insisted, should be set aside solely to honor the state's veterans and military groups. The senate president never did mention what he wanted to do with the existing portraits there of *civilian* giants of Maine history, including Governor William King, the state's first chief executive, Congressman Thomas Brackett Reed, probably the most powerful-ever speaker of the U.S. House, U.S. Senator James G. Blaine, U.S. Senator Edmund S. Muskie, and U.S. Senator Margaret Chase Smith.

It might have been thought that Pray was being partisan; a fiercely combative Democrat, he could have had it in for Republican Baxter. Yet a Democratic governor, Edmund S. Muskie, had been in office when the bust was put in place. Muskie called that event "one of the high points of my experience as governor."

The arguments of Baxter's defenders were summed up succinctly by one of its leaders. "He gave Maine Mount Katahdin. He's earned two square feet in the Hall of Flags."[1]

But it was precisely Baxter's great gift that lay behind Senate President Pray's explosion of ire, which he was venting on an inanimate sculpture.

Charles Pray's senate district included Baxter State Park. Early in 1991, some of his constituents were incensed by a vote of the Baxter Park Authority, the park's governing body, to close the West Gate, a new egress opened several years previously. The Authority argued that since only 5 percent of the park's visitors used this access to the road system, it was hard

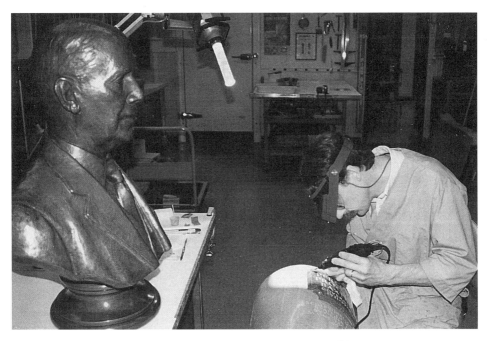

REPAIRS BEING MADE AT THE MAINE STATE MUSEUM ON
THE BUST OF PERCIVAL BAXTER, INEXPLICABLY VANDALIZED
IN 1996, BUT ALSO A SUBJECT OF POLITICAL TAMPERING.

to police against prohibited oversized vehicles and motorcycles, and it cost the Authority thousands of dollars to keep the gate open. The locals liked the West Gate because it was a shortcut for them and also a route for drivers wanting to avoid road fees charged by the Georgia-Pacific Paper Company, the largest landowner in the region.

The Millinocket-based Fin and Feather Club, a sportsmen's group long-involved in controversies arising out of the existence of Baxter Park, was in the forefront of the debate. They claimed the closing of the West Gate violated the terms of Governor Baxter's trust establishing the park and warned that the members would provoke arrest by dismantling barricades the park authorities had erected. But Park Director Irvin "Buzz" Caverly and his superiors did not yield to their pressures. A six-foot-high earthen wall was constructed and the decision made final: the West Gate would stay closed.

Senate President Pray then chose a more draconian action than simple retaliation against Governor Baxter's bronze and stone presence in the Hall of Flags. During the legislative session, he sought to eliminate the $60,000 road maintenance fund the park received from the state but had to settle for a $20,000 reduction. Pray, himself, faced criticism that he wanted the West Gate open to benefit his business—he runs sporting camps in the area—but denied the charge, pointing to the solid support he had for his actions from twenty-two representatives and three senators out of nearby Penobscot and Piscataquis counties.

Stymied by the opposition, Pray was not only unsuccessful in his vendetta against Baxter's bust but also failed to get himself re-elected the following year. Baxter's defenders, convinced the old governor would continue to stare out serenely at the world in the Hall of Flags, relaxed.

They weren't taking into account a thirty-nine-year-old man from the nearby town of Sydney named Timothy Fairfield. On February 20, 1996, in an inexplicable act of vandalism, Fairfield suddenly vaulted the brass railing surrounding the sculpture and kicked over the pedestal and its bronze bust. It was 7:20 A.M. and no one was around except a custodian, who witnessed the senseless act.

The slightly nicked bust and the broken marble pedestal were remanded to the Maine State Museum for repairs, and Fairfield was arrested for an act of criminal mischief. Even here, the past reached out. In Percy Baxter's day and even earlier, it was a Maine tradition that humorously signed pieces of doggerel poetry would comment on current political events. Some time after this incident, a plastic-enclosed missive was hung on the railing around the empty space. It contained a poem entitled: "On Former Gov. Baxter's Busted Bust."

Upon this spot for many years
a pillar of granite stood;
a noble perch for the brazen bust
of Percival B. the Good

But a vandal crude one early morn
for motives still unclear
with a mighty shove sent the former Guv.
crashing on his ear.

Now the perp's in jail (or so we hope)
while Percy's being mended.
so now you know what happened here
and our little verse is ended.

The work, true to the style of its antecedents, was signed: "Anon E. Moose."

Yet issues arising from the Baxter past can be highly substantive, too. Certainly the most momentous led to a law case—and a judgment amounting to hundreds of thousands of dollars for Maine government—that reached all the way to the Maine Supreme Court, almost a quarter of a century after Percy's death.

It was a bit of unfinished business from his years as governor, the aftermath of the most bitter political fight of his administration—the epic waterpower battle of 1923.

This contretemps erupted in full force during Percy's second term (terms were then two years long). In 1921, Percy became governor when the man elected to the job, Frederick

Parkhurst, died suddenly after less than a month in office. Under Maine's constitution, the senate president (the post Baxter held at the time) is the automatic successor. Thus Percy was suddenly in a position to apply his own philosophy toward the leading issue of the day—the disposition of the extensive waterpower resources of the state, especially for generating electricity. Briefly, he believed that the people of Maine, not just power companies and industry, should receive some of the financial benefits from the abundant flow of "white gold." But in 1923, when he demanded that the Central Maine Power Company pay for state land on which it proposed to build a dam to regulate the upper Kennebec River, he was attacked as a socialist, even a communist.

These were the conservative 1920s, the era of Harding and Coolidge. The legislature was overwhelmingly Republican (there wasn't a single Democrat in the state senate) and Baxter, himself, was a long-time loyal member of the G.O.P. Yet once he vetoed a bill pushed through by CMP to deed them the state land in perpetuity at no cost, his fellow party members easily overrode him. A contemporary account details the hard feelings on both sides:

> He (Baxter) did not stop with his disapproval of the bill, but delivered a long harangue on interests which were attempting 'to *steal* the people's heritage.... The Governor paid his respects to the shrewd lawyers retained by the power interests, classifying all of them as "sinister lobbyists" openly declaring that they had used rum to befuddle the minds of the legislators and intimating that something more useful as legal tender had been distributed.

10

Those hit by these accusations came right back calling the Governor a lot of names, of which "hypocrite," "double-crosser," and "trimmer" were mild examples. In the midst of it all, the Legislature passed a resolution censuring the Governor. Altogether, it was a heated session.[2]

That the Kennebec Reservoir Bill never became law was due to a 1909 Initiative and Referendum amendment to the Maine Constitution. It had been implemented to allow citizens, via petition, to introduce bills the legislature refused to enact or to block bills already passed. Ironically, as a freshman legislator, Baxter had voted against this grassroots measure but now he took full advantage of it, publicly calling on the general electorate to stop the Kennebec Reservoir Bill. Signed petitions flooded into his office. An alarmed Central Maine Power Company finally agreed to compromise. Baxter's opening demand for a lease payment of $40,000 a year was rejected with scorn, yet CMP eventually settled for an annual payment of $25,000.

This was an age in which lobbyists were bold enough to sit in legislators' seats and actually vote in their place. Walter S. Wyman, the canny founder of CMP, arrogantly submitted the compromise bill in his own name, although he wasn't a legislator, so sure was he of being able to control the lawmakers he thought he had under his thumb. Yet many of these legislators were outraged. Having defended the company's position, they felt they had been double-crossed. This was one reason offered for the fact that Wyman eventually withdrew the compromise bill. Another, perhaps more cogent, was that the Chicago-based giant Insull holding company, the real owners of CMP, torpedoed the idea.

After Baxter left the governor's chair, a deal was consummated in 1927 with his successor, Ralph Owen Brewster. CMP agreed on a fifty-year lease at $25,000 a year.

Echoes of this long-ago political squabble are to be found in the Maine attorney-general's 1992 brief, addressed to the supreme court:

> By Motion dated July 15, 1992, CMP seeks to have this Court issue an Order that effectively sets rental on only the timber value of the dam site and flowed land, or, in the alternative, that allows CMP to ignore this proceeding and unilaterally set the rental at the 1923 level. These efforts conflict with Maine law, the plain meaning of the statute, and the intent and clear statement of CMP, the Legislature, and Governor Percival Baxter. The Court should deny the Motion and, instead, should order that CMP is leasing the site and appurtenant power rights, and that CMP should pay an "equitable and just" rental to the State based upon the site's value with respect to the additional electricity produced as a result of the supplemental flow from the use of the site.[3]

Assistant Attorney-General Paul Stern, in charge of the case, then asserted:

> The enactment of P. & S.L. 1927, c.113, represents an important and fascinating chapter in the history of the State of Maine. CMP has conspicuously failed to bring any of this history or its role in it to the Court's attention because quite simply, this information, which includes contemporaneous admissions by CMP, establishes how specious CMP's motion really is.[4]

Stern's arguments were persuasive. On May 28, 1993, the *Portland Press Herald* reported: "After paying $25,000 annually for half a century, Central Maine Power Company will be charged nearly $600,000 a year for the use of state land along the Dead River in Stratton."[5]

An associate justice of the Maine State Supreme Court, Samuel Collins, Jr., himself a former Republican state senator, had ordered the new fee set at $597,423, made retroactive to December 14, 1990.

In commenting on the decision, Attorney-General Michael E. Carpenter stressed that Collins's decision "fulfills Governor Baxter's intent that the people of the State of Maine receive a just and equitable rental for this valuable and unique public property at Long Falls."[6]

This political battle royal had lasted seven decades. Its happy ending (for the Maine taxpayers) is simply one example of the extraordinary energy and foresight of the Baxters. They seldom appear to be far from the surface of events in Maine.

---

[1] Representative Herbert Adams, quoted in the *Maine Sunday Telegram*, March 31, 1991; page 14B.

[2] *The Boston Herald*, October 30, 1923: "The Water Power Muddle" by Thomas Carens.

[3] State of Maine Memorandum of Law In Opposition To CMP's Motion For Partial Summary Judgment. Maine Supreme Court. Docket No. KEN -92-11.

[4] Ibid.

[5] *Portland Press-Herald*, May 28, 1993; page 4B.

[6] Press release from Attorney-General Michael E. Carpenter, May 27, 1993.

CHAPTER ✳ *2*

Family History

IN THE 1996 NEWSPAPER ACCOUNTS of the brouhaha over James Phinney Baxter's bequest for a New England "pantheon," modern-day journalistic negativism could not resist a few slams at the donor, himself. *Portland Press Herald* staff writer Jason Wolfe stated that "in his writings, Baxter, a Mayflower descendant, expressed little tolerance for immigrants, other than his blue-blooded descendants."[1]

The reporter based his comments on a 1917 monograph written by James Phinney Baxter that allegedly said his dream of a New England Westminister Abbey (or the town hall, Rathaus, in Hamburg, Germany, another of his models), was "to teach 'diseased and feeble' immigrants an appreciation of American history." [2]

A closer reading of the original document, which was appended to James Phinney Baxter's will, is in order so as to better judge the man. Baxter may well have expressed the WASP chauvinism of his position in the middle to late nine-

LEFT: DR. ELIHU BAXTER: HIS YOUNGEST CHILD, JAMES
PHINNEY BAXTER, WAS BORN WHILE DR. ELIHU WAS
PRACTICING AS A COUNTRY DOCTOR IN GORHAM, MAINE.

RIGHT: SARAH CONE BAXTER: DR. ELIHU BAXTER'S
SECOND WIFE AND THE MOTHER OF THEIR SIX CHILDREN.
HE HAD NO CHILDREN WITH HIS FIRST WIFE, CLARISSA
SIMMS, WHO DROWNED WHILE CROSSING THE CONNECT-
ICUT RIVER IN WINTER ON HORSEBACK.

teenth-century Protestant ascendancy in this country, but his
target in the monograph is not non-Mayflower immigrants
per se. He indeed conceded that many foreign immigrants
made "valuable additions to our population." As a prosperous,
conservative businessman, he was, instead, aiming at radicals
among the newcomers, specifically naming the I.W.W. (International Workers of the World) and their allies. He saw

these often-violent precursors of the trade unions as destructive of the principles of the Constitution and feared they would "substitute in its place a thing of their own in which License would take the place of Liberty, Class Favoritism of Equality and the Nullification of Property Rights of Justice."[3] The reference to the "diseased and feeble" came when he predicted that the end of World War I would see foreign nations holding back their abler men and sending less desirables to the United States.

His remedy for thwarting the "dangerous advocates of false theories of government" was "to instruct the uninformed in the principles of those who created the early history of our country." This, the "pantheon" would do and, furthermore, it would be useful, he felt, in uniting "the people of New England blood who are scattered through every State of the Union" to assist in the undertaking.

Was James Phinney Baxter a WASP bigot? Certain actions of his, as well as circumstances he tolerated in his own family, seem to belie an outright ethnic "racism." For example, at their summer home the Baxters played host to "fresh air" children from the slums of New York City, particularly Jewish kids, one of whom, Abe Weinberg, became a lifelong friend of the family. James Phinney's beloved daughter Emily converted to Catholicism early in her life and, while living with her father, was an active member of the church. William Cardinal O'Connell of Boston, writing in later years to Percy, fondly recalled his visits to the Baxter home when he was a young priest in Portland. Percy, himself, epitomized public tolerance. He courageously fought the Ku Klux Klan when it briefly rode a wave of anti-Catholicism in Maine in the early 1920s, he appointed the first Jew to a public post in the state, and he was the only one of the nation's governors to say no to the governor of California who was seeking support for national legislation to exclude Chinese and Japanese immigrants.

Needless to say, the Baxters, like all Americans (including our Native Americans) came from somewhere else. But, the *Portland Press Herald* notwithstanding, they most emphatically did not arrive on the *Mayflower*.

The first of the line in the New World was apparently one Simon Baxter who emigrated to Connecticut from England at an unspecified seventeenth-century date and settled in a town called Hebron. His son Simon was born in Middletown in 1698 and, of the eight children born to him and Abigail Mann, the second oldest, William, born August 15, 1725, also at Middletown, achieved a distinction of sorts by having been captured as a colonial soldier in an abortive English raid on the Spanish stronghold of Havana in 1762. William's brothers Aaron and Nathan were Revolutionary War soldiers, as was his own son Hiram.

It was through William's first son, Elihu, born in Lebanon, New Hampshire, on December 18, 1749, that the line further descended. This Elihu was the father of fifteen children, and one of them was another Elihu, born at Norwich, Vermont, April 10, 1781. The second Elihu was the father of James Phinney Baxter.

Like many Connecticut Yankees, the family had drifted north where land was still plentiful and opportunities seemingly beckoned. These poor English immigrants led hardscrabble lives but undoubtedly more fruitful ones than if they had stayed in their caste-bound, hierarchically minded mother country. Almost imperceptibly they became Americans and shed an English mind-set that persisted only as dimly felt tradition. The Baxters had no trouble fighting their British cousins for their country's independence. One wonders if James Phinney Baxter ever ruminated on the fact that his own father was actually born before the United States officially became a nation.

Elihu Baxter, at age twenty-five, married "a young lady of high social standing" named Clarissa Simms. Two years later, before they had any children, she fell through thin ice and drowned while crossing the Connecticut River on horseback. Told of the accident on April 1, the young husband at first thought it was an April Fool's joke. The grieving widower, who had trained in Hanover, New Hampshire to be a doctor, soon left the New Hampshire-Vermont border area. A year later, he took Sarah Cone as his wife. Sarah's family was connected to many of the noted families of Connecticut, including that of a governor, Thomas Welles.

Elihu moved to Maine where he set up practice, first in the town of Wayne and then in 1812, in the town of Gorham. His choice of Gorham may have occurred because the existing local physician, Dr. Dudley Folsom, had left to become a military surgeon during the War of 1812. That Dr. Folsom returned to Gorham did not seem to bother Dr. Elihu, who, "with a large and lucrative practice," stayed in the Cumberland County community until 1832. James Phinney was born in Gorham on March 23, 1831.

He was named James for an uncle, James Baxter, of a branch that had gone to Canada. This gentleman, who had prospered in the town of Stanstead, Ontario, (he was a successful merchant and Member of Parliament) sent Dr. Elihu a $10 gold piece to be put out at interest and paid over to the boy when he became twenty-one. The name Phinney came from a closer distance, in honor of a neighbor and friend, the Deacon James Phinney, the nonagenarian son of the first resident of Gorham, Captain John Phinney. Relying on his parents' description, James Phinney later wrote of the elderly country preacher, "how with white hair falling over his shoulders and eyes sightless from old age, he took me in his trembling hands and with eyes turned heavenward blessed me after the manner of the patriarchs of old." [4]

The Baxters' house in Gorham had been built in 1797 by another early settler, Isaac Gilkey. The town, itself, settled in 1736, had originally been called Narragansett Number Seven, and it was one of seven townships granted by the Massachusetts General Court to veterans who had fought the Pequot Indians in King Phillip's War. Named for a Captain Shubael Gorham, this piece of Maine wilderness had been populated mostly by residents of Cape Cod seeking new land to farm. South Street, where the Baxters lived, was (and still is) one of the main thoroughfares of this rural community that today is an exurb of Portland.

After twenty years in one place, the restlessness of his forebears—who had moved from England to Connecticut to New Hampshire and to Vermont—once more sent Dr. Elihu packing. He transported his family, which included Hiram, Hartley, William, Elizabeth, and Sarah, in addition to baby James Phinney, north in Maine to the wilds of Stillwater, now Orono. He bought considerable land in this virgin area but lost money when he endorsed the speculations of his "scamp of a son-in-law," Henry Gooding, who had married daughter Elizabeth. Then, the family briefly settled in nearby Levant, where the father not only doctored but farmed. Two of James Phinney's older brothers stayed in the Penobscot County area, one as a doctor and one a businessman. His other brother Hartley went to sea, "much to my mother's grief," James Phinney wrote later in his journal. And, in fact, Hartley was to be lost at sea, swept overboard when hit by a swinging boom.

James Phinney also detailed childhood memories of his mother reading to him by candlelight from a New England primer and telling old-fashioned stories of her early life, showing him samplers, handbags, and purses she had made in her youth. At the time, the boy was the only one of the Baxter children at home. A particular memory, "which would make me weep," was of his mother's telling of the "sad death of her mother when she was a wee girl."

The sensitive child absorbed lessons from life, as well as from his mother's readings. An incident with a black bear that had frightened Mrs. Baxter in her yard led to the discovery by some local men of two bear cubs. They were brought to Bachelor's store to serve as amusing attractions for the local folks. But then Tim Bachelor hit one on the nose after it got into a barrel of sugar and the poor creature promptly died; the other soon sickened and also died. Little James Phinney was greatly disturbed, named his puppy Cub, and evolved into a lifelong, even fanatical, defender of animal rights.

A tragedy of more human dimensions also occurred while the boy was still impressionable. His Canadian Uncle James, for whom he'd been named, had been cheated by an agent he had sent to the U.S. to buy lands for him. So affected was this successful merchant and M.P. that he became demented. Picking up a razor, he told his wife he was going to shave and when she asked him not to, he turned toward her, cut his throat and fell dead.

Part of the worthless, swampy land he had been stuck with is now the business district of Milwaukee, Wisconsin.

James Phinney's own father speculated in land and ended up owning part of the township of Parkman. But ever restless, he soon moved his family again, transporting them to a farm on China Lake in 1837.

It was here that the future Maine historian became aware as an eight-year-old of the "Aroostook War" and the "hard cider" presidential campaign of William Henry Harrison. Maine militia regiments marched north through their village in 1839, en route to the state's disputed border with New Brunswick, and the local boys, including James Phinney, formed themselves into mimicking companies that drilled with sticks for a conflict that never took place. The "hard cider" songs of "Tippecanoe and Tyler, Too" were overheard as sung in the town taverns and imitated by the youngsters.

The following year, Dr. Elihu Baxter uprooted his family yet again and finally settled them in Portland where, at long last, the Baxters were to sink permanent roots.

By then, James Phinney was ten years old and, in his own words, "a timid, affectionate boy, not in very good health, the overprotected idol of my warm-hearted mother."

Sent to Master Jackson's school, the new kid on the block had to endure the taunts of local city kids who called him a "greenhorn" because he came from the country. Years later, James Phinney could remember with affection the names of two boys who had been kind to him—Bob Green and Albert Stephenson. Master Jackson, despite the fear he inspired in all of his pupils, treated him kindly. Two girls—Margaret Dockray and Susan Harding—likewise remained embedded in his memory from this period for, as he wrote, he fell in love with both of them.

Even within the relatively narrow confines of the "peninsula" that still forms the downtown heart of Portland, the peripatetic Baxter family did not stay put. Their first house was on the southerly side of Pleasant Street, five or six houses west of Maple Street, a house that then seemed immense to James Phinney and from whose upper windows the harbor could be glimpsed. By 1842 they had moved again twice and were living on Oxford Street. The next year they were a few blocks away at 1 Cotton Street. A more permanent relocation took place in 1849 once Dr. Elihu finally settled at 26 Brown Street, a short side street off busy Congress Street. It was here that the patriarch lived until his death; James Phinney lived with him and inherited the dwelling.

It was when the family was at Oxford Street that news of another family tragedy reached the Baxters: the death of Elizabeth in Greenville, Illinois, for which her abusive husband was blamed.

As a youngster, James Phinney was to experience more than simply the dislocation of moving from neighborhood to neighborhood. A change of schools made him very unhappy and a sojourn in Lynn, Massachusetts, with his sister Sarah and her husband Joseph Barry unhappier still. He hated "the petty tyranny of my egotistical brother-in-law" and pleaded with his parents by letter: "Send for me at once. I must come home."

When his plea was favorably answered and he joyously returned to Portland, his disgusted brother-in-law grumped that the boy was too tied to his mother's apron strings and would never "be a man." Joseph Barry, by the way, eventually died an alcoholic, which perhaps was a factor in James Phinney's lifelong dedication to the cause of Prohibition.

His formal education, completed at Portland Academy, a private school run by an ex-mayor of the city, was buttressed by his own intense reading, begun at the age of twelve with Addison's *Spectator* and some of Shakespeare's plays. One winter, at age thirteen, he devoured a hundred volumes. Sir Walter Scott, Hans Christian Anderson, James Fenimore Cooper, and even Vulpius, the Walter Scott of Germany, were among the authors.

His practically minded father did not think much of young James Phinney's literary bent. Such frivolous reading, said the doctor, was only for "cranks and good-for-naughts." Moreover, now that James Phinney was eighteen years old, he had to make his way in the world and to do so with the knowledge that he had a "deficient education." There was to be no

Harvard for him. The erudition that later earned him two honorary degrees from Bowdoin College was entirely self-gained, *in spite of*, not *because of*, the world of business and politics in which he spent most of his adult life.

His first venture was to try to become a lawyer. In those days, law schools were not the fashion; an apprenticeship with a practicing attorney was the route to the bar, and James Phinney attempted to start in Boston with one of the most prestigious barristers of the day, Rufus Choate. There are several versions of why he gave up after a short period of time. The meager salary of six dollars a month may have been a sore point. It has also been said that Choate sent him home, saying he was "not physically strong enough to take on the law."[5] But another account states pretty much the opposite, that the law was too dry and unexciting "for this young man from Maine, this robust down-Easter with the skeedaddling active mind."

His brother William had come to Portland and set up a hardware store on Middle Street, the city's main retail center. As a youngster, James Phinney had hung around the shop and done errands and, as a teenager, had worked there. After his failed experience with the law and his return to Portland, the young man, now in his twenties, tried to better his education by privately studying languages (Latin, French, German, and Spanish) and polishing his writing skills. But as for making a living, nothing concrete appeared on the horizon until his brother's former partner, Harry Bailey, offered him a place in a new firm if he could invest $3,000. On his own, James Phinney had saved $1,000. A wealthy uncle, Chester Baxter of Sharon, Vermont, lent him $1,500. And the final $500 came from his usually tight-fisted father, who decided to show his faith in his inexperienced son.

Over and above his obligation to his relatives, James Phinney had another vitally pressing motive to succeed. Liv-

JAMES PHINNEY BAXTER AT AGE TWENTY-ONE, TWO YEARS
BEFORE HE MARRIED SARAH KIMBALL LEWIS.

ing nearby was a widow and her two lovely daughters and on
a visit to them with his mother, young Sarah Kimball Lewis
had immediately attracted him, he admitted, because of her
"large eyes." Since Sarah attended Gorham Academy, James
Phinney soon found himself visiting his birthplace quite frequently. Yet until he had the wherewithal to support a wife,
marriage was still only a distant possibility.

SARAH KIMBALL LEWIS: THE YOUNG BEAUTY WHOSE "LARGE EYES" ATTRACTED JAMES PHINNEY AND WHOM HE MARRIED IN 1854.

Adding a new wrinkle to the retail business he entered (cutlery, threads, buttons, suspenders, pins, needles, etc.), he devised a catalog to circulate among Maine dealers, thus hoping to capture purchases that might otherwise have gone to Boston. Generations before L. L. Bean perfected the art of catalog shopping and retail sales, James Phinney was making a go of the combination.

Consequently, by 1854, when he was twenty-three years old, he was able to marry Sarah Lewis. After a honeymoon trip by four-wheel chaise to the White Mountains, the couple returned to Portland to live in Dr. Elihu's home. Their first child, Florence, was born ten months later, but the sickly baby died within two years. Consoling them to a degree for the loss was the arrival in 1857 of a strong, sturdy son whom they named Hartley. Then came Clinton in 1859, followed by Eugene in 1862.

For a young man on his way up, with a growing family and a budding business, Portland was an exciting place in those days. Although the "Forest City" (so-called because of its profusion of beautiful elms) had never quite lived up to a euphoric prediction made for it in the 1840s that it "might be a rival, and not a satellite, of either Boston or New York," the Maine community *had* prospered. By 1832, Portland had already outgrown its status as a town and had organized itself as a city, complete with mayor, seven aldermen and a common council of twenty-one members.

In 1845, John A. Poor, one of Portland's great entrepreneurs, traveled by sleigh through a blizzard to Montreal to persuade a group of Canadian railroaders to locate the end of its Grand Trunk Railroad in Portland rather than Boston. Portland became not only a railroad hub but a steamship hub. The waterfront developed and Commercial Street was built alongside the soon bustling wharves. In the 1850s, 246 sailing vessels and 12 steamers were servicing Portland. This decade was "a time of pronounced growth and prosperity"[6] for Portland. The J. B. Brown Company sugar factory, which used a new process to refine molasses, was the largest establishment. The Portland Company, begun in 1846, had already achieved a national reputation in the construction of locomotives, boilers, and machinery. Portland, which had had a mere

1,076 dwelling houses in 1830, had a population of 26,242 in 1860.

Its principal thoroughfare, Middle Street, was a "handsome street" of two- to three-story brick buildings, mostly stores, with stone fronts or ornamental pillars. Parallel to it ran Congress Street, containing the city hall, churches, and public buildings. Between them ran Exchange Street, the site of banks, brokerages, and auction rooms. Here, according to the nineteenth-century Portland author John Neal, "forty-nine fiftieths of the jobbing and retail business and about all of the dry goods and hardware business were done...."[7]

James Phinney worked so successfully that he was able to pay off his Uncle Chester's loan by the early 1860s. According to Chester, it was the first time a relative had ever paid him back.

Part of this success was due to a change of partners. His original partner had been Harry Bailey, but James Phinney dissolved the connection in 1856 and joined with Oliver E. Shepherd to concentrate on the jobbing business and an outlet store at 8 Exchange Street. He stayed with Shepherd for three years but declared him a "great drag upon me on account of extreme penuriousness and an unfortunate address, which prejudiced customers against us." He then teamed up with William G. Davis, a native of Limerick, Maine, and a former traveling salesman. James Phinney called him "a wholesale peddler and a man of popular qualities," and it was said "Davis was so persuasive he could sell moos to a cow."

The Baxter-Davis partnership also included James Phinney's nephew James Baxter, who was given the Exchange Street store to run. Within a few months they had doubled their business and then had to contend with Shepherd, who tried to set up as a competitor.

In 1861, James Phinney had his father's house on Brown

Street enlarged and remodeled, extending the front and adding a parlor, two other rooms, plus a small conservatory and a bay window. During the progress of the work, the family boarded in Buxton with a man named Ira J. Batchelor, who was to have a significant effect on the Baxter fortunes.

For it was Batchelor, then working as a clerk for John Winslow Jones of Westbrook in the canning business who suggested that Baxter and Davis enter the field. This did not happen until the summer of 1863, after James Phinney had completed a trip to England, Ireland, and France where he'd ordered goods made to meet a rising demand in Maine and the U.S. because of shortages caused by the Civil War.

Their original business was described by James Phinney as "the importation of foreign threads and cutlery and as agents for various American manufacturers." And, in spite of Davis's gift of slick talk, their code of ethics was to keep "goods of sterling quality with the true weight and measure marked on them." They also had goods made especially for the firm, done up in the most attractive packaging and emblazoned with unique trademarks. The solid reputation for quality they developed helped them easily outdistance such rivals as Oliver Shepherd.

At the start of the Civil War, James Phinney had tried to enlist but was rejected because of his general poor health. His father had died in 1862. "I felt greatly his loss," James Phinney wrote, "and the pleasant house was dark for a long time without him." But once the canning operation commenced, it became an immediate success and absorbed him fully. The first factory was opened Downeast in a section of Deer Isle called Oceanville, where Baxter and Davis started canning lobsters. In no time at all, they were creating such a demand for the crustaceans that the state began to contemplate imposing conservation measures.

SKETCH OF THE PORTLAND PACKING COMPANY'S FACTORY
IN PORTLAND. AN 1887 NEW ENGLAND BUSINESS
PUBLICATION STATED THAT WHILE PACKING WAS A BRANCH
OF TRADE WHICH IS MOST DISTINCTIVE OF THE LARGE
CATTLE CENTERS OF THE WEST, "THE MAINE CITY COULD
BOAST A PACKING COMPANY THAT HAD FEW SUPERIORS IN
THIS COUNTRY."

Their greatest coup took place when they decided to can
corn—"green corn," as the uncooked product they put into
tins and then steamed was known.

A process for doing this had been invented by a
Philadelphian named Isaac Winslow when he was living in
France in 1842. His brother Nathan, who resided in Westbrook, Maine, began experimenting with the idea, aided by
another local man, Samuel Rumery. The firm Nathan Winslow created to pack green corn was eventually taken over by
his nephew, John Winslow Jones.

The key to the process was a special knife, containing a
gauge that determined how deep it would cut, used to strip the
kernels from an ear of corn. This original cutting instrument,

developed by Isaac Winslow, was supplemented by another with an *adjustable* gauge, which John Winslow Jones had perfected. The patents for these knives were later sold to Samuel Rumery and he, in turn, sold shares in them to James Phinney and Davis.

The Portland Packing Company, the entity that was created to exploit the success of canned food, and especially corn, had Baxter, Davis, Rumery and George Burnham as partners. In 1866, Baxter and Davis bought out the other two. Their company became not just nationally known but in the words of a Portland Landmarks publication, "the largest food packing firm in the world."[8]

At the time, an international magazine, the *London Illustrated News*, commented: "like the famous Hudson's Bay Company, the Portland Packing Company has a 'long reach,' having establishments from the Gut of Canso (Nova Scotia) to the Gulf of Mexico."

This was a bit of an exaggeration, but it did have twenty-one plants, thirteen of them in Maine, and employed as many as 3,000 people. In 1863, they did $100,000 worth of business and in 1874, this had shot up to $750,000. Their payroll, alone, that latter year was $100,000.

Their first factory for canning corn was established in Yarmouth in the summer of 1865, and James Phinney supervised the operation while his family stayed in the country with a farmer named Hammond in West Paris. The first factory in Portland was on Richardson's Wharf, where they also had their offices, but this site was abandoned and they moved into quarters on Franklin Street, where Rumery and Burnham had had an establishment. Additional factories were soon erected in Gorham, Sacarappa (Westbrook), and Winter Harbor. When the J. Winslow Jones firm dissolved "through the mismanagement of Jones," according to James

Phinney, Ira Batchelor joined the management.

James Phinney's role was primarily to promote the business beyond Maine. He traveled west and found agencies to sell their products from New York to St. Louis and as far south as New Orleans. He would work all day and travel by train all night. His letters home to wife Sarah were mostly banal affairs—all about the weather and if he had a cold or not—but underlying them was his anxiety about her health. "Consult a physician often if your cough does not get well," he advised her. On one trip, he had his photograph taken and told Sarah how the photographer made him laugh "for the purpose of removing my too sober expression of countenance."

A rather hulking figure, now sporting mutton-chop whiskers, James Phinney was every inch the no-nonsense Yankee businessman, "whose presence was always felt," as one of his fellow Fraternity Club members later wrote. "He made no pretense to personal magnetism nor to humor," this writer went on, "but he added dignity, force, and character to any association of men." Yet dour as he might appear, he could, in his letters to his children, try (not always successfully) to appeal to them. The news from Sarah about the boys at home was that they were learning to ride bicycles (referred to as *velocipedes*) on Brown Street, Hartley on a two-wheeler and Eugene ("Genie") on a three-wheeler. From New York City, their father wrote them: "I saw a blind man on Broadway today and two Chinamen.... I was down in Wall Street. There are bears in Wall Street, lots of them, and they are not in cages but quite tame...." Whether the youngsters understood his stock market humor is doubtful. They had to have been far more receptive to the intelligence that Papa was trying to find a monkey to buy for Hartley and Clinton.

These trips had to be exhausting, as well as lonely, for a family man. In 1870, one jaunt took him to Baltimore, then to

THE SUCCESSFUL BUSINESSMAN, JAMES PHINNEY BAXTER,
AS HE APPEARED IN 1871, THE YEAR BEFORE PERSONAL
TRAGEDIES MADE LIFE "WELL-NIGH UNBEARABLE" FOR HIM.

Philadelphia en route to Pittsburgh (where he arrived at 2:00
A.M.), then Cincinnati, then Chicago. From Chicago, his let-
ter home was on the stationery of J. L. Smith, described as an
"agent for Manufacturers of Tobacco and Packers of Canned
Fruit," and a representative of the Portland Packing
Company.

His stay in Pittsburgh, which he had reached on a night
train ride through the mountains by way of Chattanooga,

"where the rebels fought us in the war," was memorable in several respects. He was staying in a hotel near the Monongahela River, and his boyhood reading about flatboats on the Monongahela bringing whiskey from the south had always stayed in his mind. He was also accosted by a little boy who had lost his leg and was seeking money to buy a cork leg. Much to his own surprise, James Phinney gave him a generous donation.

Writing Sarah during a trip to Buffalo and Syracuse, James Phinney is not only worried about her cough but also about a revolver he left on a shelf in a closet at home. He is afraid it might drop and go off and wants to be assured it is out of reach of the children.

When back in Portland, James Phinney worked mostly in the office of the Portland Packing Company, while during the canning seasons (and these varied for the different products) he had general supervision of some of the factories. The canning could go on for several months or for as short a time as three weeks. Quality was essential. Tomatoes had to be drained well; lobsters packed in as big pieces as possible and as fresh as possible; and corn in its own juice and milk, without husks, making sure it didn't ferment.

A large red-brick building in downtown Portland at the confluence of five streets—an area known as "Gorham's Corner"—is called the Cannery and allegedly was the site of one of James Phinney's factories. Yet his supervisory trips were not just within the vicinity of the Forest City. On one occasion, having to go to Oceanville, he took young Hartley with him. On another, seeking a payment he was owed, he endured the discomfort of an all-night stagecoach ride from Bangor to Cherryfield in Washington County.

It has often been stated publicly that James Phinney made most of his money by selling tinned food to the Union

Army, with hints that it wasn't always of the best quality. But more evidence lies in the fact that most of the firm's expansion occurred after the Civil War, and that it was famous for the quality of its products. Edward H. Elwell, writing in 1875, said of the company: "The packing of hermetically sealed provisions is peculiarly a Portland process and has given the city a worldwide reputation." In addition to lobsters and corn, those provisions included salmon, beans, tomatoes, meats, and soups.

The devastating Portland fire of 1866 did not seem to slow down Baxter, no more than it did the city, which rebounded quickly, led by J. B. Brown's decision to build the luxurious Falmouth Hotel on Middle Street and William Widgery Thomas's rebuilding of the Canal Bank.

The Baxter family expanded, as well. The next addition, a second James Phinney, arrived in 1867, then came daughter Alba (called Dolly) in 1869, and son Rupert in 1871. Another child, Mabel, had preceded the infant James Phinney, but she lived only five months.

In the summer of 1870, the Baxters joined two other families—that of their physician, Dr. Burr, and of Stephen Berry, a close friend of James Phinney's, in leaving Portland and spending July and August in the country. The site they chose was a farm in Gorham, ten miles from the city, owned by a Civil War veteran named Thomas Smith. So agreeable was the experience that the following spring, James Phinney purchased the property.

His intent was to reside at Smith farm for the entire next year. Sarah's health had deteriorated badly. The years of continual childbearing and child-raising, and the added burden of caring for the elder Mrs. Baxter, who had been thrown from a carriage and, as a result, suffered from bouts of mental illness, had taken their toll. It was hoped that country living might be easier for her. James Phinney had the Smith farm remodeled to accommodate Sarah's needs and those of the children, who enjoyed the animals and the chance to go sliding in the winter with their father when he was home. Still as busy as ever, James Phinney commuted into Portland every day by train.

But rural Gorham did not provide the desired health cure for Sarah. Rupert's birth, which took place at Smith farm, weakened her so much that the baby had to be sent to Portland and boarded with a nurse. On January 12, 1872, Sarah died at Smith farm.

This devastating blow to James Phinney was soon followed by others. The next was financial: the failure in business of his nephew James, whose losses he was obliged to cover. But the absolute nadir of his existence was reached when Dolly, his only daughter, "a very beautiful and bright little child," four years old, tipped over in her high chair and severely injured her spine. She was taken to Dr. Burr's and devotedly nursed by a woman from Massachusetts named Perkins, but the best efforts made to save her were of no avail. Well might James Phinney bemoan, as he did in his journal, that "life was well nigh unbearable."

In September of that year, he was still writing in his journal such heart-rending entries as: "I have a beautiful family but no home." Yet a month later, a change in his fortunes seemed in the offing. The widowed Mrs. Perkins who had nursed Dolly with such care had attracted the new widower, and he visited her at her home in Peabody. Writing to Mehitabel Cummings Proctor Perkins soon afterward, James Phinney said how much "he had enjoyed the quiet of her pleasant home over the Sabbath" and asked, with characteristic bluntness if she would like to become better acquainted. She immediately wrote back that she was ready to grant his request "but a fear has crept in that you might think me committed to more than I intend."

Wasting no time, James Phinney responded: "Doubtless I have appeared hasty and abrupt and shocked you. I always act thus, going openly to the point." He then asked her to join him for dinner at the Parker House in Boston.

By November, she was writing to "My dear James," and in December, it was "my dearest one," while James Phinney could state: "Sweet love, you are my last thought at night and first in the morning."

On April 2, 1873, James Phinney and "Hetty," as Mehitabel was called, were married. The admiring husband wrote of his new wife: "She proved to be a helpmate indeed and soon had my children fully under her magnificent influence, at the same time producing order out of the chaos of my domestic affairs."[9]

The next task was to find a proper place to live. James Phinney had soured on the country life at Smith farm. In his journal, he stated:

THE BAXTER HOME AT 61 DEERING STREET, PORTLAND, WHICH JAMES PHINNEY BOUGHT AFTER HIS SECOND MARRIAGE.

MEHITABEL CUMMINGS PROCTOR BAXTER: JAMES
PHINNEY'S BELOVED "HETTY," WHOM HE MARRIED AFTER
THE DEATH IN 1872 OF HIS FIRST WIFE. HETTY WAS THE
MOTHER OF PERCIVAL.

I have purchased a house at Deering Street, whither I
intend removing in a short time. My farm life has not
been what I fondly anticipated (mainly because of the
impossibility of finding good help). I shall leave it without regret.

The large, two-story, mansard-roofed, red-brick structure at 61 Deering Street had been built after the 1866 fire by a William H. Anderson. Prior to 1852, Deering Street, which runs parallel between Congress Street and Cumberland Avenue on Portland's west side, did not even exist. Into this new, upscale neighborhood, James Phinney and Hetty settled for what was to be the rest of their lives. They proceeded to produce their own family, "the second litter," as James Phinney playfully dubbed the three additions, two girls, Emily and Madeleine, who both survived to adulthood, and in between them, another boy, named Percival, perhaps because of his father's fondness for Arthurian legends, and Proctor, for his mother's famed New England ancestors, including John Proctor, the noted martyr of the Salem Witch Trials.[10]

[1] *Portland Press Herald*, August 24, 1996.

[2] "A New England Pantheon" by James Phinney Baxter, 1917.

[3] Ibid.

[4] *Maine's Beloved Benefactor* by Jane Veazie Nelson, Gorham Library Publication, page 5.

[5] *I Bequeath* by Arthur F. Joy, New England Homestead, May, 1949.

[6] *Portland by the Sea* by Augustus F. Moulton, Katahdin Publishing Co., Augusta, 1926.

[7] *Portland Illustrated* by John Neal, W. S. Jones, Publisher; Portland, 1874.

[8] *Portland Illustrated*, Martin Dibner, Editor; Greater Portland Landmarks, Portland, 1972.

[9] James Phinney Baxter, Journal #2, 1885.

[10] In her letters, Hetty often refers to Percy as *Proctor.*

CHAPTER ✳ 3

Public Service

EMILY, THE FIRST OF James Phinney Baxter's new line, was actually born in 1874 at the Smith farm before the family took possession of 61 Deering Street. There commenced a happy time, saddened only by the death of James Phinney's mother. The business was doing exceedingly well; in 1873 it earned a profit of $200,000, an astronomical sum in that era. The hard-driving businessman now felt he could relax somewhat, at least to the extent of taking vacations, which he had never done before. So he took Hetty and the children to the White Mountains in the summer. He fished and his wife painted and sketched, a pastime he was later to take up, himself.

It was 1876 when James Phinney started this custom of going to North Conway, New Hampshire, and that November, Percy was born. At the same time, the baby's oldest half-brother, Hartley, was entering Bowdoin College. A few years later, Hartley's ill health led to another sojourning site for the

BY HIS LATE FORTIES, JAMES PHINNEY WAS A PROSPEROUS
BUSINESSMAN WITH EIGHT CHILDREN AND A SECOND WIFE
WHOM HE CHERISHED.

Baxters—Florida. Alarmed that his college student son
appeared on the verge of developing tuberculosis, James
Phinney took the family south. Hartley revived and, completely recovered, spent part of that next summer camping
with two of his brothers in Maine's beautiful Rangeley Lakes
area.

The following year, 1879, the last of the "second litter" was born. Of his daughter Madeleine, James Phinney wrote: "...she who now queens it so over me by right of being the youngest of the family."[1]

James Phinney was now forty-eight years old. He was a rich man, eminently successful in business. He had eight handsome children, some already starting college careers, and the satisfaction of having daughters who appeared healthy and thriving helped fade the memories of those he had lost. He had a wonderful second wife whom he cherished. Everything seemed to be going his way.

Then, tragedy almost struck. He contracted pneumonia, always a tricky illness and particularly so in an epoch when medicine was fairly rudimentary. For a time, it seemed he wouldn't survive. While his family agonized, he slowly fought off the infection. Once out of danger, he took the family back to North Conway, where he convalesced, reading voraciously and taking up painting, with the aid of a prominent Portland artist, Harrison Brown, who journeyed to the White Mountains resort to give him art lessons and take him on sketching expeditions.

Given these circumstances, it is not surprising that James Phinney seemed to come to the conclusion that it was time for him to devote more attention to the things he loved to do. Foremost among his predilections was his love of history and historic research, especially the history of Maine and New England. He had already been aware, through a John Thornton of Boston, of the existence of the Trelawney papers, a voluminous collection of the seventeenth-century letters between Robert Trelawney, the Lord Mayor of Plymouth (England) and owner of Richmond Island in Maine and his overseer, John Winter. James Phinney decided to publish these documents, but annotate them, and thus create a full picture of the early settlers, rough as they were, in what is now the Cape Elizabeth area.

This love of history sent the Baxters abroad to Europe for almost an entire year in 1885, where James Phinney set out to collect the original sources, mostly in England but also in France, connected to the founding and settling of New England. At his own expense, he had copies made of all of the documents he found—twenty-one volumes. While in England, he was able to visit Sir Robert Trelawney, a direct descendant of the seventeenth-century lord mayor and to see the hiding place for two hundred years of the original Trelawney letters.

The joy of delving into the colonial past was a welcome

HETTY WAS A FINE ARTIST, PERHAPS EVEN BETTER THAN JAMES PHINNEY, WHO WAS ALSO QUITE TALENTED. HERE ARE TWO OF THEIR LANDSCAPES: LEFT: HETTY'S, A SEASCAPE; RIGHT: JAMES PHINNEY'S, A VIEW OF THEIR SUMMER HOME, MACKWORTH ISLAND.

distraction that took more and more of his time. Yet he was always practical when it came to money. And he had a lot to invest. Real estate in Portland seemed the safest bet and brought him increasing returns. He no longer had to spend long days at his business office. His partner, William G. Davis, was also able to free himself and managed to get elected to the legislature in 1875—as a Democrat! Baxter, whose father had been a Democrat, proudly described himself as a lifelong member of the Republican Party but "never a machine man," he added.

He soon became Mr. Civic Responsibility. Some of his positions, such as "President, Portland Savings Bank," merely cemented his business relationships, as did his directorships of the Portland and Ogdensburg Railroad and the Portland and Rochester Railroad (both later merged into the Maine Central); others showed his civic and charitable bent: vice-president of the Maine Historical Society, trustee of the Portland Public Library, a founder of the Associated Charities of Portland (now the United Way), a founder of the Portland

Society of Art, and a promoter of the Longfellow Association and the Soldiers and Sailors Monument Association.

In 1889, his first gift of "bricks and mortar" to the city was dedicated—a building to house its public library. Until then, the books had been kept in several inadequate rooms at City Hall, where one complainant groused that the premises were "crowded with small boys whose attire, not always clean, made the atmosphere...unendurable for older persons."[2]

The "noble structure," built Romanesque style in Connecticut brown freestone and Ohio sandstone on upper Congress Street had been an intention of James Phinney's for several years. His goal, stated openly in 1887, was to provide a home for three of his favorite activities: the library, the Maine Historical Society, and, in time, the Portland Society of Art. Included in the design, therefore, were three eight-foot-high statues representing history, literature, and the arts. Another feature was a sculpture inside called "The Dead Pearl Diver" by a local artist, Paul Akers, who had achieved a national reputation.

Using Baxter Hall, a Gothic-style chamber paneled in Georgia pine, for the dedication ceremonies, the citizens of Portland gratefully lauded their benefactor. Mayor Chapman pronounced that: "In James Phinney Baxter, the people of Portland have ever recognized an eminently cultured and high-minded citizen deserving of and receiving universal respect.."[3]

After stating that the building was the "material embodiment of one of my early dreams," James Phinney ended modestly by telling his listeners: "I have reared a structure of wood and stone. You are to build character."[4]

One small Baxter family footnote to this accomplishment: At an earlier cornerstone-laying ceremony, when the library was only partly constructed, young Percy became restless during the speeches. Slipping away, he climbed up into the unfinished walls and then, like a cat stuck in a tree, could not get down. The Portland Fire Department came to the rescue much to the mortification and, no doubt, ire of his father.

A man who was involved in so many things, who was so well thought of, who had so many friends and admirers, and who had done so much for Portland—who was so "solid," as the expression for *rich and respectable* went in that period— such a man was a natural when political leaders were looking about for candidates.

In 1892, the local Republicans needed someone strong to run for mayor against the incumbent Democrat, Darius H. Ingraham. Whether Baxter would accept, if asked, seemed doubtful.

A biographical sketch that year in a Portland newspaper, the *Post*, began with the prediction—quite accurate, it turned out—that "when the names of nine out of ten of the businessmen of this city are forgotten, James Phinney Baxter will be alive"; it ended on this discouraging note for the G.O.P.:

> Perhaps no man ever lived who had less of the politician in his make-up. He is far too straightforward, business-like and honest to be a party leader, or even an acceptable party candidate.[5]

It could be thought that James Phinney would never wish to tie himself down to the affairs of the city, even had they not been enmeshed in the political climate of the time, with its open graft, unashamed patronage, and myriad dirty tricks. So why, at the age of sixty-one, did James Phinney Baxter agree to the blandishments of his party's leaders and enter an arena for which, in later years, he expressed nothing but distaste?

A sense of duty, perhaps? The naiveté of the citizen of strong opinions who believes that he can do a better job than the bumblers in office? The *Post* interview had paraphrased a letter of his on the subject:

> ...while he made it plain that he would never be the candidate of any party for any office, yet indicated unmistakably that as a citizens' candidate, when the people should have grown tired of the rule of politicians, he could and would be elected.[6]

To some, this might look like pretty good politics, itself—being above the fray, non-partisan, an "independent." Party-bashing is not restricted to the late twentieth century.

Obviously, Baxter was a man of considerable ego, a prerequisite for tossing one's hat into any political ring. And he had decidedly strong opinions, some even a bit quixotic, such as his notion that school children should buy their own school books (the theme of an address to the American Institute of Instruction). Or that Francis Bacon was the author of Shakespeare's works (Baxter's thesis was published by Houghton-Mifflin in an enormous, 700-page book).

The non-partisan citizen's candidate went on the mayoral ballot in 1892 as a Republican—and lost by eighty-three votes! But several hundred votes were found to be missing, particularly in the Republican stronghold of Ward 1.

Baxter's opponent, Mayor Ingraham, was anything but a hack politician. A graduate of Annapolis, a well-known lawyer, ex-state representative, and one-time U.S. consul in Spain, he recognized that something was amiss and returned his certificate of election unsigned. A new election was called.

The second time around, Baxter won by 319 votes. The saga of the missing Ward 1 ballots continued with the trial in superior court of Thomas Harper, the Ward 1 election clerk who admitted burning at least sixty-five of them at the order of City Clerk John S. Russell. The clever legal work of noted Democrat attorney Nathan Clifford won a split verdict for Harper. Not long afterward, a night watchman at city hall found a missing packet of ballots hidden in a closed-off closet.

As mayor, James Phinney was popular but always controversial. To use modern parlance, he had the "vision thing" and the leadership capabilities to bring people along with him (often kicking and screaming) where he wanted to go. He truly was not a "machine man," and the niceties of attending to the political needs of his allies were not among his priorities, which often got him into trouble with his own Republican Party. The Democratic opposition, of course, seized every opportunity for attack, which was to be expected. One difference between those years and today was the media. Its politician-bashing was only on a partisan basis. Certain newspapers were Republican, others Democrat. Candidates did not run ads. The newspapers, in their columns and in notices they placed themselves, reminded people who to vote for—invariably the straight ticket of the party they championed. For example, here is the Portland *Evening Express*, the G.O.P. mouthpiece, on the eve of one of Baxter's re-election campaigns (all in all, he served six single-year terms):

> The Portland Democracy is very sick. Like the poor heathen Chinee he has shouted himself hoarse for nothing. The Republican party is in line. It will come unitedly to the polls on March 2 and the sick man will breathe his last.[7]

On the other side was the *Eastern Argus*, which never could find a good word to say about James Phinney. This Democratic voice usually dripped with sarcasm, as it did in savaging Mayor Baxter's thought process for explaining why he would run for a fifth term. Baxter, they said, had

...dived into the pellucid depths of his inner consciousness and come to the surface grasping a pearl of great
price for Portland people...that he would run again as the
only capable and progressive gentleman this town contains to complete his unfinished work.[8]

James Phinney's "vision thing" was a forerunner on a
smaller, municipal scale of the great goal his son Percival later
set for himself in acquiring Katahdin and its surroundings for
the people of Maine. His plans initially included securing for
the city the land adjacent to either end of the peninsula on
which the city sits, where it borders the ocean at Casco Bay.
These magnificent pieces of real estate were then in private
hands. Walkways, which gave the areas their present names of
Eastern Promenade and Western Promenade had been laid
out by the city in 1836 but it was Baxter who finally bought
the bordering land and saved it from being developed for
houses. For him, this action was but one piece of a far larger
master plan. Indeed, at his own expense, he had hired the
nationally known Boston landscape architectural firm of
Frederick Law Olmstead, the creator of New York City's
Central Park, to put his vision on paper. The jewel of his conception was to be a broad boulevard encompassing the Back
Cove area, then a tidal basin that filled and emptied and that
constituted, in Baxter's words, "a slimy and ill-odored waste"
and a "sink of corruption."

There is a story, probably apocryphal, of a society
woman who passed through Portland when the tide was out
and Back Cove at its most disgusting, who upbraided the
mayor and in her most imperious grande dame Brahmin manner directed him to do something about it. When she journeyed back through Portland sometime later, it was high tide
and Back Cove was a lovely, pristine-looking, salt-scented

stretch of estuarine water. "That is much better," she congratulated the mayor.

James Phinney intended more reliable improvements.
He would fill parts of the shore, enclose the water with a tide
gate, and lay out greenery-shrouded drives and walks. A model
for his improvements had already been accomplished in
Boston with the filling of its Back Bay and a green belt of a
thousand acres that extended out from it along the Fenway
and Charles River to the Arnold Arboretum.

Trying to keep up with Boston and make Portland into a
first class "residential city" did not sit well with all of the
locals. Those who had property they wanted to develop were
not pleased with James Phinney's idea. Politics being politics,
they ignored the grandeur of his vision and accused him of
merely seeking to increase the value of his own properties in
the areas to be beautified. After one of the many hearings on
the project, he wearily complained:

> It's so hard to get people owning the mud flats to yield
> their almost valueless rights. A Mrs. Knight who has a
> large tract of land treated me very badly, indeed, and was
> not only furious at the suggestion of the improvement of
> the shore but abused me.[9]

In 1897, when he was seeking his fifth consecutive term,
the vision had not been so fully fleshed out. His inaugural
address the previous year had called for adorning residential
streets with wide esplanades, open spaces with fountains, statuary, shrubbery, and flowers, and securing "as much land as
possible for parks and public playgrounds."[10] On the governmental structure side, he was also sticking his neck out, calling for an end to the system by which Portland had been run
as a city since 1832. He wanted to eliminate the bi-cameral
bodies of Aldermen and Councilors and consolidate these two

HON. J. P. BAXTER: SIX TIMES MAYOR OF PORTLAND, HE
WAS TWICE DEFEATED, ONCE BY HIS OWN REPUBLICAN
PARTY IN A PRIMARY AND ONCE BY THE DEMOCRATS.

branches into a single, less unwieldy body. Opponents, not surprisingly, accused him of trying to engineer a power grab.

Baxter's thoughts about political reform were appropriate to the "Progressive Era" in which he lived. A favorite pejorative term at the time for a political organization was to call it a "Ring." Some twenty years earlier in Portland, an anonymous, privately published pamphlet entitled *History of a Ring* circulated in the city; it was actually James Phinney's work and in play form satirized a situation in which Portland's pols were alleged to be worse than Boss Tweed's in New York City, or as stated in the preface's florid language:

> ...that we in this godly Forest City have for years had a Ring which has sapped its vitality to a greater extent in proportion to its wealth than any ring ever did in that Empire City we are ever especially apt to regard as ungodly.[11]

Baxter most likely had the Democrats in mind in presenting this rather sophomoric satire. It reveals, however, that the political life was not as far from his consciousness as it might have appeared. Indeed, there is a curious letter in the family archives from President James Garfield to a D. G. Swain, dated June 21, 1881, in which the nation's chief executive states: "I have never wavered in my purpose to appoint Baxter," and this despite an attack on him, because he had visited Mrs. Garfield during her sickness. The cryptic allusion to a federal post James Phinney obviously never received raises the question as to how much the resistance to him at the time was an intra-party matter. In 1897, when the four-term mayor announced his decision to try again, that resistance within the G.O.P. had reached the boiling point. Announcing his candidacy was another Republican, Alderman Charles H. Randall.

The *Eastern Argus* held back its fire against Randall who, to them, was the quintessential "Ring" politician, and concentrated on attacking Mayor Baxter under the time-worn rubric of *he's been there too long and has become pompous, conceited, and out of touch.* The Democratic editors even faintly praised Randall as "a man who fought in the open instead of pretending to be an unwilling candidate." Seizing on the ammunition the enemy was giving them, Randall's supporters echoed the theme that Baxter had been in office too long. Said one of Randall's workers: "He has a notion that he has a monopoly of pretty much all the capacity and spirit in the party."

The image of James Phinney as a wealthy autocrat who threw his weight around had been inadvertently reinforced by a highly publicized incident that occurred the previous fall during the presidential election of 1896. It was a particularly exciting election in Maine because a Maine man, Arthur Sewall of Bath, was the vice-presidential candidate of the Democratic Party, running on the same national ticket with William Jennings Bryan. In Bath, then as now known for its shipbuilding, Arthur Sewall owned the largest fleet of ships under the American flag and was also a partner in the growing Bath Iron Works, still in business today supplying warships to the U.S. Navy. For this small Maine city, anxious to honor its most distinguished citizen, the highlight of the campaign was a visit by Bryan to his running mate's hometown for a major rally of the Pine Tree State's Democrats.

Ten miles away, at Bowdoin College in Brunswick, a group of young Republicans decided to intrude on the gathering of two thousand people, the largest ever in Bath's history. Two hundred G.O.P. boys from Bowdoin arrived by train and marched from the railroad station to the center of town, provocatively singing a Republican fight song,

"McKinley and Gold." En route, they were stopped by the city marshal, and one of their leaders, a six-foot-tall, articulate young blond, was arrested despite his protestations that he was only trying to quiet down his classmates. This was Percival Baxter, a sophomore but well-known as the son of the mayor of Portland. Incarcerated in the city jail, he was freed a short time later through the personal intercession of Bath's own mayor, Charles E. Bibber.

There, the affair might have rested. But shortly afterward, the man who'd arrested young Baxter, Bath City Marshall Orrin A. Kitteredge, received a letter from James Phinney Baxter's attorney arrogantly demanding that he sign a paper admitting he'd wrongfully arrested Percy and apologizing for his actions. Adamantly refusing, Kitteredge argued that the boys could have "created a riot and some of the students might have been killed." James Phinney then had Kitteredge's property attached for the $1,000 he was seeking in damages.

The case came to court in February 1897, just at the very time Mayor Baxter was facing Alderman Randall in the Republican primary. The upshot was a Pyrrhic victory for James Phinney. The jury awarded damages to Percy but instead of $1,000, they were a derisive, if not insulting, one cent. Although the boy proudly took his penny and had it made into a watch charm, the political fallout could not have been worse. A Bath newspaper, remembering how Mayor Bibber had had Percy released as soon as he'd heard of the imprisonment, publicly ruminated: "Now that magnanimous person (James Phinney) returns the courtesy by suing the city. Such is the gratitude of Portland princes."

Closer to home in the *Portland Press*, there was this caricatured dialogue:

Bath Store Keeper: "Hello my little man, Who are you?"

Little Man: raising his head proudly. "I am Percival C. [sic] Baxter, my papa is Mayor of Portland."
Bath Store Keeper: "Well, Percival, what do you want?"
Percival: "I want a strip of that striped candy." (Then smiling brightly,) "Mr. Kittridge give me a cent."

The primary was held on February 15, 1897. Randall took four of the Portland's seven wards and outpolled Baxter in the choice of delegates to the nominating convention, 28-21. While the *Argus* exulted that "the 'silk stocking' backing of the Mayor is routed from the field" and prepared to turn its guns on *Ring politician* Randall, James Phinney was seemingly unconcerned by his loss, even perhaps relieved. "I felt relaxed and painted in the afternoon and wrote in the evening," he noted in his journal.

Yet, after a hiatus of almost seven years, he would once more go on in his stubborn pursuit of the vision he had for Portland.

---

1 James Phinney Baxter, Journal #2, 1885.
2 *Dedicatory Exercises of the Baxter Building to the Uses of the Portland Public Library and Maine Historical Society*, Lakeside Press, Printers and Binders, 1889.
3 Ibid.
4 Ibid.
5 *Portland Post*, December 10, 1892.
6 Ibid.
7 *Portland Evening Express*, February 20, 1896; page 4.
8 *Eastern Argus*, February 11, 1897.
9 James Phinney Baxter, Journal #6, August 24, 1904.
10 *Portland Evening Express*, March 9, 1896, page 1.
11 *History of A Ring* by One of the Governor's Wards, 1877.

CHAPTER 4

Young Percy

No evidence has been found to confirm that James Phinney Baxter chose to run for mayor again in December 1903 because of the political aspirations of his son Percy. But it is a known fact that Percy was his campaign manager in a winning effort that saw two Republican opponents demolished in the primary and James Phinney's old opponent, Darius H. Ingraham, beaten in a landslide. Three years earlier, Percy had been graduated from Harvard Law School, and in the fall of 1904, he was indeed on the ballot for state representative.

The little boy with the page-boy blond hair seen in the "Babes in the Woods" portrait had grown into a well-educated young man with an obviously promising future.

A famous story told about his childhood has the aura of legend, but is absolutely true. It happened while he was fishing with his father on a family trip to the same Rangeley Lakes where his half-brother Hartley had recuperated from his life-

YOUNG PERCY, POSSIBLY ABOUT THE AGE WHEN HE
CAUGHT HIS FAMOUS EIGHT-POUND TROUT ON
OQUOSSOC LAKE, FOR WHICH HIS FATHER PAID HIM $80.

threatening illness. They were out on Oquossoc Lake and the fish weren't biting. Seven-year-old Percy was growing restless. To quiet him, James Phinney made the boy an offer. For every trout he caught weighing more than five pounds, he would be paid $10 a pound. "I was just a small boy, sitting in the middle of the boat, holding onto a short, stubby rod with both hands," Percy later related. Suddenly, he had a strike.

Fighting the fish all by himself, he finally landed an eight-pound beauty of an eastern square-tailed brook trout. At $10 a pound, this meant a fortune for him—$80!

The boy's character and upbringing were revealed that same evening. In the Oquossoc Club lounge, the gentlemen anglers present teased the lad about his winnings. What was he going to do with them? "Bank 'em," he instantly retorted, no doubt coaxing amused smiles and nods of approval from these business-minded folks. Bank them, Percy did. The nest egg was left for almost half a century until the original $80 had compounded to more than $l,000. Only then did he spend it. Or, rather, he gave it away, as he did with so much of his money, in this case donating it to a fund to teach children about wildlife.

The outdoors—fishing, nature, and the environment—was a strong influence on Percy from his earliest childhood. But hunting was never included. Like his father, who was a noted anti-vivisectionist, Percy admired, revered, and always fought to protect animals.

He had been told a story by James Phinney that he sometimes told himself, in later years, to illustrate the origins of the Baxters' horror of cruelty to animals. It had begun with James Phinney's desire, as a young boy, to go duck hunting, to which end he had procured a rifle. Out in the field, after hunting long and hard without success, he suddenly spotted a white duck swimming peacefully on a stream. He fired and killed it, only to learn almost immediately from an irate farmer that it was a tame pet. It cost him money to calm the man down, and his chagrin was made all the worse when his mother pretended it was a game bird and cooked it with great ceremony. As Percy said, "As far as I know, my father never killed anything wild or tame after that, for he loved life and wanted to protect every living creature from pain and violence."[1]

THE "SECOND LITTER": PERCY (CENTER), MADELEINE (LEFT), EMILY (RIGHT).

A more personal experience occurred when Percy was nine years old. He then received his first dog, a ten-week-old, tawny-colored, Irish Setter puppy, which was brought to his home in a crate. Describing the scene, Percy said: "As the precious package was placed upon the grass, the tiny inmate poked her nose through the slats and lapped the hand of the one she was ready to acknowledge as her master. She knew little but loved much."[2]

The gift brought with it another lesson. Although James Phinney had paid the $3 charge for the dog, Percy had to contribute, too, and he forked over 85 cents to cover the expense of shipping the loving creature from Rockland to Portland.

An untold sequel to the story occurred that summer when the family moved to a vacation home James Phinney had bought on Great Diamond Island in Casco Bay. Unused to its new surroundings, Percy's puppy cried and cried and was eventually put outdoors so it wouldn't disturb the family. In an act of considerable daring for any well-behaved Victorian child, the nine year old sneaked out of his house in the dead of night, found his pet, brought her to bed with him, then arose before dawn and placed her outdoors again.

This particular Irish Setter female eventually had several litters of nine pups, all of whom were sold. Even here, the Baxters showed their business acumen. These pedigreed puppies from a mother who cost $3 were sold at a handsome profit—$10 for males and $5 for females. But the discrimination in price bothered young Percy and perhaps accounted— he would say half-jokingly—for his devotion as an adult to the cause of Women's Suffrage.

The departure of the puppies always moved him to tears. But on one occasion, his sorrow turned to laughter when he learned that a Baxter pup had eaten the salmon main course of a dinner party thrown by its new owner, a manufacturer in upstate New York.

It was also during Percy's ninth year, in 1885, that James Phinney took the family abroad for almost twelve months. That is, he took Hetty and the "second litter." Emily and Percy were enrolled in English schools while little Madeleine, at six, was kept with her mother. James Phinney busied himself by haunting the public records offices in London and went to Paris on several occasions to do similar work in the French archives.

Eton House School, where Percy studied, was a day preprep for Eton, the most famous public (meaning private) boarding school in England. Only one other American student was there, a grandson of the notorious Civil War general, Benjamin "the Beast" Butler (whose nickname had been earned when he was commander of the Union troops occupying New Orleans and threatened to treat the women of the city like ladies of the night if they continued to insult his men). The two young Yanks at Eton House tried to teach their school chums how to play baseball and, in turn, their classmates tried to teach them cricket, which the Americans found dreadfully slow. When it was time for Percy to go home, the English boys all flocked to sign his memory book. A number of them were to achieve prominence as judges, generals, and members of Parliament.

A trip to Europe had to have been a momentous experience for a nine year old. The family's first taste of the Continent was in Ireland, where they landed and visited many of the famous sights, such as the Blarney Stone (which they didn't try to kiss). But their tourism was also interrupted by jolts of realism not usually available to an upper middle class child in Portland, Maine. On the ship, a steerage passenger had died, and Percy observed the sad spectacle of a burial at sea. Ashore, he was confronted by what his father termed "the indescribable poverty of southern Ireland." Riding on ponies through Killarney's breathtakingly beautiful Gap of Dunloe, they needed their guide to fend off a swarm of beggars of all ages. But the worst trauma for the boy came unexpectedly during a tour of Switzerland.

"Poor Percy had a serious grief on our ride,"[3] his father wrote. While traveling on a mountain road, they happened upon a shepherd and his flock; one of the animals strayed and fell under the wheels of their carriage and had its legs broken. As the creature lay writhing, the loutish shepherd beat it to try to make it rise. James Phinney writes: "Of course, the children were greatly shocked at this cruelty and Percy cried for half an hour as though his heart would break; indeed, it was almost impossible to get his mind turned away from the subject."[4]

Before they settled in London, their route took them to Scotland, France, Germany, Belgium, and Holland, as well as Ireland and Switzerland. They boarded in a London suburb called Upper Norwood, and James Phinney traveled into the city almost every day, spending much of his time at the British Museum, to which once in a while he would take Percy. A lasting family memory of the stay was Emily's triumph over her teacher in insisting that the word *clerk* could be pronounced "clerk" and not "clark" as the English did. When the dictionary proved her right, she received the nickname of "L. D." from her school chums, standing for "Living Dictionary."

In England, the second-litter Baxter children continued a practice they had started in Portland, conducting church services at home for their parents. Emily was the chief organizer, playing the piano and conducting while Percy sang hymns and little Madeleine chimed in. Their admiring if uncritical father commented: "They are the brightest children I ever saw."

Except for his sojourn overseas, Percy's elementary education was accomplished in Portland schools (Park Street Primary, Butler Grammar), and he went on to Portland High School as a member of the class of 1894. In the days when football was played without helmets, Percy was a varsity guard on a squad that coached itself. Nevertheless, their class history

PORTLAND HIGH SCHOOL'S 1893 FOOTBALL TEAM, ON WHICH PERCY PLAYED GUARD USING EQUIPMENT BORROWED FROM HIS HALF-BROTHER RUPERT. PERCY IS IN THE TOP ROW, CENTER.

claimed that "Ninety-Four has done more than any other class to make a name for Portland High School in athletics and in football." In a postcard to Rupert, Percy spoke about one game where "we beat those fellows 68-0, making 34 in both halves...." He then said he was practicing for the Brunswick game and was chosen for guard because his competitor for the position "has the nose bleed very easily." He asked his older half-brother if he had a hat (helmet?) he could spare, not a felt one, which was too soft, and that he also needed a pair of boots with cleats. In another missive to Rupert (who was at Bowdoin) he asked to borrow a whole "football suit" (jacket and pants).

In Percy's junior year the old high school was remodeled and while they were waiting for its completion, classes were held at the City Hall, where James Phinney presided as mayor.

The prophecies in the class year book make for interesting reading. They were written by a co-educational team of Annie M. Allen and Harold A. Pingree. Considering that Percy remained a lifelong bachelor, the rather teasing tone in regard to his attitude toward girls is instructive, if not ironic. All of these prophecies were based on a time significantly in the future when these high school seniors would have reached full maturity. Here's the prediction for Percy:

> Mr. Percival Baxter, the "Golden-haired youth of '94" is a merchant in Columbus, Ohio. He also owns a large horse farm outside the city. I saw by the *New York Herald*, some time ago, that three colleges, Vassar, Wellesley and Smith, had been endowed by Mr. Baxter. Well, I'm not surprised. Percy always had a weakness for the fair sex, although he thought that other people did not know it. [5]

No forecast of a political career for him was included. This honor was given first to a Jack Dana, who was pictured as a Maine legislator pushing for female suffrage (a role Percy later filled in real life) and then to a Thomas Hannegan, prophesied to be a member of the House of Representatives in Washington, D.C. Jack Dana was the class salutatorian (and later a founder of the venerable Portland law firm, Verrill, Dana) and gave a speech in Latin at graduation. On June 27, 1894, the class banquet was held and the youngsters danced until 2:00 A.M. Paul P. Goold, the class poet, summed up their experience in a bit of schoolboy doggerel.

When first we came together
As Freshmen green and bold,

'Twas in a somber structure,
With aspect grim and cold,
But when we came our fourth year,
Strange things had come to pass;
A schoolhouse fine in grandeur stood
To greet our senior class.[6]

Then, it was off to Bowdoin College for Percy. Three of his half-brothers had preceded him: Hartley, class of 1878, Clinton, class of 1881, and Rupert, who finished in 1894, the same year Percy completed high school. So, even if his father hadn't been the mayor of Portland, already a recipient of his first honorary degree from Bowdoin, and recently made an overseer of the college, this fourth Baxter to matriculate would have entered the institution in Brunswick with a feeling of confidence. In Percy's case, one might have sensed a certain over-confidence; he brought an Irish Setter dog to the campus with him who promptly received the name "Deke" after the DKE fraternity Percy was invited to join. Apparently, the faculty had no objection to the presence of the animal in their classrooms, where he behaved himself beautifully. Except one day, during a history lecture, Deke suddenly vomited. Percy was mortified, but his professor immediately said: "Don't worry about it. The poor dog was more uncomfortable than any of us. You needn't apologize for him."

At chapel, Deke would jump right up onto the platform, greet the parson and lie quietly down by the pulpit. On a memorable occasion, Deke brought a bone which he presented to the college president while he was addressing the students.

DKE is an athletically minded fraternity and during his first two years, Percy played on the varsity football team. The DKE's did not have their own house off-campus until after

ABOVE: PERCY IN 1896, WHEN HE WAS A SOPHOMORE AT
BOWDOIN; BELOW: PERCY WITH HIS CLASSMATES, POSED AS
MUSICIANS.

Percy's graduation but kept their identity as an organization by monopolizing a group of rooms in one of the dormitories—in this case the venerable Appleton Hall, built in 1843 and named for Bowdoin's second president. It was Percy's devotion to DKE that led him to room in his senior year at 10 Appleton with a freshman Kenneth Sills, who later became president of Bowdoin, succeeding the president of their own day, the illustrious William DeWitt Hyde, who led the college for thirty-two years. As soon as Sills, a promising Portland High grad, set foot on campus, Percy had rushed to enlist him for DKE, spiriting him off with a bunch of boisterous collegians in an open electric car for a celebration at the New Meadows Inn on the road to Bath. It should be noted that just down the hall from Percy and Sills, Harriet Beecher Stowe's husband Calvin had had his quarters as a professor and a good part of *Uncle Tom's Cabin* had been written in 7 Appleton.

After two years on the gridiron, Percy turned his attention to baseball, yet not as a player. He was chosen the first non-senior ever to be manager of the Bowdoin Nine. He had also shown some definite non-jock talents, such as coming in first for the Sophomore Prize Declamation and using his musical training to become the school organist.

Under President William DeWitt Hyde, Bowdoin was slowly changing. The curriculum then has been described as "a bastion built solidly upon Greek, Latin, mathematics, and modern languages, yielding slowly to the first cautious reforms of President Hyde,"[7] who created a chair of economics and sociology in Percy's freshman year and sought substitutes for the requirement of Greek. One thing Hyde didn't try to change was the college's emphasis on recruiting Maine youngsters, with more than 90 percent of the student body coming from the Pine Tree State. In Percy's time, only six boys in the entire college were from outside New England. A

Yankee frugality in its rates had to be attractive to Mainers: tuition was a mere $75 a year and the room rent for Percy and Sills at 10 Appleton only $42.

Percy's popularity had to have soared after the episode in Bath, when he could claim to his classmates who were almost universally Republicans (except Sills, later a Democratic U.S. Senate candidate) that he had martyred himself for the G.O.P. It was a cause célèbre on campus, and a group of Bowdoin boys took part in the superior court trial when he sought vindication. They were asked by the judge to give an example of their college yell, which they maintained they were innocently expressing when set upon by City Marshall Kitteredge. To them, the measly penny Percy was granted seemed worth the effort.

A further sense of triumph for the boy, and one perhaps even more appreciated, took place at the annual Ivy Day celebration. On this occasion, young Baxter was solemnly presented by the poker-faced president of the college with a pair of shining handcuffs! No doubt, the audience collapsed into appreciative gales of laughter.

A good-deal of Percy's extra-curricular time in his later years at Bowdoin was taken up with his editorship of a brand-new literary magazine that he and a classmate from Portland High School, William Witherle Lawrence, co-founded. James Phinney not only highly approved of his son's writing activities but provided the "happy suggestion" of what they should call their publication. This title, *The Quill*, came from the lines of a Lord Byron poem.

> *Oh, Natures's noblest gift, my grey goose quill*
> *Slave of my thoughts, obedient to my will.*

James Phinney also selected the typescript used to reproduce this couplet, which always appeared on the masthead of the magazine. Lawrence was the business manager and Percy managing editor. As chairman of the editorial board, he would solicit contributions from alumni as well as students. One well-known but obviously pompous literary alumnus wrote back that he was outraged because Percy's letter had asked for "something in the line of" an article. An editorial column called "Silhouette" allowed Percy to respond to such petti-ness. In any event, this person's own literary publication (the man was never identified) presently folded.

Percy also simultaneously served as editor-in-chief of *The Orient*, the student newspaper. He continued to hone his speaking skills, and as a senior, he was one of two Class Day orators, the other being his cohort Bill Lawrence. That he was perhaps getting ready for a future political career could be dis-cerned in a speech he gave to the Political Club, entitled "The College Man in Politics." Its content has been lost but a printed comment has endured to the effect that, "The article read before the Political Club of Bowdoin recently by Mr. Percival P. Baxter was one of the ablest that has ever been heard in Bowdoin College."

On June 23, 1898, Percy was graduated at the college's ninety-third commencement. He had made Phi Beta Kappa, in addition to his non-academic achievements. This successful young man then decided to study law and headed south to Harvard Law School. Three years later, in 1901, he had his LL.B. and the same year passed the Maine and Suffolk County, Massachusetts, bar exams. Back home, he apprenticed for a while in the law offices of Libby, Robinson, and Turner.

But almost immediately his main preoccupation became his father's affairs, where he soon took on the role of an assis-tant. By then, James Phinney had been retired for more than two decades from the Portland Packing Company. Hartley had been in charge of it until 1887, when Clinton took over the firm and Hartley moved to Brunswick and started the rival canning company of H. C. Baxter and Brother (he was later joined by Rupert). An unusual letter addressed by the elder Baxter to Clinton in 1891 is worth examining as a short digression at this point because it sheds light on the father's relationship with his sons, reveals a source of tension between them, and helps explain to an extent the closeness that developed between James Phinney and Percy, the only one of the boys not to go into the canning business.

The letter is dated September 17, 1891. It is an original draft, with words crossed out and replaced, plus additions made. The opening clause of the second sentence has in its understated way, the explosive power of revealing a rankling family drama whose sting has still not diminished after more than five years. James Phinney writes:

> When I was obliged [the word *compelled* was inked out] on my return from Europe in the August of 1886 by Hartley and yourself, acting in conjunction with your [the original read *my*] other partners to leave the firm and relinquish my interest in it for no cause that I am aware of except to enlarge your shares....

In the first sentence, he had referred to "a just claim against the firm which still remains unsettled" and then in a comprehensive if rather complex manner, he proceeded to elucidate that claim.

The essence of it was that when he had given up his one-fifth share of the company, spelled out by him as "capital, good-will, and trademarks," he was to be recompensed at the end of five years by the admission of James Phinney, Jr. into the firm "to take the place vacated by me" and, in return, he was "to put back into the firm the amount of capital taken out of it by me at the time of my enforced withdrawal."

Now, five years later, he is reminding Clinton that James Phinney, Jr. never entered the firm and thus he, James Phinney, Sr., has never been adequately compensated.

Some business history is revealed. "When I took Hartley and yourself into the firm," he writes, "I owned three-fifths of it and to the acquisition of this interest I had devoted the best years of my life." A one-fifth share had gone to Hartley, one-fifth to Clinton, and James Phinney had retained one-fifth. With Hartley out of the Portland Packing Company now, James Phinney noted that his one-fifth had been worth about $75,000, plus $10,000 more for his one-fifth of the "unestimated interest." It was his own one-fifth of this "unestimated interest" that James Phinney was asking for.

"I address this to you as my former communication to the firm was unnoticed" is the terse way James Phinney ends his letter.

An undated notation, in Percy's writing, placed the missive in the family files with the comment: "Copy of Letter to Clinton. No reply received."

Thus, the question of why Percy, among the six Baxter boys, ended up as the prime heir to his father's fortune is no longer such a source of puzzlement. James Phinney's holdings were extensive, whether in Portland real estate, commercial ventures, or stocks and bonds, and he obviously had faith in the young man's abilities, came to depend on him more and more, and held great hopes for his future. He perhaps also saw him as the one most imbued with his own spirit and vision of public service.

One of Percy's duties was to travel on a regular basis to the small city of Sterling, Illinois, 110 miles west of Chicago, where James Phinney had bought a water company in 1885. The young man oversaw its operations, which included ser-

THE BAXTER MEMORIAL BUILDING IN DOWNTOWN
PORTLAND, BUILT BY JAMES PHINNEY AND NAMED IN
MEMORY OF HIS FATHER. ANOTHER LARGE OFFICE COMPLEX,
THE TRELAWNEY BUILDING, WAS ALSO ERECTED AS ONE OF
JAMES PHINNEY'S INVESTMENTS IN PORTLAND REAL ESTATE.

vicing three thousand customers in Sterling and another three
thousand in nearby Rock Falls. It was perhaps good training
for the water-related issues he would encounter in the Maine
Legislature.

Actually, the company had come into the possession of the Baxters because of a series of events that began with a loan made by Clinton to a man named W. E. Gould, an official of the First National Bank in Portland. This was followed by further loans to Gould from James Phinney and for collateral, the bonds of several water companies, including Sterling, were provided. Then, the dramatic revelation burst upon the Baxters, Portland, and the world that Gould had been embezzling from the bank. James Phinney visited him at his home just before he was arrested by the police and, in a bizarre scene, all Gould could talk about was a borrowed book that he wanted to return. Gould went to the state prison at Thomaston and the Sterling Water Company to James Phinney.

It was also in 1886, on October 3, that James Phinney dryly noted in his journal: "Made arrangements today to sever my connection with Portland Packing Company." Even earlier, he had been investing in local real estate and his friend Stephen Berry, in informing him in February 1886 about the long-awaited decision in Portland as to the location of a Civil War monument, said somewhat tongue-in-cheek:

> The vote was very strongly in favor of Market Square for the Monument and you will be obliged to have your property there raised in value. All those stores below yours will have to be rebuilt and it will make a fine square.

The Baxter Block, constructed by James Phinney on Congress Street not far from Monument Square in 1895 at a cost of $150,000, was among the major properties that Percy helped manage when he went to work for his father. To this big office complex, the Baxters added the nine-story Trelawney Building in 1909. Scattered throughout the area were numerous pieces of real estate they acquired, such as the twenty-two acres bounded by Forest and Stevens Avenues that became Baxter Woods; the Portland Pier; and the handsome Western Promenade house at 92 West Street where Eugene first lived and later Percy for the rest of his life after his stint as governor.

Incidentally, much of James Phinney's estate was handled through the Fraternity Company Trust, whose name may have derived from the famous Portland "settlement house" called Fraternity House, where daughter Emily worked for many years as a social worker. If not, its origin could have been the far more exclusive Fraternity Club in which James Phinney was an officer and hobnobbed with such Maine luminaries as former governor and war hero Joshua Chamberlain

THE MAINE HOUSE OF REPRESENTATIVES CHAMBER IN 1905. PERCY, SERVING HIS FIRST TERM, IS IN THE LOWER LEFT-HAND CORNER IN THIS ALL-MALE BODY.

and speaker of the U.S. House, Thomas Brackett Reed.

Percy's work for his father started even while he was in law school. In 1899, he was appointed treasurer and general manager of the People's Ferry Company, a commercial venture that supplied transportation to Portland's Casco Bay islands. It was an excellent introduction to local politics in the raw. When they reorganized as the Peaks Island Ferry Company, adding a prominent local Democrat, Oakley C. Curtis (later a state senator and governor of Maine) as a director, their petition for a wharf on Peaks Island was turned down by the Harbor Commission. One of the members of that commission who voted was Charles W. T. Goding, who happened to be the managing director of the rival Casco Bay Steamboat Company, which was also seeking to obtain a Peaks Island wharf site. Percy's public attack on Goding's conflict of interest caused enough controversy so that Mayor Nathan Clifford, who by then had succeeded his father, vetoed the Casco Bay lease.

More outward skullduggery was involved in another experience Percy had at the ferry company. A man from New York City named Fred F. Neal approached the young executive and offered to obtain a permit from Portland's Board of Aldermen for Baxter's company to run a street railway along the city's waterfront. For $4,000, he could swing it, he said.

Percy played along with him. Then, he contacted Judge Enoch Foster and a "sting" operation was set up. When Neal arrived at Percy's office, a number of the ferry company's "officials" joined the meeting. Among them, in reality, were a police officer named Quinn, one neutral witness, and a stenographer. Arrested after he trapped himself, and eventually convicted, Neal was sentenced to a year in prison, but he forfeited his $1,000 bail and escaped from Maine.

Percy's direct plunge into politics began in December

1903 when he managed his father's successful campaign for the 1904 mayoralty term and continued in September when he, himself, was elected to represent Portland for 1905-06 in the Maine House of Representatives. He ranked as the second youngest lawmaker in Augusta that session.

---

[1] *Maine's Beloved Benefactor* by Jane Veazie Nelson, page 18, Gorham Library publication.

[2] "My Irish Setter Dogs" by Percival P. Baxter, governor.

[3] JPB Journal #2, September 18, 1885, page 57.

[4] Ibid.

[5] Portland High School, Class of 1894 Yearbook, NPSP Souvenirs, Smith and Sale Printers, 1894.

[6] Ibid.

[7] *Sills of Bowdoin* by Herbert Ross Brown, Columbia University Press; New York, London; 1964.

JAMES PHINNEY AT A PUBLIC EVENT, SEATED NEXT TO
JOSHUA CHAMBERLAIN, WITH PERCY IN A BACK ROW,
SHORTLY BEFORE BOTH OF THEM WERE DEFEATED FOR
THEIR RESPECTIVE RE-ELECTIONS IN THE CAMPAIGN
SEASON OF 1906-07.

CHAPTER 5

A Political Baptism of Fire

WHEN PERCY BAXTER RETURNED to Portland after law school, it was a pretty safe bet that he would join the Lincoln Club, the local Republican organization. In his famous escapade at Bowdoin, he had already shown his political colors and if he still harbored resentment over the treatment his father had received from the Forest City G.O.P., it perhaps had been sublimated into an all-too-human desire for revenge, or at least vindication. By the approach of the election for the 1904 mayoralty term, it may have been apparent that the voters were tired of the "Ring" politics represented by Mayor Randall and a yearning had set in, as often happens, for the *good man* they had ousted.

Timing is everything in the political world, and Percy's timing was perfect. As his father's campaign manager, he presided over—and could take the credit for—two effortless victories. In winning the primary, James Phinney carried every ward in Portland and in defeating Darius Ingraham, he did, indeed, receive a form of vindication in the huge plurality of 1,600 votes he amassed.

The Democrats fought hard, claiming to be fiscal conservatives and complaining that Baxter's previous administrations had been the most extravagant on record. A particularly nasty attack on the man who had already proved his philanthropic devotion to the city was leveled against the well-known fact that James Phinney donated his salary to the Walker Manual Training School, which he had helped to found. The charge was made that it had only been his first year's salary of $1,500 that he'd given away and that in subsequent years, he had recouped the loss because the salary was raised to $2,000 and he'd kept the extra $500 over the next three years.

Once more, too, the cry was raised that he'd been in office too long. If he gained a fifth term, he would seek a sixth, then a seventh, then an eighth and more. "Do the voters want to establish a Baxter dynasty?" the Democrats asked.

The size of James Phinney's vote seemed to answer that question in the affirmative. The *Eastern Argus* even conceded that his win took on "the proportion of a personal compliment."

And then it was Percy's turn to go before the voters.

Statewide and national elections in Maine were somewhat different then from what they are today. For one thing, they were held in September, not November, a full two months ahead of the rest of the country. Since 1904 was a presidential year, the old adage of "So goes Maine, so goes the nation" would be in effect and the Republicans hoped to capitalize on the popularity of incumbent President Theodore Roosevelt, who was running against Democrat Alton G. Parker, an appeals court judge from New York State who has been recently described as one of "the all-time worst candidates" for the presidency in U.S. history.[1] On the G.O.P. ballot for governor was William T. Cobb, running against Cyrus Davis; Republicans were exhorted to remember that "a vote for Cobb is a vote for Roosevelt."

Most voters of that day (and they were all men) voted the "big box," putting a single check or cross at the top of the ballot that counted for the whole party ticket. It was drummed into voters' heads that if they split their tickets, they could spoil their ballots.

Roosevelt won easily in Maine, a faithful Republican state. His coattails, however, were not as long as the G.O.P might have wished. There was no problem in Portland. All seven Republican candidates running for the state house of representatives were swept into office. But elsewhere, they lost three state senate seats and ten house seats; in Cumberland County (Portland is the county seat) they failed miserably to unseat the popular Democratic sheriff, William M. Pennell of Brunswick.

Under such a system, it was hard to gauge Percy's voting pull in his first effort. He came in fifth among his seven fellows but did outpoll the Republican city chairman, Colonel Frederick Hale. An odd result of this election was the defeat of a young Republican legislator in Bangor, Harry F. Ross, who was to cross Percy's path many times in the future in connection with Percy's acquisition of Katahdin. Had they served together, their relations might have been less stormy.

The Augusta to which Percy Baxter now commuted by train during a three-month session had officially been the capital of the state since 1832. Close to the banks of the Kennebec River, the community, originally a rural hamlet in the shadow of its larger neighbor Hallowell, had grown to serve the needs of government. Entry was by way of the train station on Water Street, which ran along the Kennebec (and occasionally would be flooded), and then a climb was necessary to reach the Bulfinch-designed granite statehouse erected on Weston's Hill. The pride and joy of the city was beautiful, elm-shaded Western Avenue, then home to magnificent mansions but today turned into a "strip" of fast-food places, gas stations, and malls. In Percy's era, most businesses were down on Water Street. The center of life for the legislators was the Augusta House, a hotel first built in 1832 and later renovated and expanded, where most of them boarded. It advertised itself as "The Political Headquarters, The Social Headquarters, the All-the-year-round Headquarters."

This last exhortation may have been directed to lobbyists, who also frequented the hostelry and who yearly staged "assemblies" or dances for the elected members. The legislative sessions themselves were kept short to serve the interests of the part-time lawmakers, a majority of whom, even until the 1920s, were farmers. They had to get back home in time for spring planting. For a short period in the 1840s, a summer session had been tried but only survived six years.

In the opinion of many Augusta watchers, most real business was conducted not in the official halls of the capitol building but in the rooms of the Augusta House. "If only the walls could talk" was a statement frequently heard right until the end of the hotel's existence in the 1970s, when it was torn down to make way for a bank. The stately brick building, "painted a drab free stone color with brown stone colored trimmings" when it was remodeled by its owner Major Harrison Baker and later re-painted yellow, became Percival Baxter's home away from home from the moment he arrived in January 1905 in a place where he was to spend so much of his life.

First-termers in the Maine Legislature are known, not surprisingly, as "freshmen." They are supposed to be seen, not heard, but this unwritten rule is usually honored in the breach. Energetic members, no matter how young or inexperienced, are given leave to express themselves, both on the floor and in the submission of bills.

Because he had a law degree, Percy was assigned to an important committee, the Legal Affairs Committee.

He is mentioned early in the record as introducing a bill based on the "Petition of Agnes E. Chase and seven other members of the Women's Clubs of Maine, for the enactment of laws to preserve the beauty of the fields and forests of Maine from being defaced by advertising signs and for the preservation of the forests and planting of trees along the highways of the State."

In this regard, he was no pioneer environmentalist, pushing for highway beautification. Dozens of identical petitions were also being submitted as bills by his colleagues. The members of women's clubs, although women had no vote, still had influence and this was the only route they could take. It didn't hurt to oblige the ladies, at least to the extent of attending to their petitions.

Right from the start, Percy was given an opportunity to learn. Taking his work seriously, he wanted his petition on highway beautification to be referred to his own Legal Affairs Committee where he would have some control over it. The senate had other ideas and voted to send it to the State Lands and State Roads Committee. Such "reference fights" can be fierce. But Percy never had a chance to battle. His house majority leader, Harold Sewall of Bath, tabled the bill before Percy could move it to Legal Affairs and then went along with the senate on referencing.

The session began on January 4, 1905 and on January 17, Percy cast his first really important vote. Prior to 1913 and the adoption of the Seventeenth Amendment to the U.S.

Constitution, U.S. senators were not elected by the people. State legislatures chose them—that is, whoever had the majority. In 1905, the Maine Republicans, despite their losses on election day, held a commanding lead in Augusta. The race between Eugene Hale of Ellsworth, the Republican, and State Senator Lindley M. Staples of Knox County, the Democrat, was a foregone conclusion. There was no indication that Percy would vote any other way than the party-line vote of 101-22.

Still, he could be a maverick and not be intimidated, even as young as he was.

He showed his mettle in several ways. One was to introduce a bill for Women's Suffrage, a fairly daring and substantive act for a freshman. Of course, it had no chance of passing and yet every time he was elected, he fought the same fight until he achieved a breakthrough in 1917. An even deeper sign of courage (his opponents would call it stubbornness or pigheadedness) during his first term happened in committee. He took a stand against his own party to try to thwart an act of political mischief.

The target was the Democratic sheriff of Cumberland County, William Pennell, who had been so easily re-elected. The Republicans introduced a bill to investigate Pennell on the charge (not uncommon in that era when Maine still had its Prohibition law, passed as the first of its kind in the country in 1856) that the sheriff wasn't enforcing the ban against drinking. This measure was sent to the Legal Affairs Committee with the expectation that its nine Republicans would rubber stamp the bill with a recommendation that it "ought to pass." The lone Democrat on the committee was expected to recommend it should be killed, which he did. The surprise to the Republican leadership was that Percy Baxter, plus his G.O.P. colleague Joseph B. Reed, went their own way, calling for the bill to be killed and stating "that the evidence at the hearing was no more than hearsay and common report and not such as would be legally admissible in judicial proceedings."[2]

From another point of view—and the G.O.P. leaders might have argued this way in sparing the freshman any noticeable punishment—Percy's vote could be seen as a shrewd Machievellian move—on the record as principled support for the most popular politician in the county in which he hoped to make a career.

But in his maiden speech, which occurred on March 2, 1905, Percy also took on his elders, this time the leader of his own G.O.P. city committee, Colonel Frederick Hale, over a bill to change Portland's form of city government. By introducing a bill to end Portland's twin chambers of aldermen and a council, Percy was pursuing his father's long-term agenda. A single body composed of eighteen aldermen would result if the act passed. Hale complained about the lack of a referendum vote for the citizens of Portland. Percy, perhaps realizing that in a referendum the idea would be turned down, shot back that five of the seven house members from Portland were against a referendum. Hale asked for a roll call. In a lopsided vote of 103-28, the brash young freshman saw his bill get trounced.

But he was a quick learner. Offering a compromise, an increase of the number of Aldermen to twenty-seven, he was able to revive the measure.

This local dog and cat fight was hardly one to be memorialized. But sitting in the legislature that session was a sardonic Democrat named William R. Pattangall, a journalist who wielded one of the most acid pens in Maine political history. In his classic book, *The Meddybemps Letters and Maine's Hall of Fame*, "Patt" Pattangall satirically roasted both Percy

Baxter and Colonel Hale with an almost Swiftian use of over-statement.

> He [Hale] took a strong stand for temperance, voting promptly against resubmission and all that kind of nonsense and when he joined in debate he picked out such opportunities as were presented to tackle Percy Baxter or some other innocuous subject, instead of going up against the real debaters of the House, which showed good judgment. A debate between Colonel Hale and the Baxter boy was a great drawing card in Augusta in 1905. Nothing like it has been seen there since....
>
> But those Hale-Baxter debates were unique.... They were truly great. No one who heard one of them could ever forget it. Baxter usually opened.... Meanwhile all eyes would be turned toward Hale. Not that the assembled populace did not listen to Baxter. They did. They could not help it. He has a rare gift of eloquence and a way of speaking that would move almost any audience. In fact, had it not been that those Augusta audiences had their minds fixed on hearing Hale, Percy would have moved them. As it was they stayed.
>
> The topics selected for these great contests of oratory, argument and tact were always important. Whether the ward lines of Portland should be changed without first submitting the matter to a vote of the people, for instance, or whether the voting booths in cities over 40,000 inhabitants should be furnished with doors which swung from the outside in, or from the inside out, or something like that.
>
> With such great issues at stake even ordinary men speak well, but these were not ordinary men....
>
> Of course when the vote was taken, Hale always won.[3]

The *resubmission* Pattangall mentioned referred to Maine's Prohibition statute, which the "wet" Democrats had been trying to "resubmit" to the people for decades. Stymieing another vote was a sacred principle of the Republicans, who were all "dries." Here, Percy had absolutely no problem sticking with his party and by a 101-29 count, resubmission was crushed in the house in 1905.

With the end of his first legislative term, the young lawmaker had to feel confident about his re-election, which would take place in 1906. He must have been in a heady mood. His father, with his help, had already been easily re-elected to another one-year term as mayor. On his own, Percy had at least begun the process of making a name for himself and impressing the powers that be. The Republican leaders, in fact, had made him a monitor, or vote counter, a responsible position usually reserved for veterans. He had served on a fairly prestigious committee and had not been bashful about introducing legislation, even controversial bills. Percy Baxter was a "comer." That was evident.

The first indication that things might turn sour surfaced during James Phinney's next re-election campaign. Running for the 1906 term, he went before the voters in December 1905. His opponent was the same person he had defeated without any trouble the previous year—the Harvard-educated young Democratic lawyer Nathan Clifford, who had been the defense attorney in the Ward 1 vote scandal trial. Clifford was the grandson of one of Maine's most illustrious politicians of the pre-Civil War era, when Democrats were as much in control of the state as the Republicans were afterward. His august ancestor, another Nathan Clifford, had been President James Polk's attorney-general and then chief justice of the United States.

It was not simply that young Clifford seemed more animated than he had been in his first try against James Phinney. The elder Baxter had committed a political faux pas that came back to haunt him in the delayed fashion that sometimes happens and galvanizes campaigns.

The problem was an article he had written almost two years earlier for a Portland Board of Trade publication. Entitled "Something About Parks," the piece had promoted his green-belt vision for Portland and caused little stir. Then, someone in Clifford's camp must have re-read it carefully and come across certain incendiary phrases that could be turned against the incumbent mayor.

James Phinney's impolitic pitch was that Portland, through its parks, should become a "residential city" and forget about being a "manufacturing city."

Strange words from a man who had made his fortune by establishing a world-class canning company in Portland.

Yet here he was, stating baldly: "Portland can never be a large manufacturing city and we should not desire it."[4]

Worse, he immediately added:

What advantage can be derived from an ignorant foreign population which every manufacturing city attracts to it?[5]

And he compounded this by excoriating:

...the anarchy and strife and bloodshed which result from gathering together large numbers of ignorant men in towns where manufacturing enterprises predominate.[6]

So he was open not only to attacks as being a hypocrite and a bigot, but also anti-business.

The *Argus* gleefully editorialized: "Mayor Baxter has only cold comfort for the businessmen of Portland.... Up with the boulevard and down with manufacturing industries is Baxter's program."

The newspaper also ran its own unsigned huge ad, asking caustically:

WOULD MAYOR BAXTER
DRIVE OUT OF PORTLAND
The Portland Company
The Thomas Laughlin Company
The Portland Star Match Company
The Ayer, Houston Company
The Mecquier and Jones Company
The Portland Stove Foundry Company
and others, because they make noise
and dirt, and their workmen are
obliged to wear overalls?

Since the 1840s, Portland had received a large influx of Irish Catholic immigrants and they had become (and still are) a sizable voting bloc in the city. James Phinney's words about "foreign elements" were turned against him by a man named O'Brien.

Another negative issue was the alleged condition of the city's streets. It was claimed by Clifford that $200,000 had been appropriated to clean them but that the money had gone to James Phinney's pet boulevard project. Finally, there was Percy. Nepotism was an easy charge to make against the six-term mayor seeking his seventh term and the *Argus* did it in the lampooning country bumpkin voice so often used then for political satire:

He also says he don't want to serve but one term more and then give the rest of the terms to his son. He must think he is, before Abraham was....

The day after the election, the *Argus* ran its banner headline: CLIFFORD, THE NEXT MAYOR.

He had beaten James Phinney by 212 votes.

In the same issue of the paper, the Democrats gloated in a parody of the poem, "The Night Before Christmas," and also took a poke at Percy's future while they were at it.

Twas the night after election and all through the town,
Not a Baxterite stirring, that crowd was undone.
The City Hall stockings, done up with great care
In the hope of the graft they hoped would be there
Are moth gnawed and tattered, empty and bare
Visions of sugar plums danced in their heads.
But the days of their plundering are numbered instead.
Percy can enjoy a political nap
For a double disaster his plans did entrap...
The Boulevard tricksters will stay down and out
"We must have cleaner streets" was Portlanders' shout.[7]

James Phinney's immediate comment in his journal was: "I pitied Percy more than anything else. I would not care myself much...."[8] Once more, his son had been his campaign manager and no doubt had worked his heart out. So there had to be some excuses and James Phinney went on to indict "the largest use of money ever known in any campaign in this city,"[9] alleging that much of it came from Boston liquor dealers who paid $5 a vote. "What are we coming to if our elections are to be controlled by money?"[10] was his modern-sounding plaint. A week later, relaxed and seemingly indifferent, he was planning a trip to Egypt. But he never ran for political office again.

Some internal Republican politics may have been at work, as well. From the start of his career, James Phinney had run afoul of several powerful G.O.P. figures in Portland. Prominent among them were George P. Westcott, treasurer of the Portland Water Company, and Colonel Frederick Dow, son of the nationally famous General Neal Dow, who had created the Prohibition movement, both in Maine and the United States. James Phinney's initial tiff with Westcott had come during his first term as mayor over the seemingly trivial question of consolidating the offices of street commissioner and city engineer. James Phinney, an ardent Prohibitionist himself, believed that the street commissioner's office contained a "rum shop," from which Democratic ward heelers had been dispensing liquor to voters on election day. For reasons of his own, Wescott did not want to see a consolidated "public works commission," nor did Alderman Charles Randall, the man later enlisted to run against James Phinney in a primary and defeat him. The fight with Dow did not concern liquor but James Phinney's support for Thomas Brackett Reed against Dow in the battle for a congressional nomination. Ironically, the liquor question *was* used against James Phinney in subsequent elections—a claim that he wasn't enforcing the laws strenuously enough—but it was a charge that didn't stick.

His ill-considered remarks about manufacturing, of course, made a juicier target and were combined with his promotion of the "Boulevard" to present him as an elitist, out of touch with the common man. It was said that only those who could afford a horse and carriage would have the ability to build a home on the improved (and thus expensive) residential land that would be developed on the far shore of the Back Cove.[11] James Phinney was fond of saying that "the fine sheet of water" resulting from the dammed-up tidal flow would be ideal for "regattas" and for "sailing yachts and steam launches," without consciously realizing how much he seemed to be promoting a *playground for the rich*. His plans for widening residential streets in Portland, copying Boston's Commonwealth Avenue, with esplanades, open spaces, statuary, shrubbery, etc., also seemed self-serving, particularly after he pushed through an order to improve his own street—Deering Street—against Alderman Randall's vehement objections.

By 1905, James Phinney had accomplished many of his improvements. Portland Street, as it ran by the Deering Oaks Park, had been enlarged. Trolley service had been established from Union Station, at the foot of Congress Street, into the central city. A continual roadway existed from the Western Promenade to Deering Oaks, and most of the property for the Boulevard had been acquired.

Seven years would elapse before James Phinney's pet project would once again be taken up by the city fathers. His political enemies—both Democrat and Republican—would be alive and well in the interim, and Percy and his political ambitions would also be in their gunsights.

Percy was on the ballot for re-election that following September, and although straight-ticket voting had helped him in 1904, in 1906 it killed him. The Democrats took all seven house seats in Portland (and most of Cumberland County, for that matter). The G.O.P. vote in Maine's largest cities dropped by more than 11,000. It was a political tidal wave. Cumberland County pundits attributed the sweep to Sheriff Pennell's popularity. But a statewide consensus laid the blame for the Republican losses on something called the "Sturgis Law."

Again, the past had come to haunt the present. The Sturgis Law, which had come out of the Legal Affairs Committee with Percy Baxter's enthusiastic endorsement, had been what many individualistic Maine people regarded as a draconian infringement of their privacy rights in its attempt to enforce Prohibition as vigorously as possible. "Sturgis Deputies" were authorized to sniff out private booze and frequently overstepped their bounds. The electorate decided to send those in power "a message."

At age thirty, Percy had thus experienced both sides of politics—the heady excitement of triumph and the pit-in-the-stomach pain of defeat. Would he, like his father, drop out of the public game altogether or did he still harbor inner ambitions, an as-yet formless "vision thing" that would drive him onward to a lengthy quest, not unlike his namesake, the naive young nobleman *Percival* seeking a knighthood at King Arthur's court?

---

[1] *Civilization Magazine*, October-November 1996.

[2] Legislative Record, 1905 Session; page 519.

[3] *The Meddybemps Letters and Maine Hall of Fame* by William R. Pattangall, Lewiston Journal Company, Lewiston, Maine, 1924; page 275.

[4] January 1904 article, *Journal of the Portland Board of Trade*.

[5] Ibid.

[6] Ibid.

[7] *Eastern Argus*, December 5, 1905; page 5.

[8] James Phinney Baxter, Journal #6; page 255.

[9] Ibid.

[10] Ibid.

[11] In 1885, the separate town of Deering, which contained the far shore of Back Cove, was annexed to the city of Portland through a bill passed by the Maine Legislature.

JAMES PHINNEY'S LIBRARY IN THE FAMILY HOME AT
61 DEERING STREET.

CHAPTER **6**

The Historian

PERCY BAXTER ONCE WROTE that his father hoped to be remembered above all as an *historian*. "His political and business successes were to him as nothing in comparison with those in connection with his historical work" were the sentiments expressed in *Just Maine Folks*, published by the Maine Writers Research Club.[1] Presumably James Phinney's additional accomplishments as philanthropist, poet, and even painter of landscapes and animals, were also to be subordinated to his preoccupation with the past. "He loved the State of Maine," Percy went on, "and its history was as familiar to him as is the alphabet to most people."[2]

It is probably just as well that his penchant for writing developed mostly on the non-fiction side. His poetry and his one attempt at satirical drama (*The History of a Ring*) revealed a talent considerably less well-honed than his extraordinary capability for wide-ranging factual research and its incorporation into clear, declarative English sentences.

His three self-published works of poetry are hard to date—that is to say, when the poems were actually penned, not necessarily published. Indeed, the last of them, copyright 1902, seems like the earliest since it contains a memoir of his childhood in Portland. Entitled *Two Rhymes*, it contains exactly that—a pair of verses, one called "The First Parish Vane" and the other "All In Gools." It was the latter, dedicated to "George and Ed, my early schoolmates," that in awkward couplets paid homage to Master Jackson, the stern but kind schoolteacher of his pre-adolescent years, and reminisced about playing mumble peg, tag, Jackstones, and ball in Deering Oaks, the city's central municipal park. Every refrain ends with the children's slang cry of "all in gools," terminating whatever game they're playing. The other poem is a fairly mawkish tribute to Portland's past, based on incidents and personages in its history and kept together by the image of the weathervane atop the spire of the First Parish Congregationalist Church, where James Phinney worshipped.

Another Portland landmark was the focus of a longer single poem he published eleven years previously. "The Observatory" was about a tower-like structure of that same name, still located on Munjoy Hill, the eastern anchor of the neck of land on which the heart of the city is located. In the poem, James Phinney has taken his grandson to see it. The illustrated booklet in which he published the lengthy ode was dated 1893 and, curiously enough, by that date, he did not have a grandson—only three granddaughters, two born to Hartley and one to Clinton (whose wife died in childbirth). His fictional idea of a little boy's speech seems stilted, with the rhyme, at times, laughably stretched. Apropos of the tall building, the child asks:

Did bad men build it
so very high
That they might climb
to the sky thereby
And were they punished?
and how? and why?
Grandpapa?
Shipmasters, he is told, built it.
"They built it so that their ships might be
Espied far off upon the sea
Returning from voyages long and dree [sic]
Grandson mine.

Then, James Phinney continues in an historic mode with well-known events from the history of Portland, like the city's destruction by bombardment during the Revolution due to the wrath of British Royal Navy Captain Henry Mowatt and the epic naval battle off the Maine coast during the War of 1812 between the *Boxer* and the *Enterprise*, which was observed from Munjoy Hill—a fight in which both captains were killed and brought ashore to be buried in a cemetery close by the Observatory. A lesser known incident related by the grandfather was the wild ride of Indian chief Mogg Hegon's son, tied to "Brackett's horse" and sent to his death, a fate likened by the narrator to that of Mazeppa, a Ukrainian hero whose romantic life and sorrowful end were immortalized in a poem by Lord Byron. Perhaps in imitation of such tragic style, James Phinney finishes his tale with the story of a local girl who stood on Munjoy Hill awaiting her sailor lover.

And so for long years till her brain was
quite turned
And her long hair was white and her eye
wildly burned

And at last the foul title of witch she had
earned
    Grandson mine
And the boys hooted after her, "coot!"

This particular literary effort of his, James Phinney made it a point to tell his contemporaries, was well received and sold well.

Whether this could be said of his first effort as a bard, published in 1884 and called "Idylls of the Year," has not been recorded. His schemata, somewhat in epic form, was to construct a poem for each month, interspersed with others, reflecting a related theme: i.e., "January," "The Alchemist," "February," "Ebb," "March," "Flood," "April," "The Flight North," etc.

    Flood
Out from the east, o sea!
Dawn kisses still aglow
Upon thy breasts of snow
Thou flowest unto me.
They come—a gallant fleet
Bound home from Orient ports,
Laden with richest sorts
Of merchandise, I weet.
For all my buoyant hopes
Are ships with every thread
Of snowy canvas spread—
Slant masts and straining ropes....

The History of a Ring, already mentioned, was printed in 1877. The alleged author was "One of the Governor's Wards," which, in the dramatis personae, James Phinney identified as "citizens of Portland." It was pretty silly stuff.

The villain was Tom of the Portland and Coal-Kiln Corner Railroad Corporation who wants "to build a railroad to SOMEBODY'S Land" and wheedles his uncle, the governor, into giving him grants of money but never builds the line, even after pocketing more than $1 million. James Phinney would obviously never be a Pattangall in wit, yet his moral would later be reflected and even echoed publicly by Percy in the story he frequently cited of a giveaway of state land to a railroad never constructed in the northern part of Maine.

In the same way that the chronology of his fictional works remains obscure, it is difficult to follow the trail of his far more voluminous historical writings. The dates he worked on them do not necessarily correspond to the publication dates. We know that in 1885-86, he was in England, collecting the stupendous research base of primary documents that in twenty-one volumes still are housed in the Maine Room of the State Library in Augusta. While on that same trip, he also visited France, where he unearthed Gallic documents relating to his interests and had them copied at his expense. He had studied the French language and knew it well enough not only to understand what he was reading but to translate passages for books and articles he wrote that told of the French experience in North America and Maine.

As an aside in this regard, in the "Baxter Collection" of documents in the Maine State Library in Augusta, there is a thin, bound pamphlet that explains why it has only twenty thick volumes, not twenty-one. A 1924 letter to Percy from the Reverend Everett S. Stackpole of West Bath explains the mystery. It referred to a communication Stackpole, himself an amateur historian, had received from a George W. Chamberlain of Malden, Massachusetts, who had done genealogical work for James Phinney. What Chamberlain described was a meeting with James Phinney in 1919 or 1920 in Boston and the tale of woe the Maine historian had poured out: how he had been working a few nights previously on the "Mascarene Papers," the personal letters of Jean-Paul Mascarene, a French Protestant who became a British officer and eventually governor of Nova Scotia during the French and Indian Wars. These documents had been painstakingly gathered in Paris by James Phinney and translated by a woman who had since died. Forgetting to put them away in his safe before he left the office, James Phinney returned the next morning to find that they had been destroyed by fire. Nor could they be reproduced because there was no one in Halifax to translate them again at the time.

Two of his important works that did employ French sources were *The Pioneers of New France in New England* and *A Memoir of Jacques Cartier*. The latter has been described as a book (it's over four hundred pages long) "that illustrates Baxter's depth and thoroughness in...scholarly study."[3] The bibliography, alone, is thirty-five pages. Published in 1906, jointly in New York City and London by Dodd, Mead and Company and Henry Stevens, Son, and Stiles, it combines, as do many of his works, his own historical narratives plus original documents that had never before been printed. James Phinney, in the preface of his work on Cartier, cites his "interest in French history and especially in that part of it relating to the North American continent" and states that he has always wanted to do an English translation of the *Relation Originale du Voyage de Jacques Cartier au Canada en 1534*. Through Henry Vignaud, the assistant secretary of the American legation in Paris, he was able to procure a photographic copy of the manuscript, which had been discovered at the *Bibliotheque Imperiale* in 1867. He then adds that after translating the story of Cartier's first voyage, he wanted to translate the account of "the second and most important of Cartier's voyages," published in 1545 under the title of *Bref Recit*. Again, a manuscript was found in the French national library.

In amassing his huge bibliography, he also contacted libraries in other parts of France, as well as in Russia, Sweden, Germany, Holland, and Spain.

This wide-ranging search for knowledge—and on a dizzying variety of subjects—is the most outstanding impression that James Phinney imparts of himself to the reader. He is literally everywhere. After remarking that the French neglect the history of Canada, he proceeds, himself, to dip into French history—particularly that of St. Malo, the port in Brittany from which Cartier, a native mariner of the region, sailed to discover the Gulf of the St. Lawrence and much of eastern Canada more than eighty-five years before the Pilgrims came to New England. This background and that of the three voyages Cartier undertook form the essence of a seventy-page narrative by James Phinney that opens the book. It is followed by the translated manuscript of the first voyage, to which James Phinney has appended numerous notations (as he does, too, for the second and third voyage manuscripts), many of them fascinating and all of them quite erudite. For example, when Cartier refers to birds that he says "are very bad to attack for they bite like dogs and are called *margaulx*," Baxter is able to identify them as gannets (*sula bassana*) and report that they still "bite like dogs" when intruded upon. Other birds mentioned with French names by the explorer are recognized by James Phinney to be murres (*genus uria*) and razorbills (*alca torda*). The author has also included an extensive note on the now extinct great auk (*alca impennis*), large as a goose and just as good eating because Cartier's crews salted down four to five butts for each ship besides what they would eat fresh.

In his preface, James Phinney states that he had to study

the animal and plant life and "ethnological and lingual pecu-liarities of the savage peoples" inhabiting Canada. Yet despite his undoubtedly natural use of a pejorative term to describe Native Canadians, he is not loathe to condemn the genocidal instincts of the Europeans toward the Indians. "Their con-duct," he writes, "sinks them far below the level of savages," a "kind of barbarity that continued for 200 years," and he openly expresses his sympathy for the Beothuks, so-called "Red Paint Indians," exterminated in the north, "whose his-tory forms one of the most pathetic pages of the history of Newfoundland."

He read extensively from whatever sources were avail-able to him: Audubon's *Ornithological Biography*, (Edinburgh, 1838) for his knowledge of birds; John Josselyn, the earliest of Maine's naturalists; and George Catlin and Henry Schoolcraft, artist and chronicler respectively of American Indians. (In fact, it was the latter's ethnographic studies that were used by James Phinney's fellow Portlander, Henry Wadsworth Longfellow, in composing his epic poem, "Hiawatha.") On the linguistics side, examples of the Algonquian language of "the kingdoms of Hochelaga (Montreal) and Canada, or New France" are included in the opus. It may have raised a few eyebrows that a Victorian like James Phinney left in the words for male and female genitals and for pubic hair.

A most interesting feature of the Cartier book is the set of collateral documents that follow the reproduction of British publisher Richard Hakluyt's account of Cartier's third voyage in 1540. Five of these collateral documents were from Spanish archives, and James Phinney relates: "I had them translated by Mr. E. De Garmo from the original Spanish transcripts." They include the report of a spy sent by the Spanish Council of the Indies to France "to find out about the fleets being fitted out" in Samalo de Lila (St. Malo de l'Isle). The Council of the Indies, which controlled all of Spain's overseas activities, wanted to stop these "French corsairs" but admitted they didn't have the 150,000 ducats they figured it would cost.

An itinerary of Cartier's voyages, maps (some reproduced from James Phinney's private collection), and a genealogy of the Cartier family complete this exhaustive historical study.

Less objective and, indeed, almost a polemical anti-French broadside is James Phinney's earlier (and perhaps less mature) book, *The Pioneers of New France in New England*. It appeared in 1894 and was published by Joel Munsell and Sons, Albany, New York. The title page describes him as the author of *George Cleeve of Casco Bay and His Times*, *The British Invasion From The North*, *Sir Ferdinando Gorges and His Province of Maine*, and *Christopher Levett*.

The title, itself, is somewhat of a misnomer. His intent was not, as in the Cartier memoir, to present a balanced study of a French effort to explore North America. Rather, it was an attack on the French Jesuits who came to the New World, settled among the natives, and converted them to Catholicism. James Phinney acknowledges in his preface that a question he is examining is the "participation of many of the Jesuit missionaries in the cruel attempts of the French to ruin the settlements in New England." His especial target is Father Sebastian Rasle (Baxter calls him Rale) who lived with the Kennebec Indian tribe in what is now Norridgewock or Madison, Maine. In 1724, he was shot dead during a raid on the village by rangers from the Kittery-York area of southern Maine, responding belatedly to the 1692 massacre of settlers in York, which they blamed on Rasle.

Thus, James Phinney entered a controversy that is still continuing today. Was Father Rasle a devil or a martyred saint? As a staunch Anglo-Saxon partisan, the author naturally chose the former designation. "We cannot regard Rale as a martyr; indeed it is hard to understand how men even of his own order can so regard him." He goes on to relate that when Rasle was blasted at point blank range by the York ranger Richard Jacques in his cabin, lying on the bed was a fourteen-year-old English captive boy surnamed Mitchell who had been shot through the thigh and stabbed, allegedly by the Jesuit priest. One of the commanders of the raid, Captain Jeremiah Moulton, was absolutely furious with Jacques for killing Rasle because they had wanted to take him alive for a show trial in Boston. The French later complained that Rasle's body had been mutilated, but the English responded that it was well known he had suffered fractures in both legs during a fall and neither had healed right. Rasle's death could also be claimed by the English as just retribution for the killing of a Protestant minister at the York massacre, the Reverend Mr. Dummer, but they were hard put to defend the scalping of a man of God. Even James Phinney, for all his English chauvinism, had to admit he couldn't understand "how our forefathers could have complacently regarded the exhibition of his scalp in the streets of Boston."

Although it must have been grating to him, James Phinney did include in the book a photograph of a monument to Rasle that exists to this day at the site of the attack on the banks of the Kennebec River. But his tone in regard to the Jesuit is never even neutral, as epitomized in this utterly disdainful yet well-written description of why Rasle was so well accepted by the Indians with whom he lived.

> ...by persistent intercourse with the savages in their smoky wigwams, subjected to their rude gibes and disgusting habits of life, he finally acquired facility in utter-

ing their harsh gutturals and threading the intricacies of their bewildering idioms.[4]

Also, more than a century and a half after the fact, he used his book to continue an argument over who owned the land in Maine. An historical exchange reported by James Phinney makes the point. Meeting with local tribes at Georgetown on Arrowsic Island in 1717, Governor Samuel Shute of Massachusetts presses his contention that (in Baxter's words), "the savages must desist from pretensions to lands belonging by purchase to the English." Chief Wiwurna is quoted as replying that the Indians "embrace the English who come to settle on our lands." Shute objects to the use of the word *our*. His claim is that the English legally bought the land from them and their ancestors. James Phinney likewise makes reference to his discovery in England of "31 papers...in proof of the right of the Crown of Great Britain to the lands between New England and Nova Scotia and of several depredations committed by the French and Indians between 1720 and June 1725."

The central core of James Phinney's historical interest was the Anglo-Saxon settlement of Maine and New England; the French element was merely a framework.

James Phinney did not produce a concentrated or a comprehensive set of writings. Nor did it always stay within the bounds of the New World, evidenced by his address to the Maine Historical Society on January 25, 1908, commemorating the one-thousandth anniversary of the death of King Alfred, "from whose loins we sprang," he reminded his anglophile audience.

James Phinney Baxter was president of the Maine Historical Society for thirty years, and the amazing output of his pen was consumed in good measure by the seemingly inexhaustible flow of "papers" that he delivered before this body on subjects pertaining to Maine's past. He belonged to and spoke before other societies, as well. For thirty-nine years, he was a member of the New England Historical and Genealogical Register and for the last twenty of them was its leader. In 1890, the Prince Society of Boston invited him to present the results of his pioneer research on the historical figure often referred to as the "father of Maine," the late sixteenth and early seventeenth-century nobleman soldier, Sir Ferdinando Gorges, who played a key role in English colonization efforts throughout North America.

JAMES PHINNEY AND HIS FELLOW MEMBERS OF THE MAINE HISTORICAL SOCIETY OFTEN TOOK "FIELD DAYS"—OVERNIGHT TRIPS TO HISTORIC SITES WITHIN THE STATE. HERE, THEY ARE ON THEIR WAY TO STONINGTON-DEER ISLE.

Sir Ferdinando Gorges and His Province of Maine was also published by the Prince Society. In the introduction, James Phinney explains that one of the reasons he went to England in the summer of 1885 was to unearth material on Sir Ferdinando. It had been believed until then that no such material existed except for some papers in the British Museum on the Essex Rebellion, in which Gorges was briefly implicated. James Phinney writes that he began his search in the British Museum "where I examined every manuscript and every printed book of the 16th and 17th centuries relating in any way to America...."[5] Then, he went to the Office of Public Records and looked at all official correspondence and documents relating to colonial and state affairs. Finding material, he was then led to other locations, such as Plymouth, Bristol, Wraxall, Ashton, Arundel House, etc., and individuals who could help him, such as the Reverend Frederick Browne of Beckingham, Kent, the Marquis of Salisbury, Anthony Gibbs the owner of Charlton Manor, etc. Amid the two hundred manuscripts containing the correspondence of Sir Robert Cecil, he found letters signed by Sir Ferdinando Gorges. His indefatigable sleuthing thus brought to light an absolutely essential foundation stone to any understanding of Maine's origin.

A number of James Phinney's monographs were developed for excursions he organized to bring the Maine Historical Society to important historic sites in Maine. These "field days" followed a pattern and must have required considerable advance planning. On a trip to Fryeburg, for instance, the society members were met by a local notable, the Honorable George B. Barrows, who took them to his home to see his library and collection of autographed documents, then to the registry of deeds to inspect deeds in the handwriting of Daniel Webster (who had been a schoolteacher in the town), then lunch at the Oxford House, then by horse and carriage to Lovewell's Pond, site of a famous battle of the French and Indian wars, and finally to a meeting at the Congregational church where James Phinney read a paper on Captain John Lovewell and his fatal clash with the Pequacket Indians.

During this trip, note was taken of the fact that Eastman Johnson, the famous portraitist who had painted James Phinney's own children, was a native of nearby Lovell.

A "field day" in Kittery followed a similar pattern. The Maine Historical Society group led by James Phinney left Portland by train at 9 A.M. and arrived at Kittery Point two and a half hours later. Their stay was at the Champernowne Hotel, Horace Mitchell proprietor, where they could look across the Piscataqua River to Newcastle, New Hampshire, and seaward to the Isles of Shoals. There was considerable concentration on the illustrious Pepperrell family of Kittery Point and visits to structures relating to them, some still standing such as the Pepperrell Mansion, the Lady Pepperrell House, the tomb of Colonel William Pepperrell, the founder of the dynasty, and other places since demolished, such as Sparhawk Hall, built for Sir William Pepperrell's daughter Betsy and her husband Nathaniel Sparhawk and the home erected by Sir William for his son Andrew, who died at a young age. James Phinney's speech that evening was about the Pepperrells and the Piscataqua region, with an interesting allusion to William Screven, pastor of the earliest Baptist church formed in Maine, who, with his parishioners, was subsequently driven out to South Carolina, so violent were the feelings of the local Congregationalists against this new religion.

The next day, the Maine Historical Society outing members left for New Hampshire to visit historic sites in Portsmouth, before entraining to return to Portland.

When not in the field, the society held its regular meetings in Portland and a regular feature was a paper delivered by James Phinney. His subjects covered a wide range, displaying his catholic interests and, in several instances, unabashedly and during a period long before "consciousness-raising" in the United States, revealing a strong degree of prejudice toward Maine's native Indian population. His paper, "The Abnakis and their Ethnic Relations," read before the Society on March 27, 1890, indeed begins with a contrast between the civilized Aztecs of Mexico and the Abnakis of New England, "clothed with the skins of savage beasts to which they seemed akin."

In discussing Native Americans (and Native Canadians), the word "savage" fell trippingly from his pen. And there were often pejorative asides of a personal belief of his, as stated in these passages:

> ...on the other hand, the English regarded the savages with abhorrence. Mather denominated them wolves with men's brains, *which was by no means a wholly wrong description of them.*
>
> It was difficult for a Puritan to believe that they possessed enough spirituality to enable them to become real Christians, *and their belief was not groundless.*

No noble red men roamed New England's forests in James Phinney's eyes. The best he would begrudge the Abnaki was that they had certain useful arts, were gentler and more docile than the Iroquois, and exhibited sexual restraint. As he wrote, "perhaps the most favorable thing to be recorded in favor of the Abnaki warrior is the fact that no female prisoner ever had occasion to complain of him in this respect."[6]

Today, sentiments such as those expressed so readily by James Phinney come under the rubric of "racism." A century ago, the terrible lessons of the end result of similar thinking, as expressed by Naziism and the Holocaust, had not been made manifest to the world. Even the very scientific biological notion of race was confused with ethnicity. Nowhere was James Phinney's Anglo-Saxon chauvinism more on display than in another of his duties as a local historian of note: delivering an address on a public occasion—in this instance the centennial celebration of the adoption of the U.S. Constitution. Speaking at the Portland City Hall, James Phinney titled his talk "A Period of Peril."

The *peril* is never specifically enumerated, but may be guessed at in the use of the word, itself, so often associated with the word yellow to designate the perceived challenge of the so-called Asiatic hordes. James Phinney commences his WASP boosterism by noting that all of the North American continent, except Mexico:

> ...is in the possession of the Anglo-Saxon race; a race whose influence in the near future will control the world. This race is animated by ideas, which make it invincible, and the chief of these are the ideas of civil liberty and the universal brotherhood of man, the latter of which is the underlying principle of Christianity. As these ideas have proved to be the germs of all true progress in the past, this race, which is their exponent, must exercise a controlling influence upon the world's future."
>
> Two centuries ago, this race numbered but about five millions; today it numbers more than one hundred millions, and is increasing with a remarkable rapidity. Yet its power is not in numbers, but in its indomitable spirit; for although it comprises but a fifteenth of the world's population, it rules one-third of the globe and about that proportion of its inhabitants.[7]

James Phinney next asks: "What relation to this wonderful race do the people of the United States sustain?"

His conclusion, based on the growing number of Americans, is that the U.S. is destined to be the center of Anglo-Saxon influence—an influence that will inspire *men of every race* to make the best and highest use of all powers, "not only for the individual, but for the common weal" and further, that the Anglo-Saxons had been entrusted with "the ark of Christian civilization" and the establishment of God's kingdom upon the earth.

Given the milieu—both societal and mental—in which he lived, it is hardly surprising that James Phinney would hold these views. His membership in organizations such as the American Antiquarian Society, the Colonial Society of Massachusetts, the Old Colony Historical Society, state historical societies in Maine, Massachusetts, and Rhode Island, plus institutions such as the Portland Club (a Republican political club), kept him in a fairly rarefied atmosphere that the melting pot of American life barely reached. It is only a bit surprising that his *imperialist* hopes for the Anglo-Saxon race did not put him at odds with his favorite local politician, Congressman Thomas Brackett Reed, who was notoriously *anti-imperialist*. But, then again, Reed's objections to the U.S. acquisition of the Philippines, were based in part on his unwillingness to have the country absorb additional quantities of "little brown men."

It had been a stated intention of James Phinney Baxter, historian, not only to supplement William Willis's pioneering history of Portland but also to produce an overall history of Maine. But his desires on this score were never fulfilled, and perhaps the fault was strictly his own. He became engrossed in an enormously time- and mind-consuming project that was not really historical, although it commanded all of his ability and attention as a researcher and involved him in an exhaustive search of the Elizabethan and early Stuart periods in England.

In his own mind, it was a "literary" work and was to make his reputation in the literary arena. His masterpiece of close to 700 pages of closely reasoned and densely researched exposition on a single theme was entitled: *The Greatest of Literary Problems, The Authorship of the Shakespeare Works.* Argued *ad nauseam*, with the concentrated guile of the lawyer he might once have become, was the conviction that Sir Francis Bacon was the true author of the writings attributed to William Shakespeare.

James Phinney actually went even further and ascribed to Bacon the authorship of works by other noted Elizabethan writers, such as Christopher Marlowe, Robert Greene, James Peele and even the epic poem, "The Faerie Queene" of Edmund Spenser.

Moreover, according to James Phinney, the nobleman Francis Bacon, Viscount St. Albans, Baron Verulam of Verulam, was, in actuality, the secret illegitimate son of Queen Elizabeth and Lord Robert Dudley, Earl of Leicester. Also allegedly born of this illicit union was Robert Devereaux, Earl of Essex, the Queen's ill-fated favorite who was eventually executed for treason.

Devereaux and Bacon, as the story goes, were farmed out to different discrete noble couples to be raised; in Bacon's case, to Sir Nicholas Bacon and Lady Bacon of Kent, who were devoted Puritans. After studying at Trinity College, Cambridge, young Francis spent time as part of an English mission to the court of Henri III of France, where he reputedly became enamored of Margaret of Valois, later a Queen of France. Then, back in England, he passed the bar and entered Parliament at the age of twenty-four.

With exquisite irony (if the story of his birth is true), Queen Elizabeth forced him to be the crown's prosecutor in the trial of Devereaux, who was also his personal friend as well as his supposed brother. Afterward, under James I, Bacon held important posts: as solicitor-general, attorney-general, lord chancellor and privy councilor. Ultimately, a conspiracy of the Duke of Buckingham forced him from office on a trumped-up charge of bribery and he devoted the rest of his life to his intellectual and scientific pursuits. As a philosopher, Bacon is known for his promotion of the inductive thinking method of modern science in opposition to the dogmatic a priori rigidity of medieval scholasticism. His *Essays* are his most noted writings, distinguished by his literary style and striking observations, and *The New Atlantis*, published posthumously in 1627, his most enduring work. It is a utopian tale in which science is the hero and the antidote for human ills, and it served as an inspiration for the founding of the Royal Society.

Early in his book, James Phinney sets out his premise, having established William Shakespeare to be a country boy of doubtful reputation, a convicted poacher, and a hell-raiser of little or no formal education. Consequently, he can then state:

> It really seems too much to ask us to believe that a man past his majority, bred to the rudest of trades, and absolutely ignorant of books, who was according to tradition a frequenter of taverns, and a participator in drinking bouts...would apply himself to the study of literature, law, medicine, science, philosophy, languages....[8]

Much of what follows is merely a repetition, in innumerable forms, of the same argument. Several specifics, amid this torrent of backup, are striking:

1) That in *Henry VI*, there is a dialogue between Joan of Arc and the Duke of Burgundy, in which the Maid of Orleans convinces the Duke to desert the English cause and rally to

the banner of France. James Phinney's point is that until 1780, it was not publicly known that this encounter was based on historic fact and that "it would seem impossible for the actor to know of this secret history, but to Bacon, student and poet at the French court, it would strongly impress and leave its impress upon his sensitive memory."[9]

2) That shortly before the appearance of *The Merchant of Venice*, Francis Bacon was imprisoned for debt by one Sympson, a Jew of Lombard Street, and was rescued by his older brother Anthony, who paid to have him released from jail. It is no coincidence, James Phinney thinks, that in the play attributed to Shakespeare, Antonio comes to the rescue of Bassano who is being prosecuted for debt by Shylock.

3) That Yoricke in *Hamlet* is based on the real-life personage of John Heywood, Court Jester to King Henry VIII, who was a friend of Bacon's father, Sir Nicholas, and often stayed in their home when Bacon was a boy.

4) The famous "Bohemian coast" conundrum. In *The Winter's Tale*, Antigonus speaks of his ship's touching the ocean shore of Bohemia, an area in today's Czech Republic that is totally landlocked. The answer to the obvious question of how could Bohemia have a coastline is answered by the fact that in the fifteenth and sixteenth centuries, it was part of an empire that did reach the Adriatic Sea, an empire formed by a complicated series of marriages among the Hapsburgs. James Phinney's claim is that only a courtier like Bacon, "whose association with royalty and court life rendered it incumbent upon him to know the intimate history of the royal families of Europe" would have been aware of the extent of Bohemia, knowledge presumably unavailable to an obscure actor like William Shakespeare.

In venturing into these literary waters, James Phinney

could not entirely desert his penchant for explicating the past. He had to set the historic scene and he did so with some fine writing, as in this excerpt from his prologue:

> The action of our drama lies within the meagre compass of a half-century, between the meridian splendor of the last Tudor reign and the waning of that of the first Stuart, a period crowded with events of more real import to the English race than any other in its annals. It was an era of feudal splendor—emblazoned banners—plumes—purple and cloth of gold—the glint and clangor of steel—ruthless emblems of autocratic rule. It was one, too, of cruelty and corruption....[10]

And, in another passage, he comes close to one of his own true loves in history, the overseas saga of the English explorers, bringing Anglo-Saxon values to the rest of the world.

> Yet this epoch had its heroes—Drake, who through fire and blood encompassed the world; Gilbert, who sang his swan song amid tempest and gloom, triumphant in the thought that heaven was as near him as in his beloved Devonshire; Frobisher, who drove his frail keel through the ice-locked portals of Boreal seas; and scores of others, who, on sea and land, proved the invincible courage of the English heart....[11]

Still, overall, James Phinney had to be disappointed as well as exhausted by his labors. Despite his monumental, four-year-long effort, the "obscure actor" from Stratford remained unbudged as the author of Shakespeare's Works.

Although the *Portland Daily Press* (in which James Phinney had a large financial interest) declared that "in this book, Mr. Baxter has made his literary reputation," others were less kind. Perhaps best expressing the thoughts uppermost in the minds of interested Maine people were the comments of "The Saunterer," an unsigned column in the *Eastern Argus*. There was no attempt in this Democratic newspaper to ridicule their former political opponent for spending so much time and talent on such a seemingly quixotic literary quest. There was merely an almost plaintive note of regret as 'The Saunterer" said:

> While Mr. Baxter's contribution to the Bacon-Shakespeare controversy is a notable one, many of his friends would have been better satisfied if he had put his time and labor into the preparation of a History of Maine.

---

[1] *Just Maine Folks*, Maine Writers Research Club. Lewiston, Maine, 1924. This chapter was later published as a separate pamphlet titled "James Phinney Baxter, Historian, Portland, Maine, 1831-1921, A Short Biography, Written for the Maine Writers Research Club."

[2] Ibid.

[3] *Maine's Beloved Benefactor*, by Jane Veazie Nelson; page l3.

[4] *Pioneers of New France in New England*; page 36.

[5] *Sir Ferdinando Gorges and His Province of Maine*; page vi.

[6] "The Abnakis and Their Ethnic Relations," paper read to the Maine Historical Society, March 27, 1890.

[7] "A Period of Peril," Centennial Adoption of the U.S. Constitution, address by James Phinney Baxter, April 30, 1899.

[8] *The Greatest of Literary Problems*; page 51.

[9] Ibid.; page 491.

[10] Ibid.; page xix.

CHAPTER 7

Back In Politics

WHEN JAMES PHINNEY BAXTER voted on the statewide election day, September 10, 1906, he wrote in his journal that he was surprised to find the ward room "occupied by men mostly strangers to me." It was his first inkling of the Democratic tide that would sweep Percy from his state representative position and bring the Baxters their second defeat at the polls within a year. "I feel blue over Percy's defeat as he could have done good work this winter in the Legislature," the elder Baxter sorrowfully concluded.

Life went on, of course. Four days after the election, Percy took the afternoon train to New York to join his half-brother Hartley and sail home with him in Hartley's new yacht. This was the *Kanawha*, originally built for a founder of the Standard Oil Company, H. H. Rogers, and auctioned off by the U.S. government, which had commandeered her during the Spanish-American War. Hartley had bought the 150-foot luxury vessel for a rock-bottom bargain price of $10,000.

AFTER GRADUATE SCHOOL AND HIS DEFEAT AT THE POLLS IN
1906, PERCY LIVED AT HOME AND WORKED WITH HIS FATHER.
IN 1908, HE ENTERED POLITICS AGAIN AND WAS ELECTED TO
THE MAINE STATE SENATE.

116

But the question of a political future still hung over both Baxters. As a new mayoralty election neared in Portland, pressure mounted on James Phinney to run again. On November 1, his journal records:

> People are begging me to accept a nomination for mayor, but I must not think of it. The *Argus* is evidently alarmed fearing that I may do so, and is beginning its old time abuse of me.
>
> What a saint I should be if I was only a Democrat.[1]

Firm in his decision to avoid future political battles, he put his determination in writing to the Republican Mayoralty Convention, "declining to permit my name to be used as a candidate for nomination."

However, there was one public issue in which he still maintained a lively interest and, since it would come to a head in the next legislature, it perhaps underlay part of his regret that his son would not be there to do "good work." This was nothing less than a scheme he had helped promote in 1889 to move the state capital from Augusta to Portland, where it had been on a temporary basis from 1820 to 1832. In 1907, yet another—and final—attempt was made to move the capital (with James Phinney chairing the effort), which failed by a narrow margin and then faded into history after Augusta partisans were able to insert an amendment into the state constitution that the capital would remain where it was.

There is no indication that this issue had any bearing on Percy's decision to run for the state senate in 1908. Why the senate and not the house again? The obvious answer might be that Portland had become too Democratic and that it would be easier to get elected as a Republican by running at large in Cumberland County. And why was Percy running? Was it sheer ambition? Or had he already latched on to the one issue that he was to develop and solidly identify with his name for the rest of his career—the disposition of the state's water-power resources?

In the intervening two years between his defeat in 1906 and his victory in 1908, Percy lived at home, worked with his father (particularly on ferry transport matters), traveled, spent time at the family summer home on Mackworth Island (which was kept open all year), went sledding with his nephew James Phinney III (and was thrown off the sled), and, in general, led a pleasant life in the closeness of a large, lively family.

On June 9, 1908, James Phinney wrote in his journal: "Attended the County Convention in forenoon. Percival was nominated Senator." Then, he went for a drive with his wife Hetty and daughter Emily in one carriage and daughter Madeleine and her husband Fenton Tomlinson in another.

On September 14, 1908, the elder Baxter wrote: "Shortly after supper, I had a message from Percival that the Republicans had won and that he was elected Senator."

If it had indeed seemed less risky for Percy to run county-wide, his hunch paid off handsomely. All four G.O.P. senate candidates won in Cumberland County. That a branch of the Baxter family had been established in Brunswick by his half-brothers was a factor, too, plus his Bowdoin connection. Also elected on the same ticket with him was John E. Warren of Westbrook, whose family owned the S. D. Warren Paper Company. Percy and Jack Warren decided they would share rooms at the Augusta House once the session began in January 1909.

Although he had never served in the senate before and this was, in effect, his freshman term, Percy apparently felt that his previous service in the house entitled him to veteran's status. At least, he was bold enough to run for leadership and for no less a position than president of the senate. At the

Republican nominating caucus, the brash newcomer and another challenger were easily defeated by Senator Luere B. Deasy. "Patt" Pattangall, ever sarcastic, later wrote, "Disregarding Hastings' little strength and Baxter's great weakness, he (Deasy) became an eleventh hour candidate and won."[2] Yet despite his presumption in bucking tradition, Percy was not punished by being exiled to one of the lesser committees. He was named, instead, to the Judiciary Committee, which, if anything, had more prestige than the Legal Affairs Committee on which he'd served as a house member. And he went right into the thick of an all-out legislative battle by introducing a rather radical measure, "An Act to prohibit corporations from transmitting power beyond the confines of the State," that soon had him pitted against one of the corporate giants of Maine, the International Paper Company.

Teddy Roosevelt was no longer president of the United States, having ceded the G.O.P. nomination to William Howard Taft, whom the voters put in the White House in November, 1908. Teddy Roosevelt's influence on Percival Baxter is hard to assess. But it was Roosevelt, prodded to an extent by his Chief Forester Gifford Pinchot and by the naturalist John Muir, who had exposed the country to the concept of conservation. The idea that America's natural resources were no longer inexhaustible and needed to be harvested in a sustainable fashion was as new as it was controversial. The socialism of Karl Marx's philosophy had already become a force in the world, and opponents of Teddy Roosevelt's idea that America's natural resources belonged to its people were quick to try to link the two notions. Business—particularly big business—was not prepared to concede any limitations on what it considered its birthright to exploit.

In May 1908, Roosevelt galvanized the nation by holding a major conference at the White House on the subject of conservation. Not only were all of the U.S. governors invited but other notable citizens such as Andrew Carnegie, railroad magnate James J. Hill, labor leader John Mitchell and ex-presidential candidate William Jennings Bryan were on hand. *The New York Times* called it "...one of the most notable gatherings that has ever met to consider a great public question in that historic mansion."[3]

Maine sent a delegation headed by former Governor John F. Hill, Forest Commissioner Edward E. Ring, and Professor Austin Cary. All three were described by the Maine press as "strong advocates of proper restrictions upon the cutting of forest trees." Commissioner Ring's paper was printed in full in Maine. It included a discussion of the state's waterpowers. Also printed was Teddy Roosevelt's eloquent plea that the time had come "to inquire seriously what will happen when resources like the forests, coal, iron, oil, gas, etc., have been exhausted, when the soils have been still further impoverished and washed into the streams, polluting the rivers, denuding the fields, and obstructing navigation. These questions do not relate only to the next century or the next generation...." It was an event that Percival Baxter, with his love of nature and the outdoors, had to have followed.

Somewhat earlier, an effort had begun in nearby New Hampshire to set aside a portion of the White Mountains to be a "forest reserve" (known today as a national forest). Congressman John W. Weeks of Massachusetts was pushing a bill to use surplus funds from the "Western National Forests" to buy up the area, and the Society for the Protection of New Hampshire Forests was rallying public support. James Phinney was one of those in Maine who were interested. On November 13, 1906, his journal reports: "Attended a meeting of citizens to promote forest reservations in the White Mountains region." It was a region dear to him from his vacation stays in Jackson and North Conway and no doubt his feelings were known to his son.

Percy's no-export waterpower bill was aimed at a different kind of conservation, the fear that large companies would monopolize Maine's abundant water resources, sell the power out of state, and reap the benefits without a cent of profit remaining for the people of Maine. Although the bill ran into a buzz-saw of opposition, Baxter also had significant support, including that of Governor Bert T. Fernald. The opposition's main argument was signaled during the opening debate by Senator George E. Macomber of Kennebec County. He claimed the notion of prohibiting export of power from Maine was as silly as it would be to stop Aroostook County farmers from sending their spuds to other parts of the country. Echoing him was Percy's own roommate, John E. Warren, who added lumber and Poland Springs water to the mix and then called for the bill to be killed. But such homespun Maine logic failed to carry the day. His opponents may have had a good analogy, but Percy, playing on Downeast nationalism and frugality, had the votes.

A similar bill of his, also passed in that session, established an independent Water Power Commission whose task was to survey the state's waterpower potential and develop plans for its use in ways that would benefit all Maine people. Unlike its companion, it "went under the hammer"; that is, without a vote or discussion, with a single bang of a gavel indicating unanimous consent.

Even if the no-export of power legislation was forever afterward referred to as the Fernald Bill, in honor of the governor, everyone knew that Percy Baxter had taken the lead on waterpower. He had been gutsy—and successful—and his friend Jack Warren liked to tweak him, lest he get too swelled a head.

Referring to another of Percy's accomplishments, an omnibus bill on the National Guard that he safely steered through the legislative process as chairman of the Military Committee, Warren said teasingly on the floor of the senate:

> I understand that there has recently appeared along the coast of Maine a sea bird unknown before, which the naturalists have been unable to classify and for which they must find a new name; and they have decided to call it the Baxter bird, because it has such a big bill.[4]

A bright future had to be predicted for the young senator and yet, once again, the vagaries of politics stepped in and conditions beyond his control put a dent in his plans. Problems were developing within the Republican Party nationally and were felt in Maine even earlier than the final rupture in 1912 between Teddy Roosevelt, representing the Progressive wing, and his one-time protégé, William Howard Taft, representing the Old Guard. The "conservation" issue was one of the biggest points of difference. Yet for Percy and James Phinney, who as good party men later stuck by Taft, the rift was more a matter of local personalities. And for the average Maine voter in the election of 1910, it was simply the feeling that the time had come for a change, and that the party in power almost uninterruptedly since the 1850s had grown stale and unresponsive and should be voted out.

Which is exactly what the electorate did on September 12, 1910. In an overwhelming landslide, the Democrats captured the governorship and both branches of the Maine legislature. It was advertised that the new chief executive, Frederick W. Plaisted of Augusta, a former Kennebec County sheriff, was the "first Democrat elected on the Democratic ticket since Governor Hubbard in 1851." There had been other Democratic governors since then, including Plaisted's own father, but they had run on *fusion* tickets in tandem with other parties.

And in the great slaughter of the G.O.P., Percy Baxter went down with the others. In fact, he ran last among the Republican senate candidates in Cumberland County. So much for waterpower as a vote-getting issue, he must have thought.

James Phinney had his own spin on the debacle. Even two days before it happened, after attending a final Republican rally, he commented, "Frederick Hale presided and showed his incompetence in many ways," adding his pronounced relief that Hale earlier had failed to receive the G.O.P. nomination for Congress.

Hale, the Republican boss in Portland, had of course been a constant thorn in the Baxters' side. He had fought them, both in the city and in Augusta, on the issue of changing Portland's form of government. Even worse, in James Phinney's eyes, he represented an historic strain within the Party that could be lumped together as "a bad ring of bosses that has dominated legislation for a number of years."

In his extensive analysis during the days following the election, James Phinney was more explicit. He talked about the "old gang" headed by James G. Blaine, Joe Manley, George P. Westcott, and the Burleighs and how Frederick Hale's father, U.S. Senator Eugene Hale, had taken over as "consulting chief" upon Blaine's death.

Fred Hale, he said, had "a small part of the ability of his father" and he further abused him for his tactics in his unsuccessful bid to win the party's congressional nod, "spending money without stint."

Of the "gang," he noted, perhaps thinking of himself: "Any man showing independence in any conspicuous manner has been turned down summarily and nobody could hope to get an important office without subscribing to its interests, unless he was a man of such marked power as to fight his way to success."[5]

And then he added several men he thought had filled the bill as attempted reformers in Maine, namely the Ricker brothers of Poland Springs fame, who had begun one of the earliest and most successful tourist businesses in the state. The entrance of the Rickers into G.O.P. politics, James Phinney wrote, "startled the old ring and they resolved to down them at the start." What he apparently had in mind was an intra-party squabble that had eventually involved Percy's backing, as a first-term legislator, of the Rickers' candidate for governor, Bert Fernald, as opposed to the establishment's choice. It may even have been that Fernald's backing of Percy's waterpower bill was a return favor, although James Phinney is silent on this score.

Yet it is plain that the moral issue of "unrest caused by boss rule in the party" loomed large in his mind as a reason for the G.O.P.'s rout, alongside more practical motifs such as the Sturgis Law, the failure to allow the people to vote on resubmission, and a misunderstanding of the tariff revision. For he baldly stated on election night, "The defeat of the Republican Party is so complete that I am not sorry that Percy went down with the rest, as much as I was interested in his success."[6]

As a man completely out of politics, himself, James Phinney was having a good time. His routine was busy, but hardly stressful. His "forenoons" were often occupied with affairs at the Portland Savings Bank, on whose board he seemed particularly active. He made frequent trips to Boston for regular meetings of the New England Historical and Genealogical Society, whose finances he helped to manage. In 1910, he helped them purchase the Ashburton Hotel property for the society's new headquarters. On occasion, Percy would join him and they would go to the theater together. James

Phinney was usually critical. He thought *Peter Pan* with Maude Adams was a "non-descript affair" and that the famous actress played the title role in "an amateurish way." As for *The Girl of the Golden West*, also seen with his son in Boston, it was "a most wretched affair, coarse and silly."

Another fairly habitual trip was to Worcester for meetings of the Council of the Antiquarian Society, where James Phinney enjoyed meeting eminent Yankee gentlemen such as the famous writer and clergyman, Edward Everett Hale. He also went abroad. On a trip to Bermuda, he even ran into Mark Twain, whom he knew from having shared the speakers' platform with him at the town of York's 250th anniversary celebration. They had a mutual friend in Congressman Thomas Brackett Reed (also on the stage with them at York), and they briefly chatted about him. James Phinney, then seventy-nine himself, wrote of Twain, "Although nearly an octogenarian, he is alert and bright as a man of much fewer years."

In the weeks following the disastrous election, James Phinney's routine continued as before, only now his son had more time to accompany him. For several days, they traveled Cumberland County together, looking to buy cows for the farm at Mackworth Island. In Cape Elizabeth, infuriated by the filthy conditions they found at some barns, James Phinney fulminated that the farmer "ought to be prosecuted by the Board of Health." Percy now had his own automobile and was constantly driving his father around the state on this and other errands.

During a train trip in November that the two of them took to Boston, there might have been an embarrassing moment when they encountered Hugh Chisholm, the founder and president of the International Paper Company, which had taken such umbrage at Percy's waterpower bill. But the time passed pleasantly in a long discussion of world conditions, and Chisholm could illustrate the need for high tariffs (a strong Republican platform plank) by telling how his company had previously supplied Japan's paper needs but now Japan not only supplied its own needs but competed with the U.S. for business in China. These important capitalists could thus regale themselves in denouncing "labor agitators shouting for free trade."

Six years were to pass before Percy once more decided to re-enter politics. He was then forty years old. In his father's journal, he appears always as the dutiful son. Yet one of the constant mysteries about Percival Baxter was the status of his relationship with the opposite sex. That he was one of the most eligible bachelors in Maine was certainly no secret. He not only had his own car as a young man; he had his own speedboat, as well. There are stories and rumors, to be sure— that he was smitten by an actress named Alma Tell who simply hated the idea of marrying and living in *Hickville*, Maine, or that his father selfishly refused to allow him the freedom of leaving his roof and control.

One piece of documentary evidence as to what might have happened can be found among James Phinney's letters. It is undated, even unaddressed, except to "My dear boy" and whether it transpired during Percy's hiatus from politics is only a supposition.

It is signed "Your loving father," and it is indeed in the tone of a stern yet warm-hearted parent who feels that his trust has been misplaced and will not let his affection permit his judgment to be swayed.

That it concerns an episode such as the rumored romance with an actress or at least a woman of whom James Phinney did not approve seems evident in one of the opening phrases: "...for you were certainly for the time bewitched." And at the end, the elder Baxter is more explicit, yet without revealing the exact nature of the events. He writes:

> You speak of marriage and perhaps the modern way seems better than the old, but it has not proved to be. My prayer is that when you marry, you may marry in accord with the old design, to secure a *helpmate*, according to the original design and not merely someone who is temporarily agreeable. I think it was Solomon who said: A *wise woman maketh* a glad husband.

A rift between father and son had certainly occurred because James Phinney states that one of his motives in writing is to restore the old conditions of two years ago. "That you have disappointed me grievously is true," he adds, and also, "It is enough that you have been my pride and the exalted object of my love." Then, the businessman that he is, he proposes a deal:

> If you will apply yourself to your profession faithfully, I will let you employ someone to take the burden of my affairs sufficiently from your shoulders to enable you to work for your own advancement and I will restore you to the chief place you have ever occupied in my confidence and hopes.

Your profession is presumably Percy's political career.

Then, two more fatherly admonitions:

> You have done wrong and this must be undone. You must cultivate studious habits and application to your business of life.... The man who works wins.

We will never know exactly what soured their relationship nor how they were reconciled to each other. In March 1913, on the occasion of his father's eighty-second birthday, Percy was on a trip to China, but sent a telegram of congratulations from Canton. Then came 1914 and an event that, if nothing else would do it, brought the father and son together—the death of Hetty in November of that year.

James Phinney, despite his seemingly phlegmatic Yankee exterior, was a man of strong emotions. Nowhere are they more poignantly revealed than in another letter he wrote to another son a quarter of a century before. Written from a Boston hotel, it was a letter of condolence to Clinton whose wife had just died in childbirth.

James Phinney wrote how the news had opened old wounds for him "in the death of Florence, my first daughter, then of Mabel and later of your mother and Dolly." This was sixteen years after Sarah Lewis Baxter had died and fifteen years after James Phinney had married Hetty, yet the pain of losing his first wife was still vivid for him. He told Clinton:

> Many times when you were playing happily at Gorham, I would wander into the desolate home on Brown Street and walk the rooms in the bitterest agony, almost beside myself, calling at the foot of the stairs or through the deserted rooms the name of your mother; or sit alone under a tree at the farm feeling that life, but for you children, was of no value to me.

He told of walking the streets of Portland, hoping he might see her and momentarily gladdening when he saw a woman in the distance who resembled her.

> Even shop windows gave me pain because I saw in them those little feminine things which I so much liked to purchase for her but now could not....

Unlike the extant letter to Percy, which was a draft with corrections and words crossed out, this finished missive in the collection may never have been sent, for it also contains some venting of parental spleen that he may not have considered appropriate on second thought. He refers to a letter from Rupert complaining that he is cold, and an accusation from Rupert that he opposed Clinton's marriage, which he denies, only admitting that he had asked for a short postponement. He speaks of indifference toward him from the older boys and of "selfish demands" made upon him. Then, part warmly, part reproachfully, he ends: "I want you to come home as much as you can and get acquainted with your sisters whom you hardly know, I fear."

His final ordeal with Hetty, who had been ailing for a number of years, began in October 1914. Early in the month, she was strong enough to go for rides with him and he was cheered by the visit of his great-grandchild, the offspring of Clinton's daughter Carrie, whose mother had died giving birth to her. But he was also depressed by the war news from Europe, "the slaughter of men, women and children, the destruction of great cities, centers of learning...."

On October 22, he writes: "Greatly troubled over Hetty's condition and fear paralysis of the left side."

She lived for another seventeen days.

On October 25, he writes: "Hetty talked with me while I sat by her this morning and recalled our happy life together. A sore trial for her and me was this talk. Her love for me is so touching that I cannot restrain my tears...."

On October 26, Dr. Burrage reported an improvement in Hetty's condition and James Phinney was able to spend nearly all day at the bank and in his office. The next journal entry is November 8.

> Sunday. One of the bitterest days of my life. My dear wife after many days of suffering died this morning just as the seven o'clock bell on the church near us rang for

HETTY, PHOTOGRAPHED IN 1913, ONE YEAR
BEFORE HER DEATH.

Mass. She has been to me the most precious gift that God has given me. I have just come from her chamber after kissing her cold forehead good night. I do not know how I can drag out the days that may lie before me. God help me.[7]

In the next few weeks, Percy was with his father continually—at the cemetery, at church, and at the bittersweet Thanksgiving dinner they had with all of the family in attendance. Hartley did his bit by arranging a picnic in the winter woods near Brunswick and serving broiled partridge and roasted potatoes—James Phinney's favorites—around a roaring fire. The children knew that Christmas would be difficult for him, as it was for them, but all did their best not to show it. Memories were everywhere. James Phinney went to pieces when a shopping list in Hetty's handwriting slipped out of a book he picked up. But whatever problem he had had with Percy seemed vanished.

After the New Year, he wrote:

Emily's loving care is beyond praise. She and Percival leave nothing undone for my care and consolation. Their devotion humbles me for I am not worthy of it.[8]

Yet solid as the father-son reconciliation seemed, there was tension beneath the surface—at least on Percy's part. Since his earliest days, his half-brother Rupert had been his confidante and the closest of his friends among the "first litter." A sibling-to-sibling missive, written by Percy at age fifteen to "Rupie," contains frequent references, in the way of young boys, not to mention certain of his concerns and doings to "mamma or papa." But twenty-four years later, as an adult, while about to embark on one of his regular inspection trips to the Sterling Water Company, Percy unloaded a host of pent-up family frustrations and followed this with an even longer and more agonized complaint from Illinois. On February 6, 1915, writing from Portland, he begins:

> Dear Rupert—Believing that frankness is better than reserve, I told father and Emily that I probably would be away 10 days longer than was absolutely necessary for my Sterling trip. You would have thought I had disgraced the family...!

The next day, his father at breakfast, he said, had been "pale and sad: had passed a 'very bad night'" and, since then I've almost felt guilty of a wrong." He had been on trips by himself already, like the one to China, but now he was starting to feel he was being "kept under restraint." His P.S. to his big brother is like a *deja vu* of those teen-age years as he states: "Like a schoolgirl's letter, I want this DE-stroyed."

But within two weeks, a far longer and unhappier letter was sent from Sterling on the water company's stationery. It seemed that Percy had wanted to go to San Francisco for those extra days. Madeleine, Emily, and his father had begged him not to do so. As Percy saw it, he was being told that "to go away alone is nothing short of a crime against filial affection and love of home." Having written back from Boston that he wouldn't go, he was now upset that they didn't relent and tell him to go, anyway. He was feeling extremely sorry for himself, living under a regime of what he deemed "complete submission and sacrifice of independence," given a difficult time even if he went out to supper or to work in his studio in the evening.

> I shall be 39, think of it, and I've never done a thing really worthwhile, really manly, to make a place for myself in the world. I know now I never shall. Sur-

rounded by all the comforts, with all the money I ever shall need...with no family of my own, I yet seem to face a blank wall.

Another postscript, following this cry of pain, enjoins Rupert to destroy this letter, too, but with the ambiguity typical of his natural politician's bent for zigging and zagging, he concludes by seemingly accepting his fate, saying "perhaps I can do the most good by trying to make father's last years as

JAMES PHINNEY AND HIS CHILDREN: FROM LEFT TO RIGHT, STANDING: EUGENE, HARTLEY, JAMES PHINNEY; SEATED: RUPERT, CLINTON, MADELEINE, JAMES PHINNEY JR., EMILY, PERCIVAL. AT THEIR FEET, THE INEVITABLE IRISH SETTER.

happy as possible and that is certainly worth living for. He is...very lonesome."

The following year, sometime in 1916, after who knows what discussions between father and son, Percy decided he would run for the legislature again, this time for the house. Concurrently, Rupert also decided to run, but for the state senate and from Sagadahoc County, since he had moved to Bath.

In September, they were both elected.

But meanwhile, another terrible drama convulsed the Baxter household.

In late summer, the family was at Mackworth Island. On September 1, James Phinney was awakened by the "bird-like voice" of his grandson Edward, the youngest of Madeleine and Fenton Tomlinson's two sons, crying "Mama! Mama!," but he didn't know that anything was wrong until a distraught Fenton appeared with the boy in his arms. The child had somehow managed to set himself on fire. Burned over two-thirds of his body and judged too sick to be moved to a hospital, he was not expected to live.

Three days later, he was still alive and asked to see "Grandpa." James Phinney leaned over his bed and asked him, "Do you feel better, Edward?" "Yes, Grandpa," he manfully replied. Grandpa wrote: "I had to go to my room for a cry."[9]

His varying prognoses had a roller-coaster effect on everyone's emotions. On September 7, Dr. Small thought he might recover. On September 11, he took a turn for the worse.

September 12 was Election Day. There can have been only muted celebration over the fact that Rupert was elected to the state senate and Percy to the house. Yet Edward was more comfortable, and soon his wounds began to heal around the edges and his skin grafts were taking.

With a few more setbacks, Edward steadily improved, impressing everyone with his quiet courage. On November 2, he was well enough to leave Mackworth Island for his parents' home in Portland.

The legislative session in which the two Baxters were participating began on January 4, 1917. But on New Year's Day, Percy headed for Augusta and was joined en route by Rupert. A Republican caucus to choose the G.O.P.'s leadership was scheduled for January 2 and, once more, Percy had rather presumptuously decided to offer himself for the top position—in this case, speaker of the house. He had even written an acceptance speech ahead of time. But later that day, as James Phinney would note in his journal, "On my return to Youngs Hotel [his favorite stopping place in Boston], I found a message from Percy, which he had promised to send me, announcing his defeat for the Speakership (which caused no great regret)."

Despite his aside in the parenthesis, the elder Baxter dutifully consoled his son with a telegram sent to the Augusta House which Percy kept ever afterward. It said: "FAILURES ARE STEPPING-STONES TO SUCCESS. YOU WILL YET WIN— FATHER."

On January 4, when Governor Carl Milliken spoke to the assembled lawmakers, Percy was in seat number one in the house, the first row, farthest right-hand corner. In later years, this place was specifically reserved for the majority leader of the house and throughout this session, Percy seemed informally to serve in the role of the G.O.P.'s chief spokesman. It was perhaps a consolation prize for his failure to win the speakership.

Carl Milliken had almost singlehandedly brought the Republican Party back to its former place of domination in Augusta after its collapse in 1910. While the national party was dissolving in the Roosevelt-Taft split of 1912 that had allowed the Democrats to elect Woodrow Wilson, Milliken's work in unifying the Maine G.O.P. had ousted Governor Plaisted. A conservative Democrat, Oakley C. Curtis, an erstwhile partner of the Baxters' in the ferry business, managed to slip in for a term as governor in 1914. But in 1916, with Milliken heading the ticket, the Republicans resumed their virtual monopoly of power in the state, pretty much in uninterrupted fashion until the Depression (and then were only sporadically displaced during the next three decades).

Part of Milliken's speech must have been music to Percy Baxter's ears as the chief executive outlined his intended program.

> The water power of the State should be preserved for the benefit of all of the people.... You must prevent the placing of obstacles in the path of progress and at the same time guard the people's interest in the water powers so that it will not be released without adequate compensation.[10]

Indeed, much of Percy's time and attention during this session was taken up with the promotion of his philosophy about waterpower. In a sense, he was having to play catch-up. His bill—the Fernald Bill of 1909—had categorically forbidden the export of waterpower beyond Maine. But, as so often happens, a loophole had been found in it by the companies who had been opposed. They made sure that clauses in their charters would allow them to circumvent the law.

To forestall them, Percy now began to attach what became known as the Baxter Amendment to every re-licensing or chartering bill proposed by any organization that might have anything to do with waterpower.

The battles commenced right out of the starting gate. Typical was the fight at the start of the session over which committee should receive "An Act Relating to the West

Branch Driving and Reservoir Dam Company." Baxter wanted it sent to his own committee—the Judiciary Committee; the lobbyists—and the senate—wanted it in the Committee on Interior Waters. This time, a more savvy Baxter actually won his initial reference fight in the house but ultimately lost it when it was pointed out that the powerful Reference of Bills Committee—of which Percy was a member—had *unanimously* recommended sending it to Interior Waters.

With his soon-to-be-famous Baxter Amendments, he was far more successful. In the end, they were attached to thirty-three separate measures: electric company bills, reservoir bills, log driving bills, dam bills, boom bills, etc.

But on his first attempt, he ran into a storm of powerful opposition. A bill allowing the Oxford Electric Company to extend its lines to Hebron was in a position to be amended. Percy arose and offered his addition. Then, the man who had beaten him out for speaker, William L. Bonney of Bowdoinham, ruled that the amendment was not germane to the bill, effectively preventing the Baxter proposal from even being considered. Striking back, Percy took a very rare and extraordinary step. He appealed the ruling of the chair. To win, he would have needed a two-thirds vote; furthermore, he risked angering his fellow Republicans by creating open disunity.

So, having grown wiser politically with experience, he tactically retreated and withdrew both his challenge and his amendment. And he lived to triumph another day. Within two weeks, he had mustered enough support to stick his amendment onto the Charter of the Washington County Light and Power Company, overcoming the efforts of his perennial opponent on the issue, Charles P. Barnes of Houlton, by an almost thirty-vote margin. Helping out immensely was Governor Milliken who let it be known he wanted the Baxter Amendment on all electric power charters.

The senate remained a problem. Percy would put on his amendment in the house, and the senate would send the bill back without it. But since the senate, more attune to the needs of the companies, had no desire to see these bills killed, this put Percy in the perfect position to play hardball. He would call for the house to *adhere* to its position of supporting the bill *with* the Baxter amendment, and it would. Under parliamentary rules, the senate had no choice but to agree with the house or the bill would die.

The senate chairman of Percy's own Judiciary Committee was a fellow Republican from Yarmouth named Howard Davies. In later years they became allies, but throughout this session, Davies not only fought the Baxter Amendments but also sought to stymie Percy's attempts to revive the old Water Storage Commission that he had helped create in 1909 and that since then had had its purposes subverted by the power companies and their interests.

During the debate on this issue, Percy gave a very curious speech. On the surface, it was simply pretty good rhetoric in an emotional, personal, anecdotal style that always has appeal for the Maine legislature. Percy began to talk about his friend, the late John E. Warren, and the thrust of his argument was that if Jack Warren were still alive and representing Cumberland County in the senate, the vote against Percy's Water Storage Commission bill "would have resulted very differently."

Percy went on to say: "The last time I saw him only a few days before he died, he told me that he hoped sometime to return to Augusta to help this cause in which he took such an interest."[11]

Very touching. But, of course, not true. Had Percy forgotten that Jack Warren had been one of the strongest opponents of his no-export of power legislation? As for the Water

Storage Commission, there was nothing in the record to indicate Warren's support for it, since there had been no debate.

Another oversight (or whopper) in Percy's speech had been when he said, apropos of how well-loved Jack Warren was in his community, "there were never any strikes or labor troubles among the people in his mills."

Yet in a journal entry a mere eight months before, James Phinney praised the Warren Company's tough position on a strike at their Westbrook plant, "fomented by foreign mischief-makers."

Was Percival Baxter being a deceitful politician? "Patt" Pattangall once charged him with "an inability to make an accurate statement," saying also that Baxter believed it was possible to fool all of the people all of the time. As an exaggerator, Pattangall was hardly one to talk. Selective hyperbole is perhaps a kinder way to put it, apparently an affliction to which no politician, no matter how principled, is immune.

There is a charming story told about a visit to Percival Baxter when he was in his eighties by then-Governor Kenneth M. Curtis who had come to tell the old gentleman about all of the improvements made at Baxter Park, while showing him slides. But within a few seconds, Baxter fell asleep and remained so as Curtis talked on and the projector flashed its images on the screen. As soon as Curtis finished, Baxter awoke, opened his eyes, smiled, and said: "My, wasn't that wonderful!"

No one ever called Percy on his speech about John E. Warren.

As the 1917 session drew to a close in April, the house member in seat No. 1 was a busy man. Attempting to promote the idea of conservation among his fellows, he arranged to have Gifford Pinchot, the country's most famous forester and the inspirer of Teddy Roosevelt, visit Augusta and address the Maine lawmakers. He had been trying since February but then had to postpone the finally scheduled talk because of an illness in Pinchot's family. Before it could be re-scheduled, world events intervened. On April 7, President Wilson asked Congress to declare war on Germany. Three months earlier, Percy had presented a resolution asking for bi-partisan unity to support the president in breaking off diplomatic relations with the Kaiser's government. Now, in the house chamber, there was nothing but patriotic fervor. The loudest cheers were for Representative Frank E. Stanley of Dixfield, the only Civil War veteran among them, who declared, "I am young enough to go again if necessary."

The final feather in Percy's cap in this productive session was his leadership of the successful struggle to pass an amendment to the state constitution allowing Women's Suffrage. It needed a two-thirds vote before it could go out to the people and, since it was a plank in the Republican platform, Percy's prime opponent this time was the Democratic floor leader, Edward Murray of Bangor, who tried to slow its passage. Percy's victory in the House was resounding, 113-35. And then the senate passed it, 31-0.

The forty-one-year-old state representative from Portland was mastering his "profession."

---

1 James Phinney Baxter Journal #7, November 1, 1906.
2 *The Meddybemps Letters* et al; page 221.
3 *The New York Times*, May 13, 1908; page 13.
4 Legislative Record, 1909 Session; page 1,243.
5 James Phinney Baxter Journal #7; page 278.
6 Ibid.; page 275.
7 James Phinney Baxter Journal #9; page 66.
8 Ibid.; page 88.
9 Ibid.; page 270.
10 Legislative Record, January 4, 1917.
11 Legislative Record, April 3, 1917, page 1,250.

✳

CHAPTER 8

Prelude To Power

"YOU HAVE BEEN MY ENEMY since 1883 and the reason is burned into your brain as it is into mine." So wrote a hopping-mad, eighty-seven-year-old James Phinney Baxter in a letter to Colonel Frederick Dow, in Dow's capacity as owner and publisher of the *Portland Evening Express* and *Sunday Telegram*.

Note that he was not writing to the *Eastern Argus*, the city's Democratic newspaper. The *Express* was eminently an orthodox Republican institution—but in this instance, too orthodox to suit James Phinney.

For he was writing—on April 5, 1918—to protest an article in the *Sunday Telegram*—on March 31, 1918—"false in fact and malicious in spirit, attacking Mr. Percival P. Baxter," and demanding an apology.

The present was duplicating the past. Political enemies who had harassed James Phinney during his own career were now striking at his son. Ever the historian, James Phinney

THE OPENING OF THE MAINE STATE SENATE IN 1921 WITH
PERCIVAL BAXTER PRESIDING AS PRESIDENT. WITHIN LESS
THAN A MONTH, HE WOULD BECOME GOVERNOR.

began by dredging up a bit of hidden dirty linen from the
city's G.O.P. archives. The particular "reason burned into"
their respective brains focused not on Dow's rivalry with
Thomas Brackett Reed for a Republican congressional nomination, but his attempt to defeat Reed's re-election in 1883.
This was a full decade before James Phinney's own entry into
politics. To him, Tom Reed was "a statesman beyond the
reach of schemers who wished to exploit the public for their
private interests," and Dow, the "lieutenant" of such self-

seeking plots, "then as now." James Phinney recalled how he had been pressed to join an anti-Reed coalition because of his influence with the important Republican newspaper, the *Portland Press*, but instead, "to secure Reed's election," had invested $40,000 more in the *Press* and also had raised a considerable sum for Reed among the businessmen along Commercial Street.

"I have often wondered what your feelings were when you passed Mr. Reed's statue, facing the sunrise on the Western Promenade," James Phinney concluded in his excoriation of Frederick Dow.

All of this seems at first blush to be far removed from the spring of 1918 and the issue of waterpower, on which Percy had been attacked by the newspaper.

Yet there was a certain consistency to this octogenarian father's ire, and he spelled it out at times in his journal as the battle raged around his son's public positions. In a sense, at least to him, the waterpower fight was simply a continuation of other bygone splits in Maine Republican politics, whether it was the failed attempt to dump Tom Reed or even the more successful efforts made on two occasions to dump himself as mayor, or the continuity that he saw between the old Blaine "Ring" he had long railed against and the "Octopus," as he called it, that was now thrashing its tentacles about to try to defeat Percy.

This connection of the past to the present in his mind had begun shortly after the start of the legislative session of 1917 and Percy's failure to win the speakership. Despite his initial stated indifference to Percy's loss, James Phinney dug more deeply into the affair through his contacts in the Republican Party. A conspiracy theory was soon forthcoming and, needless to say, it fitted well with his own personal experiences in earlier times.

Of the old "Ring," he wrote, only Frederick Dow and a Seth Carter were still alive. But Fred Hale and a nephew of George P. Westcott were conniving with Dow and Carter "to revive the old regime." In an almost Populist outburst that seemed odd coming from a man who regularly railed against labor unions, James Phinney went on:

> Behind them are the railroads, the lumber and water-power interests, so valuable now to furnish electric power for lighting, transportation and manufacturing purposes. They knew they could not influence Percival, hence their effort to defeat him as Speaker.[1]

According to James Phinney, Percy's opponent, William L. Bonney, whom he considered a "weak and dissipated man," did not have the votes to win; however, the treachery of fellow Portlander Fred Hale and "a few of his tools" was enough to scuttle his son's chances. He learned that Hale had offered to support Percy only on the condition that he would not seek the speakership in any future session, a condition that Percy indignantly turned down.

Throughout the 1917 session, James Phinney closely followed his son's activities, his anger mounting toward the press once he realized that there was "a conspiracy of silence" about the waterpower issue and Percy's role in it. Only two newspapers in the state gave Percy any real coverage, and it had to be especially galling to James Phinney that one of them was the *Eastern Argus*, his old Democratic nemesis, which was quite supportive. (The other paper was the Republican *Lewiston Journal*.)

At the end of February 1917, unable to contain himself any longer, James Phinney actually went to see Frederick Dow at the *Evening Express*. He wasn't above playing hardball, himself, and hinted that if the two Republican papers in

Portland, the *Express* and the *Press*, wouldn't give his son legitimate coverage, a third Republican paper might be started. Then, he went to the *Press*, which he had once controlled and which was now controlled by Fred Hale. The editor, Harry M. Bigelow, was sympathetic and the upshot of these visits was that articles appeared about Percy's Water Storage Commission Bill and his picture was actually published. Even the *Boston American* picked up the story.

Once the 1917 session was over, Percy did not let the waterpower issue die. In January 1918, he fired off an open letter to Governor Milliken, asking him to call a special session during their down time to deal with waterpower. There was little chance that Milliken would agree, but this was a good way to get publicity. And particularly so, considering the proposal Percy wanted to offer—nothing less than amending the state constitution to give Maine government the authority to take over developed and undeveloped waterpower sites, as well as great storage reservoirs provided by lakes and dammed rivers; in effect, to go into the power business.

"Socialism!" His enemies now had a seemingly credible reason to hurl this charge at him.

But, tough and articulate, Percy could defend himself. On March 6, 1918, he spoke to the Colonial Club of Bath and told them how he had brought a power expert from Canada named Yates to Augusta to talk about the Province of Ontario's program of developing and selling its own power. To frugal Yankees, it should have sounded like a good deal. A total of 225 municipalities and 1.5 million people were being served at rates half of those in the United States. But in the audience, to use Percy's words, "were fourteen leading corporation lawyers...ready to annihilate Mr. Yates and tear his arguments and facts to pieces."[2]

Three weeks later, Percy initiated a wild scene at the

Republican State Convention by submitting a platform plank for "conservation and control of the improved waterpowers of the State." Every effort was made to defeat him. According to James Phinney, "Fred Hale, Howard Davies, [former governor] Cobb, and others representing the Octopus" unsuccessfully tried to keep Percy off the platform committee and even to prevent him from speaking. In the process, Cobb made a fool of himself and Percy pushed through two of his propositions—no export and the Water Storage Commission—while failing only on the third, the highly explosive notion of government ownership of a resource. The next night, at a reception for Theodore Roosevelt, who had come to Portland, Percy was congratulated by many present for "his brilliant contest against such violent opposition."

That opposition continued. Two days after the convention, the *Sunday Telegram* leveled what James Phinney termed "a despicable attack on Percy, even attacking his character by innuendo." And it was this broadside that led to the old gentleman's blast at Colonel Dow, whom he described as "past seventy and the same shuffling, deceiving schemer as ever."

While realizing that Percy was fighting against difficult odds, James Phinney always maintained his confidence that Percy would "succeed in his efforts to conserve Maine's great inheritance." Before them both at this period was the example of what persistence in a seemingly unattainable political goal could produce. The "Boulevard," the ex-mayor's controversial and quixotic pet project, was coming into being. In October 1917, James Phinney and the Portland commissioner of parks in one car and Percy in another entered the construction site at Tukey's Bridge and drove along the nascent thoroughfare to exit at Bedford Street. "I never expected to see the Boulevard, for which I have been so long waiting, in the forward state of construction which it now exhibits," James Phinney declared.

It had been eleven years since he had been in office and the finished road would not be ready for another four, but his dream was becoming a reality and certainly an object lesson in vision, patience, and stick-to-it-iveness for his son.

America was at war. As a male in his early forties, Percy Baxter could consider enlisting, although somewhat beyond ideal fighting age. But Governor Milliken requested that he serve in a different capacity—as head of one of the draft boards in Portland. James Phinney smelled a rat. He saw it as a ploy by Percy's enemies to make him unpopular with the local voters, since he would be sending their sons off to war and possible death. However, Percy accepted and, afterward, his father would write:

> His appointment as head of draft board No. 2 was intended to defeat his election to the Legislature, but has made him many friends instead of enemies as was intended.[3]

The Octopus, James Phinney estimated a month before election day, had already spent $50,000 and would spend $50,000 more to keep Percy and his allies out of Augusta. To lead their effort and give it a bi-partisan tinge, they chose a well-known Democrat, former Cumberland County Sheriff William Pennell. In a public statement, Percy called him "an able man, a fighting man, an antagonist to be watched and matched," but not one to be feared. Indefatigable in his public relations outreach work, particularly in subsidizing the state's newspapers to present the Octopus's point of view on waterpower, Pennell was nevertheless unsuccessful in preventing Percy Baxter's re-election.

The vote on September 11, 1918 had Percy second among the Republicans in Portland in his quest to return to his house seat, 127 votes behind the front-runner, George H.

Allan, and 76 votes ahead of a political newcomer of whom a great deal would be heard in the future. His name was Ralph Owen Brewster and he would be both one of Percy Baxter's strongest allies and most bitter foes in the years to come. In Sagadahoc County, Rupert Baxter was voted back into the state senate.

It was during the following session in 1919 that Percy added another arrow to the quiver of attention-grabbing issues that he was presenting to the Maine electorate. He introduced a bill to create Mount Katahdin Centennial Park in honor of one hundred years of Maine Statehood, 1820-1920.

No one has ever been able to pinpoint exactly when this vision of preserving Katahdin appeared to Percy nor has he, himself, left any documentary evidence. The long-time director of Baxter State Park, Irvin "Buzz" Caverly, has traced the moment back to 1903 when Percy and two friends allegedly stood in nearby Staceyville, looking up at the majestic peak, and the young Portlander said: "That mountain should belong to the people of Maine." The notion was not an entirely new one. Early in the 1890s, a mayor of Bangor, Dr. Augustus Hamlin, had proposed that a game preserve should be established on and around Katahdin. In 1905 the Maine Hotel Proprietors advanced the thought of a state park. The 1909 session of the legislature had had a bill, initiated by the Federation of Women's Clubs, for a commission to look into the costs of acquiring Katahdin. Percy's original Water Storage Commission, created that session, did exactly that, contacting the local landowners to see if they would sell and at what price. In Washington, D.C., interest was also aroused. Congressman Frank E. Guernsey of Dover-Foxcroft submitted a bill in 1913 to create a National Park and National Forest Reserve containing Katahdin and its surroundings.

The 1913 Maine Legislature (Percy was not a member) signaled its approval, but Guernsey's bill died in committee, both in 1913 and again in 1916.

Now, Percy Baxter picked up the ball again and introduced a bill appropriating $20,000 to buy 115,000 acres of cut-over land to be made into a Mount Katahdin Preserve.

But in the 1919 session, Percy's principal preoccupation was still waterpower. The furor over the Water Power Commission had diminished and Percy's bill to create it was passed with no trouble. Apparently, the Octopus no longer found a study of waterpower resources as threatening as once feared. Although there was no need for a speech on the floor, Percy felt he needed one for the record—and a long one. Calling his bill "the most important piece of legislation before the 79th Legislature," he was his historian father's son in going all the way back to 1869 to detail the history of attempts to survey the state's waterpowers.

It was his struggle to move beyond a mere study and have Maine imitate Ontario and enter the power generating business that caused him his difficulties. A major objection, raised right at the outset, was that Maine had no constitutional authority to do so. Percy's response was to offer an order requiring the lawmakers to declare a "solemn occasion"—an opportunity to ask the state supreme court to rule on the question.

Here, the flak really began to fly. The strongest opposition came from Charles Barnes, now the Republican floor leader. The two of them assailed each other with unusual heat. The affable and gentlemanly Percy Baxter showed a side of himself that was rarely seen—a nasty side. In the floor debate, he attacked Barnes personally:

> I have often thought that perhaps the worst enemy of the gentleman from Houlton is his own bitter tongue and

believe that he must sometimes regret the caustic remarks he makes in the House."[4]

Known for its decorum and collegiality, the Maine legislature severely frowns on such sour expressions. Jumping to his feet, Barnes protested to the speaker, who admonished Percy to follow house etiquette.

Rather unbelievably, Percy refused, nor would he apologize. He continued his huffy statements.

> When this session is over I want to be able to look every member in the face and have him say to me that I never once tried to win applause or momentary triumph by indulging at another's expense in sallies of wit or sarcasm.[5]

And then, lo and behold, he did just what he said he abhorred. When Representative Walter A. Cowan of Winterport, an opponent of his order, badgered him with some technical questions, Percy's reply was dripping with sarcasm, telling him to submit his queries to the Supreme Court "rather than to a humble member of the 79th Legislature" (a sally of wit that brought applause.)

What part this uncharacteristically boorish behavior played in the defeat soon afterward of Percy's bill for a Mount Katahdin preserve is not known. Ostensibly, the cause of its failure was its price tag. After killing the original bill, the lawmakers resurrected it in a totally watered-down version that allowed the State of Maine to accept gifts of land—anywhere in Maine— not just in the Katahdin region.

At least Percy could say he'd gained something, but it assuredly wasn't much.

He had other more solid accomplishments to his credit during this session. One boast, to perhaps a limited but devoted audience, was that he had pushed through the first anti-vivisection legislation in the United States. A much larger group would certainly have applauded his leadership in bringing Maine to ratify the Nineteenth Amendment to the U.S. Constitution, establishing Women's Suffrage. And, surprisingly, given the huge vote he'd received previously, it hadn't been easy. What had intervened was a statewide referendum in which only men had voted and Women's Suffrage had been defeated. Now that the U.S. Congress had sent the idea out to the states to be approved, there was strong resistance, many of the lawmakers saying that their towns were on record against letting women vote.

Percy answered this particular argument by saying that despite local sentiment "if any of us have strong convictions in favor of it, our convictions must govern our actions.... On questions of this sort, I prefer to stand upon my convictions, and if my constituency disapprove of my action, I must submit to such punishment as they may see fit to give me in the years to come." His next few arguments raised hackles, as he said:

> Why, gentlemen of the House, it is only 56 years ago—a brief space of time—that there were men in this country—thousands and perhaps millions of them—who honestly believed that the black man should not be freed. Such a state of mind is unbelievable today....

And then he continued by attacking disbelievers in universal manhood suffrage (i.e., letting all men vote).

> Such people are fearful of extending human rights but, gentlemen, they are bound to be left behind in the progress of the human race.

He ended with a flourish that drew applause:

> If you believe that woman is entitled to a place by the side of man, in fair weather or in foul, or whether the

path to be trod together is one of roses or of thistles, vote today according to your convictions. Give women such suffrage as it is in your power here today to give them.

Then up jumped Representative Benedict Maher of Augusta, an inveterate foe of Percy's on waterpower issues, as well as on this matter. He, too, drew applause when he referred to "the very discourteous thought" expressed by the Gentleman from Portland, Mr. Baxter, "when he attempted to compare the womanhood of Maine, per argument, with the black man of the South—as an opponent of this matter, I resent it."

Maher had made the motion to amend the Women's Suffrage bill. He wanted the question sent to referendum (again, where only men could vote), rather than for them to ratify it here. By four votes, Maher's sabotaging motion was defeated and Maine went on to join the other states in ratifying Women's Suffrage.

Despite his somewhat maverick positioning, Percival Baxter was becoming a force in the Maine G.O.P. With the arrival of the national election year of 1920, he further enhanced his prestige by being elected a delegate to the Republican National Convention in Chicago. Such plums were usually preserved for hoary veteran politicos. Moreover, he was also included in the Maine delegation that joined the throngs flocking to Marion, Ohio, to inform Warren G. Harding that he had been nominated. In those days, candidates did not personally appear at conventions (the first to do so was Franklin Delano Roosevelt in 1932). There was a certain irony in the fact that Percy went with his fellow delegates to Ohio, since he hadn't backed Harding. His vote had been for Herbert Hoover (the only one in the delegation). Notwithstanding, he was soon caught up in the partisan fervor, like all the other 75,000 Republican faithful who were present.

It was particularly exciting for him to note a banner carried in the parade through town that dated back to 1884 and bore the names of Blaine and Logan, plus a portrait of James G. Blaine, "decorated with flags and gold lace and braid."

Back home, James Phinney followed the events through Percy's letters. The choice of Harding hadn't pleased him, either. He, too, had been for Hoover, his second choice General Leonard Wood, then a third and fourth choice excluding the Ohioan, but his utter dislike of Woodrow Wilson and the Republican hoopla boiling up out of Marion soon reconciled him to the G.O.P. standard bearer.

It was during the train ride home from Chicago that Percy and other delegates came up with a splendid idea. They would organize a trip to Mount Katahdin, led by Percy and also by none other than Charles Barnes, his antagonist on waterpower but a strong supporter of saving Katahdin. Burton Howe, a lumberman from Patten, said he would set up the expedition, which would proceed by buckboard, horseback, and foot. In later years, Percy was to credit Howe with having been "the man who first brought my attention to the beauties of Katahdin." Another enthusiast was Arthur Staples, the influential editor of the *Lewiston Journal*.

Although trips to climb Katahdin had been arranged by the Appalachian Mountain Club since 1916, this one gained major media attention. The presence of Staples and one of his reporters, plus Charles Fogg, editor of the *Houlton Times*, was part of the reason; also along was an official of the Bangor and Aroostook Railroad, which annually published *In The Maine Woods*, a small magazine touting Maine's north country. Percy, by then (August 1920) an announced candidate for Maine's senate president, and Charles Barnes, an equally open candidate for speaker of the house, assured the interest of politically minded readers.

The expedition covered seventy-two miles in five days. Calling his ascent of Katahdin "the hardest thing I ever undertook," Percy climbed to the summit over the harrowing Knife Edge Trail. At lunch, the participants in this "surveying trip," as the newspapers called it, eagerly discussed plans for a future park. They informally decided to call themselves the "Katahdin Club." Percy solemnly promised himself: This shall belong to Maine if I live. More publicly, Arthur Staples wrote: "Katahdin got me as nothing else did." Burton Howe went to see Frederick Parkhurst, soon to be elected governor, and received his support for the park concept.

As 1920 drew toward September and Maine's first-in-the-nation election day, the media had already been rumoring that Percy might run for governor. Whatever the machinations within the State G.O.P. about seeking a candidate—and Percy and Rupert allegedly had their own man—the rising representative from Portland was able to judge that his time hadn't quite come for the top spot. So he finally issued a statement that he would be content to return to Augusta as a legislator. Then he added: "as a member of the Senate," where, he continued, he "could do more for Maine waterpowers than by holding a more exalted office."[6]

One translation might be that he knew he didn't have the votes for a gubernatorial nomination. Frederick H. Parkhurst of Bangor was the man who did. The voters elected them both that September and by substantial margins. (Rupert won his Senate seat again, too.) Percy's campaign ads had stressed twin themes:

SAVE AND DEVELOP MAINE'S WATER POWERS FOR MAINE PEOPLE SO THAT EVERY HOME, FARM AND INDUSTRY IN MAINE SHALL HAVE ELECTRICITY AT REASONABLE RATES.
STATE PURCHASE OF WASTE AND BURNED-OVER

TIMBERLANDS, REFORESTATION AND MOUNT KATAHDIN
CENTENNIAL STATE PARK.

Parkhurst breezed to a 2-1 victory. And for the first time
in his career, Percy led the ticket, both in Portland and
Cumberland County. The G.O.P. blowout in Maine, which
saw all thirty-one state senators elected as Republicans, was
repeated all over the country, with Americans tired of Wilson
and the Democrats and longing to return to normalcy and iso-
lationism.

When the newly elected lawmakers gathered in Augusta
at the beginning of January to choose their leaders, Percy was
the sole candidate for senate president.

It was said that one of Baxter's Cumberland County running mates, Senator Charles E. Gurney, had toyed with the
idea of running for senate president but had dropped out
when he realized Percy had too much support. It was also
bruited about *sotto voce* that the party leaders had allowed this
still unreconstructed young Turk to be elevated as a way of
"kicking him upstairs," keeping him so preoccupied that he
wouldn't have time to speak too much or to introduce too
many mischievous bills.

If so, the old guard should have been disappointed by his
acceptance speech. After Senator Matthew C. Morrill of
Cumberland County escorted him to the president's chair,
Baxter delivered himself of a Teddy Rooseveltian blast at the
ways of government often associated with the old guard. He
didn't mince words:

> Any government of the whole by a class or group would
> mean the end of the Republic. The paid representatives
> of classes and groups of special interests and special priv-
> ileges are always present during Legislative sessions.
> These Legislative Halls are frequented by selfish, plausi-

ble men who often attempt to control those of us who are here to represent all of the people. We must stand firmly against these group or class interests whoever they are and whatever they represent.[7]

The date was January 5, 1921. As he delivered himself of his feelings to the assembled members of the senate, there was no way that Percy or anyone else could foresee what would happen within a little more than three weeks. He had reached a pinnacle of power, not *the* pinnacle, but the second most powerful position in state government, according to the Maine Constitution. For if anything dire happened to the reigning governor, his successor would be the senate president.

Percy no doubt had ambitions to reach the very top, and there was a lot more planning to do in the next two years, with concrete goals to accomplish for himself and the Republican senate. With an energy that must have been disconcerting to those who thought he'd be hobbled by a role in leadership, he plunged right into his work.

---

[1] James Phinney Baxter Journal #9; pages 273-274.
[2] Volume 15, Baxter Scrapbooks; page 76.
[3] James Phinney Baxter Journal #10; page 71.
[4] Legislative Record, 1919 Session; page 357.
[5] Ibid.; page 358.
[6] Volume 15, Baxter Scrapbooks; page 111.
[7] Legislative Record, January 5, 1921; pages 4-5.

CHAPTER **9**

Governor Percy

TRADITION IN THE MAINE legislature dictates formal dress for its presiding officers—striped pants, cutaway coats with tails, pearl-gray vests, etc. Tradition also—and the size of the respective chambers—makes it necessary to hold a joint assembly—house and senate together—in the house, itself, but the senate president wields the gavel in place of the speaker. Thus was the scene set for the swearing-in of Governor Frederick Hale Parkhurst on January 6, 1921.

It was a happy, bustling event. Family members, friends, political supporters, and officials of the incoming administration crowded the galleries overlooking the hall. Down front sat the governor's wife and young children. Senate President Baxter administered the oath of office and sat in the speaker's chair while Parkhurst, dressed in a dark-blue suit of Maine wool,[1] spoke.

For a Republican, the speech was a curiously liberal-sounding one. But, except for a Baxterian note when he said

A POSTCARD FEATURING THE MAINE STATEHOUSE
AND THE NEW GOVERNOR, PERCIVAL BAXTER. IT WAS
COMMON PRACTICE THEN FOR SUCH GUBERNATORIAL
POSTCARDS TO BE ISSUED.

that waterpower "must be used in Maine," it contrasted with the tone of Percy's past (and future) orations in that it seemed to promise generous spending. The actual word "liberal" kept cropping up: liberal toward road building, toward school funding, toward salaries for state employees, toward fishermen, farmers, factory workers, and even child laborers, who shouldn't be under sixteen, he said. No one recorded Percy's facial expressions but surely a smile must have appeared when the new governor openly expressed himself as committed to a state park and forest reserve.

Had Parkhurst lived to serve out his term, a much different political agenda might have resulted, despite his reputation for being too amenable to the party bosses. And Percy, if those same bosses had "kicked him upstairs" to inhibit him, showed no sign at all of deviating from his campaign promises. Back in the senate, once the session began in earnest, he stepped down from the podium and had Frank Farrington of Augusta act as president pro-tem while he presented (out of order) "An Act to Amend an Act to Create the Maine Water Power Commission." He was likewise sponsoring "An Act Establishing the Mount Katahdin State Park." To ensure that he didn't lose the bill in committee without a single vote in its favor, as had happened in 1919, he exercised his prerogative as senate president to appoint brother Rupert to the Committee on State Lands and Forest Preservation, and he also arranged for William F. Dawson of Lynn, Massachusetts, to regale the lawmakers with an "illustrated lecture on Mount Katahdin," scheduled for February 2.

Three days before that date, Percy was at Portland's Union Station, preparing to entrain for Augusta to meet with Parkhurst, who had been ill but was getting better, when he received an emergency message. At 9:12 A.M. on January 31, 1921, Governor Frederick H. Parkhurst had died.

Under Maine law, Senate President Percival P. Baxter was governor, or he would be, as soon as he was sworn in.

His train left at 10:00 A.M., but it was not until 5:05 P.M. that Chief Justice Leslie C. Cornish of the Maine Supreme Court could arrive and administer the oath of office to the forty-four-year-old new governor.

Poor Parkhurst had taken sick five days after his swearing-in. Allegedly, the cause was an unsterilized thermometer put in his mouth when he had gone for an insurance exam; this had given him a "diptheritic infection." His private secretary, Gilbert R. Chadbourne (later Baxter's, as well) has left a chilling description of his illness. At times, Parkhurst's tongue was swollen so badly he could hardly close his lips. But the day before he died, he greeted his assistant cheerfully, saying, "Hello, Chad. I've had a bully day."

The shock of the tragedy paralyzed Augusta. On February 2, instead of listening to William Dawson's lecture on Katahdin, the legislators were filing past Parkhurst's body, laid out in state in the capitol rotunda. They had adjourned until February 7. On February 3, Parkhurst's funeral was held in the Augusta Congregational Church.

It was not until February 9 that Percy publicly commenced his duties with an address to a joint convention of the house and senate. As he stood where Parkhurst had stood a little more than a month previously, the tragic irony had to be apparent to all. In a touching, sensitive preamble to his governmental message, he recalled that past moment for everyone.

Those of us who sat upon this platform always will remember the smile of love and approval which his brave wife gave to him as, anxious for him to do his best, she sat with her little daughter in these seats before us and kept her encouraging eyes fixed upon him. Those of you who looked into his face will long remember the reassuring smile returned by him to her. What faithful wife ever had more reason to look into a future bright with hope and promise? The heart of Maine in these days of loneliness and grief goes out in sympathy to her and her children.[2]

Then, he followed up this tribute with a gallant gesture. Mrs. Parkhurst was to have lived with her husband in the state's newly acquired governor's mansion, the Blaine House, and the legislature had already appropriated $32,500 for its operation. Percy told the assembled lawmakers that he didn't want the money for the Blaine House account. Instead, they should repeal the appropriation and give $5,000 each year for 1921 and 1922 to Mrs. Parkhurst and her children.

Furthermore, the widow and family were to be allowed to stay in the mansion for another two months. Meanwhile, Percy and his brother Rupert would keep their rooms at the Augusta House and take their meals at the hotel, although an office would be available for them in the Blaine House.

The gift of James G. Blaine's home to the State of Maine by his daughter, Harriet Blaine Beale, had first been offered in 1919 when Carl Milliken was governor. He accepted and moved into the magnificent white structure across from the statehouse in January 1920. Mrs. Beale had made her gesture in memory of her son, Walker Blaine Beale, to whom the Blaine House had been willed by his grandfather, but who had been killed in action as an infantry officer in France in 1918. The Blaine House had been in the family's possession since 1862, when James G. Blaine had bought it and presented it to his wife as a birthday present. For a time, after the deaths of the elder Blaines, the premises had been rented—in 1897-

1902, to Governor, John F. Hill, and in the 1905 session to "six wealthy young legislators," led by Representative Fred Hale. Percy was not among them, but Oakley C. Curtis was (although a Democrat), and a "superb chef from one of Bangor's leading clubs" was brought to the capital to cater to these privileged solons' appetites.

Percy's generosity to Mrs. Parkhurst was a pronounced example of a trait that he exhibited throughout his public life; he was always openhanded when it came to himself or his own money and, as would soon be seen in his maiden gubernatorial message, he was, to use a good old Maine expression, "tighter 'n' a tick" when it came to expending taxpayer funds.

As the new governor, Percy lost no time in imparting his philosophy of government to the legislators. "It is now our duty to enter upon a period of reasonable retrenchment and true economy," he stated bluntly." No slinging around of the word *liberal* here. He had a whole string of conservative clichés to dish out. One of the favorites—a comparison with past spending—was immediately invoked: in 1906, Maine government was spending $2.5 million with a mill rate of 2.5 mills (the state then funded itself with a state-wide property tax); in 1920, the outlay was $13.3 million (almost six times as much) and the mill rate was at 7.5 mills. "The time has come," Percy declared in the most shopworn of analogies employed by politicians, "when the state, like the individual, should strike a trial balance and determine whether or not it lives within its income."

But "reasonable retrenchment" or not (and the phrase had struck a chord with the press), this was not the message of your run-of-the-mill mossback. While on the one hand pounding home his theme of Maine waterpower for Maine and warning the federal government not to interfere, he was also reiterating his "socialist" idea of public power, that Maine government should enter the power business. A state-owned Katahdin Park could be deemed equally populist. Percy said, like the pragmatic Yankee that he was, that the park would be a good investment, letting Maine derive "direct and indirect income," but he showed, too, a bit of his father's poetic nature, waxing eloquently on an intangible good, producing a nature-lover's hymn to the benefits of conservation:

> This mountain raises its head aloft unafraid of the passing storm and is typical of the rugged character of the people of Maine.
>
> The establishment of this park will lay the foundation of a policy whereby the present generation will deliver a great inheritance to the generations to come.[3]

If the big landowners of northern Maine were already nervous about this "Katahdin nonsense" of Baxter's, his message gave them even more cause for concern. They might have loved his words about cutting back on government spending, but they could only have shuddered when he specifically asked for one small appropriation, which he justified by claiming it would make the state more money. For Percy, the arithmetic was clear. By paying out $90,000 since 1905 for assessing the wild lands, the state had taken in $575,000 of added taxes; yet only 263 townships out of 441 had been surveyed. So there was a lot more money to be gained from those landowners.

A conservative, to be sure, but—

It was clear from Governor Percy's very first state message that Maine would be governed for the next two years by no ordinary politician. For the old guard, a worst nightmare had perhaps come true. For others, like James Phinney Baxter, a lifelong dream had been fulfilled. And for the people of Maine, an adventure was starting, whether they realized it or not.

On February 1, 1921, a day after Percy had taken the oath of office, his sister Madeleine wrote him from New York City where she had been staying while her husband, Fenton Tomlinson, gravely ill, was receiving specialist medical treatment not available in Maine.

> My first thought was how overjoyed Papa will be, and how thankful I am that he is alive and well enough to enjoy it all. I knew perfectly well that you would be something wonderful before long but was afraid Papa would not be here to see you fulfill his ambition, and be Governor of the State. Fenton said that Papa told him once that his ambition was to have you Governor.

James Phinney, himself, could hardly have imagined what came to pass. Exactly a year before Madeleine's letter to Percy was written—on February 1, 1920—the anxious father wrote in his journal about his deep concern over his son's health. Percy, who was subject to bouts of neuritis, had been in bed for more than a week and was running a high fever. Illness that winter was continually on James Phinney's mind. His son-in-law Fenton was seriously ill—possibly with leukemia (the disease is never named in the journals)—requiring regular blood transfusions and a protracted stay in New York City. Also a worry for James Phinney was his grandson James Phinney III, who had tuberculosis and kept up a running correspondence with his grandfather from a sanitarium in Colorado. In time, James Phinney III would not only recover but go on to become the president of Williams College and deputy director of the OSS during World War II. But in 1920, he was of college age, newly married with a child, a budding historian who liked to exchange his views on American history and politics with his grandfather.

On February 12, 1920, James Phinney received a stun-

JAMES PHINNEY'S BOOKPLATE AND HIS MOTTO.

ning blow, one to set alongside the deaths of his wives and daughters and the horror of his grandson Edward's accident. That night Emily, the oldest of the "second litter," quietly and undramatically revealed to him that she had to go to the hospital for an operation. When he pressed her for more information, she said, "An operation on my breast." Later came the news that her breast had been removed. "I sat propped up in bed and thought of her as my little yellow-haired girl of whom my dear wife was so proud," the devastated father wrote in his journal.

One of the very last entries in his ten volumes of journals described his observation of a recuperating Emily (she had come home from the hospital after two weeks) and her kid brother, who was less than a year away from becoming the governor of Maine.

From the sun room where he was breakfasting, he could see them through the windows out in the garden together, gathering vegetables.

Side by side they looked over their work, apparently considering their successes and failures and my heart went out to them with deep affection. It was a beautiful sight of brotherly and sisterly sympathy and love and I prayed God earnestly to bless them. Could their mother see them? I thought how her heart with mine must go out to them.[4]

The journals end in August 1920. Whatever James Phinney may have felt about the events that enfolded his son, or about Percy's dealings with the legislature during their first session together, remain unexpressed. That he gave up his almost daily practice of writing down his thoughts and impressions was most likely due to deteriorating health. He began to complain of a crippling pain in his knee, and he spent time in the hospital. Approaching ninety, he clearly lacked his former energy and zest. His last public appearance was as the featured speaker at the Maine Historical Society's celebration of the state's centennial in June 1920. He even admitted in his Journal that he was concerned about his performance and perhaps wished he didn't have to do it. A distinguished crowd attended, including Governor Carl Milliken, to listen to him talk about old Portland and, in particular, the First Congregational Church (where the event was held) and the Reverend Thomas Smith, its famous eighteenth-century pastor.

Percy had been quite anxious about the strain of this effort on his father and openly relieved when it was over. James Phinney recorded: "My address was well received...." But he had been irked by having to deal with a "cramped pulpit, insufficient light and the pounding of the cars as they passed the open door of the church."[5]

The next day, he still felt spry enough to take his grandson James Tomlinson to Deering Oaks Park and introduce him to chiefs of the Passamaquoddy and Penobscot tribes who were holding an encampment there. The following month, he was well enough to enjoy a garden party on the lawn of his old home in Gorham, which he had bought and given to the town for a museum.

If infirm six months later when Percy assumed the governorship, he no doubt still closely followed what his son was doing. Cheering him on in his battles was probably the best he could do at the time. And battles, there certainly were!

"LIVELIEST HEARING FOR THE SESSION" proclaimed a headline in a Lewiston newspaper, announcing the public session held by the Committee on State Lands and Forest Preservation on "An Act Establishing the Mount Katahdin State Park."

What the G.O.P. old guard had failed to do—silence Percy Baxter by elevating him to senate president—his assumption of the governorship succeeded in doing. Governors simply did not testify at hearings. A packed audience was on hand and the spacious House chamber had to be used to accommodate all who wanted to participate or listen. Percy had his allies. Charles Barnes, now house speaker, led off for the proponents. Former Senate President Taber D. Bailey began the parade of opponents.

In Percy's corner was the Cumberland County Audubon Society, the American Federation of Labor, and a "timber cruiser," one William Arnold of Houlton who marked trees for a living and testified that he hadn't found much merchantable wood in the area. Following ex-Senate President Bailey on the other side was ex-Congressman Frank Guernsey, who once had tried to get the federal government to take over Katahdin but who said Percy's bill was flawed. Its $100,000 price tag was roundly attacked. A particularly negative foe was the president of the Maine Chamber of Commerce, James Q. Gulnac, who scoffed at the notion that

Katahdin could become a tourist attraction. He was rebutted by the dean of Maine tourist operators, the famed Edward Ricker of Poland Springs.

But it was all an exercise in futility. When the bill emerged at long last from committee, only three members had signed the ought-to-pass report and, even then, it was for a woefully watered-down version. Rupert spoke on the bill, which had its first reading in the senate. Unlike Percy, Rupert hardly ever said anything on the record; indeed, in his first four years as a senator, he spoke only twice and during the 1921 session, less than half a dozen times and almost always on banking matters, since he was chair of the Banks and Banking Committee. With the Katahdin Bill, he was almost apologetic, citing a petition favoring the park signed by 1,400 Republicans at the previous G.O.P. convention in Bangor and stating:

> My conscience would not permit me to repudiate that resolution. I still have the still, small voice of conscience within me. I am going to raise my feeble voice as the voice in the wilderness.[6]

The new draft he was defending left the principle of a state park, but that was about all. The money had been stripped out and a park could be considered "only if hereafter the legislature appropriates or receives gifts."

Behind the assault on Governor Percy's bill, which was defeated 19-8, the fine hand of the Great Northern Paper Company could be discerned. Their lobbyist had pretended GNP was neutral, provided an eminent domain provision was removed, but at least one opposing legislator slammed the park's proponents for their hostility towards a wonderful company that did such wonderful things for the people of his district.

And at least one newspaper, the *Bangor Commercial*, picked up the same theme and specifically raked the new governor over the coals for his remarks about Great Northern.

> ...he has been unfair in his comment regarding the action of a great manufacturing corporation, which is seeking only to protect its rights and its property.[7]

Interestingly enough, the *Commercial* was owned by Harry F. Ross, the Bangor Republican representative who had not been re-elected in 1904 and thus had never served with Percy. The son of one of the earliest lumber operators in the north Maine woods, Ross had hired his own lobbyist to oppose Percy's bill, fearing for the lands he and his sister had inherited, including the township containing Mount Katahdin.

Percy's criticism of Great Northern was that this paper-making colossus of the north was being hypocritical. They railed against eminent domain yet had used eminent domain powers granted them by the legislature to build their industrial complex.

Ross's newspaper hammered away at Baxter on another issue, as well: his advocacy of public power, a concept they called "dangerous both in theory and practice."

The *Bangor Daily News* put the matter succinctly: "GOVERNOR SETS SAIL ON THE SEA OF SOCIALISM." Both publications were reacting to a special message Percy had sent to the lawmakers, requesting—among other things—his pet project of an amendment to the Maine constitution to allow the state to take over waterpowers and storage basins, "destroying private property rights at a single blow," as the *News* thundered. They were equally against his plan for better assessment of land values in the unorganized territories, calling it "a great taxation scheme to raise enormous revenues...."[8]

Even his goal of economy in state spending drew scorn from the Republican press. The *Lewiston Sun* derided Percy's request to buy Katahdin, saying it would be:

> ...better economy to put it into the University of Maine than into the mountain. Better pay for something useful and necessary than something pretty in imagination for the entertainment of foreigners.[9]

The editors were possibly grousing because Percy had announced he was opposed to picking up the university's deficit of $214,035.

His "reasonable retrenchment" aimed at cutting $1,275,506 from the state budget.

Legislators, no matter how conservative, become very angry when projects in their districts are eliminated. And Percy's list of cuts was a long one. Cut was the proposed superintendent's cottage at the Central Maine Sanitarium, no schoolhouse at the State School for Boys, no dormitory for women on the Orono campus, no nurses' homes at the Bangor and Augusta mental institutions, a slash of $75,000 in the university's budget, a slash of $50,000 in new construction at the men's reformatory, etc.

Then came his vetoes, more than any other governor, before or since. Each one created new enemies.

The explosive Cleaves situation next burst upon the scene, creating headlines and a controversy that never seemed to end.

Benjamin Cleaves, an ex-York County judge, was the executive secretary of the Associated Industries of Maine, big business's lobbying arm. At the same time, he was one of the three members of the Public Utilities Commission, which controlled power rates (theoretically) on behalf of the consumers.

Apparently, no one but Percy saw a conflict of interest in Cleaves holding these dual positions. Angered by Cleaves's vocal opposition to his waterpower amendment, Percy demanded that he resign from the PUC.

With fairly breathtaking arrogance, Cleaves not only refused; he even stated the only conditions under which he might leave the post.

> I would prefer to have you understand that my resignation would be handed to you at such time as you had decided on the right kind of man to be my successor.[10]

Moreover, he continued to appear at legislative hearings as a lobbyist for the AIM.

In this open fight, public opinion quickly swung behind the governor. Percy was wildly applauded by 250 of Portland's leading citizens, including businessmen, when he declared he wouldn't be satisfied until the seat was vacant. Mutterings of impeachment of Cleaves were heard around Augusta. The *Lewiston Journal* backed Percy (as it often did). But even the less friendly *Lewiston Enterprise* labeled Cleaves's attitude "unadulterated gall." The *Portland Herald*, often antagonistic to Percy, said that this time he was right.

Maine's traditional political satire, couched in country bumpkin speech, entered the fray:

> I asked Ben [Cleaves] if he was the man that killed the "What-A-Power" bill and he said he was not but that he did put the "Ax" in Baxter.
>
> Baxter: I am the man that is going to put the "leaves" in Cleaves.
>
> P.S. When Percy was leaving my office the other day, I called after him: "Has Ben...?" "Has Ben is right," said Percy and closed the door.

Within three weeks, Cleaves caved in and resigned unconditionally.

This maiden crisis behind him, Percy concentrated on his vetoes. They could be large or small: a claim from a Michael Burns for the value of liquor allegedly illegally seized from him; $100,000 to continue the medical school at his alma mater, Bowdoin College; $10,000 for fire damage caused by an inmate from the Bangor Mental Health Institution.

The Bowdoin veto meant the medical school would close (which it did); it was exercised despite the plea of his old roommate Kenneth Sills, who by now had become president of the college. Percy's veto message in this instance said, rather off the point, that Maine "should not establish a State Medicine anymore than a State Religion." Unspoken in Percy's disapproval was that the med school practiced vivisection.

In verse, the press poked fun at Percy's proclivity.

Vetoes
Our Governor sits down at his table
And writes in a message so gay
A Message to House and to Senate
Oh, what will he veto today?
Chorus: Vetoes, vetoes, our Governor's writing away, away
Vetoes, vetoes, Oh, what will he veto today?
He's vetoed Mike Burns and his liquor
He's vetoed a bill for a school
He's vetoed a bill for a fire
Although it was set by a fool.[11]

These earliest of his vetoes were easily sustained. Of the fourteen items he vetoed during the session, three, however, were overridden, including $250,000 to fund the deficit at the University of Maine. One bill he defeated did not have a price

A SURE HAND AT THE WHEEL.

OUR NEW SKIPPER HAS INSPIRED STATE-WIDE
CONFIDENCE IN RECORD TIME.

A NEWSPAPER CARTOON REFLECTS THE FACT THAT
GOVERNOR PERCY SOON PUT HIS IMPRINT ON STATE AFFAIRS.

tag but reflected his strong feelings about cruelty to animals; it would have encouraged the killing of sea gulls.

Among the sustained vetoes was one for $20,000 to build a cottage at the boys reformatory in South Portland. Yet the project was resurrected when a member of the state senate, in a Baxter-like gesture, offered to pay half the money, himself, (that is, if the building were named for him). He was Senator Arthur Gould, an Aroostook County railroad and power company magnate, and the man who would later put an end to Percy Baxter's political career.

Since there were practically no Democrats in the legislature that session, all of Percy's problems were with his fellow Republicans. In attacking his waterpower amendment, as opposed to his spending cuts, they found themselves on surer ideological grounds. One wonders what James Phinney, the quintessential union and left wing basher, thought of the cries of "socialist" constantly hurled against his son. Percy's old nemesis, Representative Benedict Maher, even mixed in both of America's recent favorite enemies, the *Kaiser and the Reds*, claiming that the governor's waterpower plan "goes right straight back to the great Central Empire of Germany, and has its beginnings with Karl Marx."[12]

Percy had his defenders. Ralph Owen Brewster, in the house, did what he could for the governor's amendment, and Senator Patrick Gillen, although he said he couldn't vote for the measure, descried the personal attacks made on the chief executive, insults to "a gentleman whose delicate courtesy to a beautiful woman and her sorrowing children when they were under a cloud of sorrow and distress marks him as a gentleman." Despite an even split on the committee report, Percy lost by almost 2-1 in both branches.

His next fierce public fight was with the executive council. A relic of colonial days, this institution's purpose was primarily to check and balance the governor's appointive powers. He could nominate but he also needed a majority of their seven votes to confirm. When he nominated former Senator Howard Davies of Yarmouth to the position on the Public Utilities Commission vacated by Benjamin Cleaves, a bruising conflict erupted.

Baxter's choice of Davies might have seemed puzzling. As his own Judiciary Committee chair in 1917, Davies had often opposed him on waterpower issues. But this former G.O.P. senate floor leader was a distinguished person, too distinguished for the councilors, who were mostly career politicos

GOVERNOR AND COUNCIL, POSING FOR THEIR OFFICIAL PICTURE IN 1921. THIS EXECUTIVE COUNCIL REFUSED AGAIN AND AGAIN TO CONFIRM PERCY'S NOMINATION OF HOWARD DAVIES FOR THE PUBLIC UTILITIES COMMISSION.

chosen by the party to look after its interests. A pet peeve of theirs regarding Davies was that he had been the legislative father of the direct primary, which had taken nominations to offices out of the hands of the bosses.

Four times, the council refused to consent to Howard Davies's appointment. Despite his stubbornness in sending back the name again and again, Percy finally had to admit defeat. After the session ended, the *Portland Herald* published "Abel Skrubb's view of Governor Baxter and his Council."

> ...The Kouncil's attitood seems to be that Governor Baxter ain't their boss, not bein' regoolarly elected to the office uv Chief Magistrate but only fillin' the place uv Governor Parkhurst who is dead.

But the people's view of the governor may have been colored most of all by the fact that he had lowered the tax burden. The state tax bite had dropped by almost half, from $4.1 million to $2.1 million and the mill rate had fallen from 7.37 mills to 4.60 mills. It was a stunning fiscal performance, the best, Percy boasted, since 1835 when the state was flush from having sold off so much of its land.

Nevertheless, rumblings were heard that a G.O.P. "Battalion of Death" was forming in Augusta to thwart Percy if he were to seek re-election in 1922. Harry F. Ross's *Bangor Commercial* repeatedly predicted Percy would have opposition in the primary.

If these rumors bothered him, he never showed it. He took courageous stands, such as loudly condemning the death penalty for being a "relic of medievalism," preaching peace and disarmament to an American Legion gathering, and, above all, refusing (alone among U.S. governors) to back a request from the governor of California to urge Congress to halt all Japanese immigration. Percy had been to Japan several times and said he admired the Japanese people. According to Max Cohen, a Republican official, Percy was the first Maine governor "to ever give an appointed position to a Hebrew."

In running the Blaine House, Percy kept within the confines of his salary. When parties were given, they were at his expense, and in 1922, he inaugurated a Blaine House New Year's Eve reception for the statehouse executives and clerical help.

While a string orchestra played and his military staff in full uniform flanked him, Percy greeted his guests as they entered an interior tastefully decorated with pink roses, red carnations, and other flowers; they dined on lobster salad, harlequin ice cream, and fancy cakes. Legislators and their wives were invitees, too, and on one occasion, in March 1923, they were fed cold turkey and scalloped oysters and then led across the street to the statehouse to view a motion picture called *Blazing Barriers*, made by a Maine film company. That June, the Blaine House grounds were used for a massive charity fair Percy helped organize: more than two thousand people circulated among booths while a ten-piece band played and a barbershop quartet sang. The governor, himself, sold hot dogs and Poland water—all for a worthy cause.

It was in 1923, too, that his widowed sister Madeleine arrived with her boys to live in the mansion. In December, Santa Claus was played by Uncle Percy.

The previous year, with the help of U.S. Senator Fred Hale, the governor had been instrumental in recovering for Maine the silver service presented by the state to the battleship *Maine* upon its commissioning. When the ship sank in Havana, the soup tureen and dishes decorated with pine cone and pine needle designs and the state seal had gone down with her, but had been retrieved by divers. These recovered items are still on display in the Blaine House.

No doubt they were shown by Percy to a distinguished guest, Vice-President Calvin Coolidge, when he visited the Blaine House on July 2, 1923. A month later, under circumstances similar to Percy's rise to the highest office in Maine, Calvin Coolidge became president of the country.

PERCY WAS THE FIRST MAINE GOVERNOR TO VISIT THE ACADIAN FRENCH COMMUNITIES OF NORTHERNMOST AROOSTOOK COUNTY. HIS VISIT TO ST. AGATHA, PICTURED HERE, WAS SO MEMORABLE THAT HE LEFT ITS SCHOOL $25,000 IN HIS WILL.

A word portrait of Percy as governor has been left by the writer Frederick L. Collins in his 1924 book on the nation's governors, *Our American Kings.*

"The Governor is a character. Bachelor. Tall, strong and pink," Collins begins. The description continues that he is a "low-voiced, pink-cheeked, boyish man," but no hail-fellow-well-met. An Augusta policeman named Reilly on duty out-side the Blaine House is quoted as saying that when the chief executive "walks along with a sack-suit and a dog and soft hat, you'd never guess he was governor...everybody calls him Percy...but nobody calls him 'Percy, old bean.'" Collins writes that he is "46 or 47 in the record books, but much younger with his hat on."

His desk in the governor's office is described as contain-ing "23 ivory images, dogs, elephants, lions, rabbits, ducks, lizards, eagles, horses, cats...." Lunch at the Blaine House was presided over by a Mrs. Mallet, the sole person Percy would allow on the state payroll to serve him. His recreation seemed confined to long treks with his dog over the hills that bound the Kennebec Valley, and Collins found him "a picturesque talker—on any subject."

Collins also captures in his description of Augusta in the 1920s a sense of the parochialism of Maine at the time. It was still an incredibly rural state. Writes Collins:

> Augusta, Maine's State Capital, is a great place for the country people. To the confirmed urbanite, Water Street may not stack up with Fifth Avenue or State Street as a retail center—but for many a down-east family the old town in the beautiful Kennebeck [sic] Valley is a verita-ble Yankee Mecca. The governor showed me a cliff over-looking the little city on which a lad from Piscataquis

County recently stood and said in an awed whisper: "Now I know what the world is like."

Perhaps responding to that sense of isolation, Percy found time, once the legislators had left the capital, to travel around in a way no other governor before him had ever done. He became especially known for his visits to schools and to places where no other chief executive had ever been before, like the northernmost tip of Maine, the St. John Valley, where the language until recently was almost exclusively Acadian French. In this region, it is traditional to call governors by their nicknames and Governor Percy must have been heartily welcomed by these warm and friendly folks. He apparently never forgot his reception at the school in St. Agatha for he remembered the school in his will with an unexplained bequest of $25,000.

This unofficial campaign had hardly begun when, on May 8, 1921, James Phinney died.

---

[1] He made much of the fact that the wool came from sheep raised in Vassalboro, had been woven in Skowhegan, and tailored in Augusta.

[2] *Legislative Record*, February 9, 1921; page 127.

[3] Ibid.

[4] James Phinney Baxter Journal #10, August 6, 1920.

[5] Ibid., June 27, 1920.

[6] *Legislative Record*, March 23, 1921; page 629.

[7] *Bangor Commercial*, March 10, 1921.

[8] *Bangor Daily News*, March 18, 1921.

[9] Baxter Scrapbooks, Personal, Vol. 1; page 82.

[10] Ibid.

[11] Baxter Scrapbooks, Vol. 16; page 113.

[12] *Legislative Record*, 1921; page 1,275.

10

Alone, and Then "Regoolarly" Elected

PERCY BAXTER NOW HAD TO FIGHT his battles alone. Whether political battles or simply the battles of life, the reassuring presence of the august gentleman at 61 Deering Street, Portland, was no longer available to counsel him. That James Phinney had been a guiding light to his son was probably never clearly articulated between the two of them, but their public personas certainly matched. To paraphrase Bobby Kennedy in a later age, they both saw things that never were and asked "Why not?"

When death arrives, one begins to think of lasting memorials. The Boulevard would serve for James Phinney, and it was nearing absolute completion at the time of his demise. A month afterward, the Portland City Council unanimously voted to change the existing name of Back Cove Boulevard to Baxter Boulevard.

In the mini-biography pamphlet that Percy published about his father, he alluded to James Phinney's never-flagging

JAMES PHINNEY BAXTER. UPON HIS DEATH, HE WAS CALLED "MAINE'S BELOVED BENEFACTOR."

interest in the Boulevard. His father's disillusion with politics, however, was also cited. There was likewise reference to the fact that James Phinney's family was his "hobby," and that he believed the greatest single factor in success was "the ability to control one's surroundings." The elder Baxter's love of animals, imparted to his children, was traced to his upbringing on a "rugged Maine farm" where he "came to know and love domestic animals and he never tired of telling of his horses, dogs, and other animal friends." No limit was ever placed on the number of pets allowed his children, Percy wrote, and he, himself, soon to be famous throughout Maine for his attachment to his Irish Setter, once had had five of them at the same time. Percy called his father a "Progressive" in politics and emphasized his support for Women's Suffrage, "a point of view unusual for a man of his age and training."

The funeral, held in the large, red-brick house James Phinney had bought for raising his second family, was almost a state affair. A delegation of legislators attended; so did the mayor and ex-mayors of Portland, the state librarian, the Portland superintendent of schools, representatives of the many organizations to which James Phinney had belonged and, of course, the governor of Maine who, along with his half-brothers, served as a pall-bearer. Adding to the sense of sorrow appropriate to the event was the tragic knowledge that Emily's cancer had returned, and that only seven weeks earlier Madeleine had lost her husband Fenton.

As he listened to the service conducted by the Reverend Henry S. Bradley of the State Street Congregational Church, what grim determination was being reinforced within Percy to be his father's son, to push to the extreme his own conception of the public good, no matter what the political consequences?

It is unlikely that he was thinking ahead to the implication that he would presently, because of his inheritance, have the financial means to accomplish the most ambitious of his goals, the Katahdin park. But he later did reveal that, in regard to his father's will, dated October 8, 1919 and probated July 18, 1921, "I was in his confidence at all times and aided in its drafting."

From the vantage of the end of the twentieth century, an assessment of James Phinney Baxter poses a somewhat awkward task. As evidenced by the reaction to his proposed pantheon to New England's exclusively WASP heroes, initiated in his last will and testament, there is an instant recoil now at an idea seemingly so natural in the cultural climate of 1921. James Phinney was a man of his time, his support for Women's Suffrage notwithstanding. How intolerant of others was he? One has a sense that his bigotries were in the abstract and, therefore, inconsistent when he was faced with living people. While his anti-unionism would certainly be respectable in certain quarters today, a remark he made in his journal aimed at Woodrow Wilson could be construed as anti-Semitic. To wit:

> Wilson has catered to the unions, the Jews and all the discontented elements in the country."[1]

Yet, conversely, there is this statement made while he was mayor:

> Laid the foundation of the Jewish synagogue. Dr. Kaplan, a Jew, made one of the finest addresses I have ever listened to.[2]

And lest his use of the word Jew in the latter instance might seem pejorative, he was to write a revealing expression of his personal sentiments less than a week later.

> Abe Weinberg and Fanny Rosenberg, two Jewish children who have been spending the summers with us went

back to New York in the boat. Emily and Madeleine went to the boat with them. Poor little things. They have been brought up in dire poverty and dread going back to their homes.[3]

Furthermore, he noted that he had wished to keep the girl with them, "a beautiful little child," but her father wouldn't consent.

Abe Weinberg not only became a lifelong friend of the family but summer after summer, came to stay at Mackworth Island, and his letters to James Phinney continued until the elder Baxter's death. Indeed, James Phinney had to have been a father figure for him. When Hetty died, he wrote to Emily that, "You will have to do all in your power to make things easier for that splendid gentleman" and his condolences to James Phinney emphasized that Mrs. Baxter had been like a mother to him. "Can I forget the early summers at Mackworth when I had the benefit of her training?" he wrote and ended, "I hope that you will recover from the shock as soon as possible; if you don't, I am afraid it will have some effect on your longevity and God knows that we all want you to be with us for a great many years to come." When Madeleine and her husband came to New York City because of Fenton's illness, Abe Weinberg visited them and his fondest wish, he said, was to have a Baxter visit the home he had just built in New Jersey, whose financial details down to his tenant's rental fee, he happily shared with a kindred businessman soul like James Phinney.

A seemingly anti-Native American bias on the part of James Phinney has already been mentioned. His constant use of the term "savages" to describe them is definitely a clue to his prejudice, as well as his undisguised scorn for the primitiveness of their way of life. One of his poems (dozens of them, not published in book form, have been left in elegant notebooks and hand-written in someone's neat, meticulous style) extols General George Custer, a hero in his eyes. But another of these poems, called "Natahda," is a sensitive epic of the original Abnaki inhabitants of Maine, revealing an extensive and sympathetic knowledge of their culture. Included in the notebook is a sketch done by James Phinney of "the ancient site of an Abnakian summer village at Meneeko, now Mackworth Island." An additional complicating ambiguity in his attitude toward these local Indians is expressed by a note prefacing his verse, where he states that there is a "remarkable resemblance" between Scandinavian lore and Abnaki lore, which cannot be satisfactorily explained, implying, however, that the red men may have inherited a white men's influence in the dim past.

In James Phinney's era in Maine, the primary prejudice was neither against Jews nor Indians. Since the arrival of boat-loads of immigrants fleeing the Irish potato famine, it had been against Catholics. The 1840s had seen a wave of Know-Nothing violence Downeast, churches burned, and at least one priest tarred and feathered, and the 1870s had added a new target: French-Canadian Catholics. The 1920s saw an explosive growth of the Ku Klux Klan in Maine, a fortunately brief reaction to the slipping of the once-overwhelming "Protestant ascendancy" in the state.

When James Phinney took his family to Europe in 1885, their first sight at their first stop, which was Ireland, revealed a "pitiful crowd of human beings," returning from the New World. "They had fled to America," he wrote in his journal, "paradise for the idle lazy—then still paupers were shipped back home."

Anti-Catholic? Maybe. Maybe not. Or consider his comment, on October 15, 1907, that he had gone to the Roman

Catholic Cathedral in Portland to witness the consecration of Bishop Louis Walsh and wondered if Christ would approve of all the ceremony, although he added that he had given up criticizing forms of belief.

Exactly when his daughter Emily converted to Catholicism isn't clear, nor did he reveal his thoughts about her action. The subject is simply never raised in his journals, but her spiritual mentor, Father John O'Dowd of Sacred Heart Church, seems to have been a regular visitor to the household, as were a succession of Protestant missionaries traveling through Portland on their way to and from foreign lands.

The tributes that poured in upon James Phinney's death would hardly acknowledge even the hint of any dark side. He was "Maine's Beloved Benefactor," and a long string of bequests in his will was soon revealed: money to buy art objects and his collection of antique watches to Bowdoin, money for a scholarship fund and his collection of Indian pottery to the Portland Society of Art, money to the Baxter Memorial Library in Gorham, money for a fountain in a public place in Portland. Alfred Johnson of The New England Historical and Genealogical Society, to which he had donated so much time and effort, wrote a long article in their monthly publication devoted to his memory. First, a description of him:

> In height above the average, possessed of a strong, massive frame, his large head well planted on his square shoulders, his figure was to the last an erect and commanding one. His voice, though gentle and low-pitched in conversation, was capable of filling the largest auditorium.[4]

Then, a perceptive comment:

> It might almost be said that half his time was spent in acquiring power and the other half in using it for the

benefit of his contemporaries and of posterity.[5]

And a snapshot biography followed, with a listing of his accomplishments and memberships, plus the little known fact that at age eighty-five, he had decided to rebuild his home on Mackworth Island, built by him thirty years before, moving the old structure and replacing it with a "thoroughly modern brick and tile structure," designed by Portland architect Frederick O. Thompson.

About James Phinney, Johnson concluded:

There was never the slightest pretense of the self-anointed autocrat or of the snob.[6]

With his father laid to rest, Percy went back to the business of being governor. Given the fairly minuscule scope of Maine government in those days (a biennial budget not more than $4 million), his administrative duties were far from those demanded by today's $3 billion-plus behemoth. He had time in the summer of 1921, acting as James Phinney's executor, to have his father's will probated. And then, almost before he had caught his breath, another blow hit him. On September 4, 1921, his sister Emily died.

A Solemn High Mass of Requiem was held for this daughter of one of the eminent Protestant families of the state, who had been graduated from Abbott Academy in Andover, Massachusetts, an exclusive girls finishing school, and Wellesley College, and who had devoted her life to social work and the care and companionship of her father and brother. She was only forty-seven years old. One of the condolence letters to Percy said, "...for I know how much Emily loved you, felt the care and responsibility that had come to you. And how she looked forward to this election...."

No one effectively challenged Percy for the nomination, and he ran for re-election. His Democratic opponent was

MARBLE BUST OF JAMES PHINNEY IN THE PORTLAND
PUBLIC LIBRARY.

THE ORIGINAL "COTTAGE" ON MACKWORTH ISLAND,
MOVED BY JAMES PHINNEY IN 1916 AND REPLACED BY A
"THOROUGHLY MODERN BRICK AND TILE STRUCTURE."

TWO PORTRAITS OF JAMES PHINNEY IN HIS LATER YEARS:
ABOVE WITH A DOG AND A GRANDCHILD; BELOW: WITH A DOG.

William R. "Patt" Pattangall. A couple of singular Downeast political expressions are appropriate to the campaign that followed. Since "Patt" had been *bad-mouthing* Percy since 1904, it was perhaps fitting that Percy should *clean his clock* for him once they were on the hustings together. In other words, the incumbent scored a solid win: 103,713 to 75,256. "Patt" was his usual sarcastic self. A vintage Pattangall thrust was when he chided Percy and his top assistant, Gilbert Chadbourne, for not being at a certain meeting in Boston.

> Perhaps he and Chad and the dog were taking a stroll through Ganneston Park. You could tell the difference between Chad and the dog because Chad wears clothes.
>
> If you had any doubt which was the Governor, he'll tell you.[7]

Percy wasn't known for his humor, but he did shoot back that it wasn't necessary for him to say anything funny since being a Democratic candidate for governor in Maine "was itself enough of a joke."

The 1923 session of the legislature was pretty much a repeat of 1921; Governor Baxter vetoed a lot of bills. He pushed for Katahdin—in vain. And waterpower was once again a major issue—even more so—since the furor over the Kennebec Reservoir Company legislation dominated the headlines and the state's political attention.

We have already seen the aftermath of that epic fight, how seventy years later, the state's citizens received full value for the waterpower resource that had been rented to the Central Maine Power Company. It had been Percy's tough persistence, his willingness to go to the people with an initiated referendum, that had stopped the giveaway of public land and water rights owned by the state with no direct recompense to the treasury.

Over the fireplace in the home at 61 Deering Street where Percy was raised, a frieze of tiles depicted the story of Jack and the Beanstalk. How much of that tale of giant-killing had sunk in while Percy had stared into the fire as a child? Probably a good deal, if his political behavior is any criterion, for in this instance he was taking on the giants of Maine: not only Walter Wyman of the Central Maine Power Company but also Garrett Schenck of the Great Northern Paper Company. Both these CEO's were incorporators of the company that the giveaway legislation was to create.

Percy had been struggling against long odds throughout his career in Augusta and his victory here was his greatest. Yet it was essentially a *defensive* victory, in that he had merely kept something from happening; i.e., preventing the handing over of two public lots on either side of the Dead River with no payment in return and a deeding away forever of water rights for free. The effort to score an *offensive* victory—creating something new, like the Mount Katahdin Park—was once more thwarted and would be forever, it seemed, because of the enmity he had created by opposing Garrett Schenck.

The legislature departed at the end of the 1923 session in April with no action whatsoever taken on the Kennebec Reservoir issue, but this did not end Percy's involvement in fierce public controversies. Another big one started quite innocently when he was attending a National Governors Conference at West Baden, Indiana, in October 1923.

It was the first time the nation's governors did what has since become exceedingly common at their get-togethers: pass resolutions urging actions by the federal government. Leading the effort to adopt a seemingly motherhood-and-apple-pie request—namely, better enforcement of Prohibition—was Governor Percival Baxter of Maine. He was even mentioned in the headlines of the *Cincinnati Inquirer*, which along with

RUPERT BAXTER: THE SIBLING CLOSEST TO PERCY—HIS ALLY AND CONFIDANTE—WHO SERVED BOTH IN THE MAINE STATE SENATE AND ON THE EXECUTIVE COUNCIL WHILE PERCY WAS GOVERNOR.

proclaiming that "Prohibition" was the dominant issue at the conclave, added a subhead: "MAINE CHIEF ASSERTS TWO FAST DESTROYERS COULD PUT AN END TO LIQUOR SMUGGLING ON COAST."

So far, so good. The State of Maine, where the first Prohibition law in the nation had been passed in 1856 and kept on the books ever since, could hardly fault its chief executive for being vocally tough on booze.

But the always hostile *Lewiston Sun* took umbrage at Percy's rather smug assertion that Maine was carrying out the Volstead Act effectively on its own soil and merely needed federal help offshore. The editors stated baldly that Percy's enforcement record at home had been none too good.

On his return from Indiana, Percy replied to their criticism by going to Bar Harbor and publicly lambasting the county sheriff, Ward W. Westcott, whom he had previously warned about lax enforcement. It was common knowledge that Hancock County was notoriously "wet" and that the Sheriff and his deputies were more than soft on smuggling. At the end of his tirade, Percy demanded Westcott's resignation.

Not receiving any satisfaction, the governor then had Attorney-General Ransford W. Shaw bring an impeachment action against the sheriff.

The court that heard this sensational case was the governor and executive council, meeting in the statehouse on November 16, 1923.

After his experience with the Davies nomination, Percy perhaps felt he needed an ally on the council more than in the senate, so Rupert gave up his legislative seat and managed to be chosen for that "advise and consent" body by the Republican lawmakers from his area. But he was the only sure vote on which Percy could count.

The story that came out of the hearing was unquestionably shocking. A "rum ring," led by one Daniel Herlihy, had already been broken up in Bar Harbor by the U.S. attorney and Herlihy sent to Atlanta Penitentiary, but many of the witnesses before Percy and the council had worked for him. For example, Clifford Willey, a Bar Harbor contractor told how he had picked up liquor in Canada and landed it on Mount Desert Island and at Blue Hill where it was transshipped through Ellsworth (Sheriff Westcott's headquarters), and that he had never been stopped by the sheriff or his men. He had also seen Deputy Clark at the Lenox Club, which handled $150,000 to $200,000 worth of liquor a year.

Witness after witness told similar stories. But when the verdict was issued, only Percy and Rupert had voted against acquitting Westcott. The anti-Baxter *Bangor News* exulted:

STINGING SNUB TO BAXTER DYNASTY
King Percival and Prince Rupert Alone Vote for Removal of Sheriff Westcott of Hancock County, Who Triumphs Over the Royal Inquisition.[8]

Entirely unrepentant, Percy kept on swinging, delivering speeches attacking "the old alliance of business, politics and rum" of Hancock County. Vindication of a sort may have come when a full-scale liquor scandal broke out in Aroostook County less than a month after the Westcott trial. This time, the county sheriff, plus a former deputy and one of the most prominent attorneys in Houlton were indicted for liquor dealing. Now, Percy's demand for a sheriff's resignation could not be ignored.

The next huge battle embroiling Percy decidedly was not his fault. In fact, it came about because he decided to follow Maine's unwritten tradition against a third gubernatorial term and announced he would not seek re-election in 1924. The way was thus open for a G.O.P. nominating race between Ralph Owen Brewster, who was sometimes seen as a protégé of Percy's, and State Senator Frank Farrington. This Brewster-Farrington primary contest developed into one of the dirtiest, most corrupt, and closest elections in Maine history.

And Percy was inadvertently caught in the middle.

Owen Brewster *had*, indeed, been an ally of his. Throughout the battle on the Kennebec Reservoir Company bill, Brewster had remained in the governor's corner and, at one point, when a compromise was worked out with Central Maine Power, he had acted as Percy's negotiator. Yet an unspoken issue had begun to create a division between these two

Portlanders. Brewster was a fanatical opponent of state aid in any form to parochial schools, which in Maine at the time, meant Catholic schools. Because of this stand, the newly organized and quickly growing Ku Klux Klan whose main target (in the absence of all but a handful of Jews and blacks) was Catholics, gave him their backing in the primary and Frank Farrington emerged as the anti-Klan candidate. Percy, of course, had never made any secret of his hostility to the Klan and its demagogic head Kleagle, F. Eugene Farnsworth.

The election, held on June 17, 1924, ended with Farrington ahead by 315 votes.

But Brewster wouldn't concede. The first public indication that his relationship with the governor might be frayed occurred when Baxter was asked by a reporter if he would order a recount. Percy replied that it was up to Brewster to request one. Brewster's snippy response to him was: "I had no intention of asking you to assume my responsibilities."

An inspection of ballots showed irregularities in a number of places, mostly in the French-speaking St. John Valley but also in Ward 4, Portland, and Ward 4, Lewiston. These were heavily Catholic areas, and the St. John Valley had given Farrington an extraordinary plurality of 2,036 to 26.

The recount brought to light some odd goings-on. The chairman of the Board of Assessors in Eagle Lake Plantation complained of how his claim had been ignored that 75 percent of the voters in that district were illegal since they had never been given a reading test in English, as the law required. In Ward 4, 228 Republicans had voted, but there were only 161 G.O.P. enrollees on the voting list. In St. Agatha, 30 people had voted after the polls were closed. In Ward 4, Portland, 400 votes allegedly had been "stuffed" into the ballot box after hours.

As the recount progressed, relations between Percy and

Primary Recount July /1924

PHOTO TAKEN DURING THE FAMOUS (OR INFAMOUS) RECOUNT BETWEEN OWEN BREWSTER AND FRANK FARRINGTON FOR THE REPUBLICAN NOMINATION TO SUCCEED PERCY.

Owen Brewster worsened. The governor was accused of delaying the count and hoping for a stalemate so he could continue in the Blaine House. The bad feelings led to this terse public exchange:

> Baxter: "Do you make any charges?"
> Brewster: "I make no charges."
> Baxter: "Do you make any innuendoes?"
> Brewster: "No."
> Baxter: "Do you think I have been unfair?"
> Brewster: "I do not think you have any right to ask that question."

The decision finally came down to Ward 4, Portland. Farrington had beaten Brewster there by a whopping 718-153, which was a suspicious total in Brewster's own hometown.

At this point, Percy intervened and instead of throwing out Ward 4, he announced that Ward 4 voters would be allowed to come to Augusta and announce whom they had voted for. It seemed a strange decision. Previously, St. Agatha's vote had been thrown out—costing Farrington 250 votes—on the grounds that people had marked their ballots in the open, without benefit of booths. Now, they were to publicly declare themselves. Was Percy merely trying to smoke out any "stuffed" ballots, or was he secretly hoping to preserve Frank Farrington's reduced 42-vote margin? If the latter (and Brewster may well have believed it), he failed. Of the mere 214 Ward 4 voters who bothered to come to Augusta, 86 said they hadn't voted on June 17, 86 said they'd voted for Brewster, and 42 had voted for Farrington. With Farrington's net loss of 623 votes, he was out of the race and Brewster became the G.O.P. nominee.

During the general election campaign, the harsh words between Percy and Owen appeared forgotten and the governor went on the stump for his fellow Republican, perhaps all the more willingly because his opponent was "Patt" Pattangall, whom Brewster easily trounced.

Some of Percy's final spleen while in office was reserved for the still unresolved matter of payment for water rights. The companies that had pushed for the Kennebec Reservoir Company bill had hardly given up. With Baxter out of their way, they would be back, and to that end they had formed a "Fact Finding Board" under the auspices of the state Chamber of Commerce whose duties were to tell the truth about waterpower to Maine people. Percy strove to expose its membership, attacking the chamber's James Q. Gulnac as the foremost foe of waterpower rights, his own friend Senator Guy Gannett as a vice-president of CMP, and Senator Arthur Gould, a power company owner who had won significant water storage rights from the 1921 legislature.

These strong forces ignored him. When Percy proposed calling a special session if they would agree to the compromise they had once supported, they did not even deign to reply. To put things in modern parlance, they figured he would soon be "history."

---

[1] James Phinney Baxter Journal #9, September 7, 1916; page 242.

[2] James Phinney Baxter Journal #6, September 14, 1904; page 149.

[3] Ibid., September 20, 1904; page 150.

[4] *The New England Historical and Genealogical Register*, July 1921; page 171.

[5] Ibid.

[6] Ibid.

[7] Baxter Scrapbooks, Volume 12; page 28.

OUTGOING GOVERNOR PERCIVAL BAXTER SHAKES HANDS
WITH GOVERNOR-ELECT RALPH OWEN BREWSTER ON
INAUGURATION DAY, JANUARY 7, 1925. NOTE THE IRISH
SETTER PERCY HAS BROUGHT WITH HIM TO THE STATE-
HOUSE STEPS.

11

En Route To A Magnificent Obsession

THE TWO MEN LOOKED FRIENDLY
enough in January 1925, when outgoing Governor Percival P.
Baxter posed with incoming Governor Ralph Owen Brewster
for a photograph on the steps of the Maine statehouse.
Brewster was about to extend a political career started in Portland that would eventually lead him to the U.S. Senate. And
Percy, having come out of the same milieu in the state's biggest city and having reached the state's top job, no doubt could
still see a bright future for himself in politics, despite the enemies he had made. He was not yet fifty years old.

The press bruited about a number of possibilities for him:
Congress, the U.S. Senate, a cabinet position in the administration of Calvin Coolidge (whom he resembled physically
and had always loyally supported), even a possible bid for
Vice-President.

One thing was clear; for good or for ill, he had made an
incredible imprint on the State of Maine during his four years
in office.

He is of the type which America knows so little, but which is so common in the public life of England—the rich man's son, who selects politics as his profession, just as one brother selects the law, another medicine and a third the clergy.[1]

Thus did an editorialist typecast the retiring governor as the closest Maine had to an hereditary aristocrat, perhaps with the knowledge that young Percy had once attended Eton School. In a book about governors of the period, Baxter was called: "...a rich man's son who has offended every rich man in Maine."[2]

Yet here was no Franklin Delano Roosevelt patrician liberal. His conservative credo had been spelled out in the inaugural address starting his second term. Barry Goldwater or Ronald Reagan wouldn't have said it any differently.

The modern tendency is toward governmental paternalism.... We should have the minimum of government and the maximum of personal effort. Citizens should become self-reliant, they should not lean upon the State or town....[3]

In this instance, the bedrock of his thought was not Adam Smith or some other free-enterprise guru. "Maine is my inspiration," he declared. And he went on to deliver a paean to the qualities of his native state, quoting from an unidentified author:

"It [Maine] is the last stronghold of the Puritan.... It is distinctive from its neighboring States.... More than most parts of the modern world, Maine has kept its native quality, moral and physical.

"Whatever may be left of that famous old New

England will be found today more purely and abundantly here in Maine than elsewhere."

He could have been quoting James Phinney. Perhaps he was. That Maine historian par excellence had given much of his life (and a good bit of his money) to perpetuate the notion of an ethnic goodness related to the perceived values that had brought his ancestors across the sea. It was a bit ironic that Maine had not originally been a Puritan stronghold—quite the opposite—and James Phinney, with his intimate knowledge of the state's past, was certainly aware of the fact. Yet the Baxters represented, somewhat belatedly, the immigrants from Massachusetts and Connecticut who had transformed Maine from an Anglican, Cavalier beginning to a Congregationalist, Roundhead continuation. Then, too, for Percy at least, there was the Proctor influence—quintessential Puritans from the Salem-Peabody section of Massachusetts. His most famous ancestor was John Proctor, of Salem Witch Trial fame, the model for the protagonist of Arthur Miller's play, *The Crucible*.

His father had steeped Percy in this heritage, and it had been reinforced by an anglophilism made real during his stay in England. Despite a tolerance always exhibited toward other ethnic and religious groups in his public life and his fierce opposition to hate groups such as the KKK, he could not forego exhibiting his pride of ancestry and the political lessons of thrift, self-reliance, and an obligation to the commonweal that he drew from it.

Such notions, carried out to their logical conclusion, often brought him trouble and lost him friends. His attitude toward the University of Maine is a case in point. He did not see why the state should continue to fund the institution.

If State aid is withdrawn will not our public-spirited citizens for the sake of principle make an heroic effort and forego State aid for their private institutions? Our citizens are generous and an appeal made to them on these grounds would meet with ready response.... Is not the sense of personal responsibility the vital factor behind the success of any institution?[4]

Despite his well-known support for Women's Suffrage, his philosophy managed to infuriate the first woman elected to the Maine State Legislature, Representative Dora Pinkham of Fort Kent, when he used it against her to veto her pet bill. What Mrs. Pinkham wanted to do was have Maine participate in the federal Sheppard-Towner Act and match U.S. funds for maternal and child health care. His veto message insisted that Maine "would return to the fundamental doctrine that the State is sovereign and will brook no interference in its internal affairs." Cried Mrs. Pinkham during the floor debate: "That sounds almost like a declaration of Civil War. We once had a war to decide the same question of States rights." Her appeal to sectional patriotism was in vain, however, and Percy's veto was sustained.

Not many of them were. Some were overridden by huge margins. And each new one made him more political enemies.

But Percy could be extremely charming. On his last appearance before the legislature, his blue eyes were twinkling when he told them about the "several boxes of vetoes" he had brought with him and he soon had them openly laughing.

Those vetoes are my children, all I have [laughter] and I hope that you will treat them kindly. If you do not take to them, if their complexions are not what you like, why there is no need of saying anything bitter about them.

Just give them a merciful burial and say that you hope they will rest in peace. [laughter]

They presented him with a silver loving cup to show that there were no hard feelings and he told them that Augusta would be lonely without them and that if they didn't drop by his office to see him when they were in the capital, he would be deeply disappointed.

A gracious, if teasing, reference to the legislature's sole woman member was his parting shot. He imagined a future session in which there were 181 women and one man who had been elected and he said:

> But when your granddaughters and great granddaughters are sitting here legislating for the State of Maine and this one man whom I am speaking of is surrounded by them, I am sure they will treat him with the same courtesies and kindliness with which you have treated Mrs. Pinkham.

The record states that the governor left "amidst the hearty applause of the members standing."

As Mainers, themselves, the legislators were bound to appreciate his performance. Wit and kindliness mixed with sharp intelligence and fiercely independent integrity were qualities that all Maine people appreciated. Never mind that he was a rich man's son. He was *smaht* and he was *down-to-earth. Nothin' snooty 'bout Percy.*

Even his eccentricities, much as they annoyed some people, were definite assets on the whole.

His devotion to animals, particularly to his dogs, was probably the best known fact about him.

To be sure, he made plenty of enemies among veterans and other patriots, and not only in Maine, when his Irish

Setter Garry Owen died and he ordered the state's flags lowered to half-mast in mourning. The resultant furor reached the national press, but Percy brazenly defended his act, contrasting the faithfulness of his pet to the inconsistencies and deviousness of humans in public life. Although Madeleine and her two sons had come to live with him at the Blaine House, his most constant companion was his dog. The Irish Setter went to work with him every morning and, to this day, Garry Owen's paw scratches remain on the door of what was then the governor's office. Percy's official portrait in the statehouse has him posed with the russet-colored canine on a couch.

When he sent another dog (not an Irish Setter) at his own expense to the state prison at Thomaston to be a "softening influence" on the inmates, he received more national press. One headline read: "THE DOG THAT WENT TO JAIL FOR LIFE." A well-known writer of dog stories, Albert Payson Terhune, eventually wrote a novel based on Percy's gift.

So identified was Percy with Garry in the public eye that just as he was leaving office in January 1925, an advertisement appeared in the *National Geographic* magazine with the following copy:

> Pictured here is Governor Percival P. Baxter of Maine. With him is his dog "Garry." They are inseparable, as anyone around the State House can tell you.
>
> But the Governor has another constant companion. One who holds a high place in his affections. One whose faithfulness is also unswerving. This companion is his Hamilton watch.

Governors don't sell watches these days. And probably many of them wouldn't do other things that Percy did—and received publicity for—like pulling an exhausted red squirrel from Moosehead Lake or stopping traffic in Portland during a rainstorm to rescue a dove that had fallen from a tree or writing to a fellow governor (Al Smith of New York) asking him to stop a rodeo scheduled for a state fair.

One thing Percy didn't do vis-à-vis animals while in office was try to cancel the ox-pulling contests at county fairs in Maine. But he was falsely accused of doing so and the reaction against him was so strong that the fair director had to make a public statement saying Governor Percy had never tried to interfere with this incredibly popular sport. Later, though, Percy pronounced himself against it.

Like every politician, Percy had to confront untrue rumors. The Klan spread the falsehood that he was secretly a Catholic—perhaps based on the knowledge of Emily's Catholicism, certainly no secret after her funeral where Bishop Walsh, himself, had delivered the eulogy. The "wets" in Maine launched an accusation that Percy, the ultimate public "dry," secretly drank. Some people swore he always had a bottle with him. The closest claim to hit home was from a man who said he saw Percy take a nip while he was climbing Katahdin. Yes, Percy admitted, he had swallowed a concoction of quinine and whiskey to combat a fever. Ah, but where had he gotten the prohibited liquor? The lame-sounding answer was that years before a sealed bottle had been placed into a cairn of rocks.

As for his relations with women, everyone wondered. All sorts of stories about girl friends, mistresses, fiancees, etc., proliferated and even a few dark whispers that he had no interest in the fairer sex.

His admirers, on the other hand, lionized him. Even before he became governor, Percy had served as the real-life model for the hero of a novel, published by Harper and Brothers in New York. Its author was a prolific Maine writer, Holman Day, who admired Percy's political stands. Entitled

ABOVE: THE GOVERNOR AT HIS DESK; BELOW: MADELEINE
AND HER TWO SONS, JAMIE AND EDWARD, WHO CAME TO
LIVE AT THE BLAINE HOUSE AND CONSTITUTE HIS "OFFICIAL
FAMILY." THEY ARE PICTURED IN THE BLAINE HOUSE;

ABOVE: PERCY REVIEWING THE MAINE NATIONAL GUARD AT
CAMP DEVENS, MASSACHUSETTS. GENERAL JOHN J.
PERSHING IS TO HIS RIGHT; BELOW: PERCY AT THE HISTORIC
POLAND SPRINGS HOUSE WITH VICE-PRESIDENT CALVIN
COOLIDGE AND FAMED HOTEL OWNER AND FELLOW PIONEER
ENVIRONMENTALIST, HIRAM RICKER.

ABOVE: THE DOG THAT CAUSED ALL THE TROUBLE—GARRY II. WHEN HE DIED, PERCY CREATED A NATIONWIDE FUROR BY ORDERING ALL FLAGS IN MAINE LOWERED TO HALF-MAST; BELOW: A STILL FROM *WINGS OF THE MORNING*, THE MOVIE STARRING MARY ASTOR IN WHICH PERCY HAD A CAMEO ROLE, PLAYING A GOVERNOR.

LEFT: THE HAMILTON WATCH AD; RIGHT: TABLES SET FOR
THE FAREWELL DINNER TO GOVERNOR BAXTER.

All Wool Morrison (the hero, surnamed Morrison, ran a wool
factory), it was all about waterpower, and the dedication was
to "Percival P. Baxter: A Consistent and Courageous Champion in the Protection of the People's White Coal."

Holman Day also was a pioneer movie maker in the years
when Hollywood was just beginning. One of his films, *Wings
of the Morning*, was based on the same waterpower theme as
All Wool Morrison and required a scene with a governor. So the
cameo role went to a genuine governor—Percival Baxter of
Maine. A film clip with Percy in it from this long-lost cellu-
loid potboiler is still extant.

Undoubtedly, his strongest open admirer in the press
(and there weren't many) was Arthur G. Staples of the *Lewiston Evening Journal*, with whom he'd climbed Katahdin.
Staples published a sketch of Percy that went beyond any

THE LOVING CUP GIVEN TO PERCY BY THE LEGISLATURE.

usual superficial journalistic treatment. Entitled "On Percy," it is not pure hero worship; there are touches of humor and some true-sounding insights. A few excerpts help paint a rounded picture of the man.

> He has an enormous head. I went into the woods with him once and he bought a hat—for it was hot weather. He chased over the shops for a common haying hat and could not find one large enough...Mr. Baxter wears an eight and something. I dropped it on my head and it went to my belt buckle—in eclipse of my diminished Ego. If I had a head full of good brains to that size, I would try to emulate Aristotle.

Percy is a persistent person. He is the most patient and persistent person I ever knew. He has certain arts of retreat from difficult positions but he always takes his weapon with him when he retreats. He never throws away his ammunition. I have followed him through all of the windings of the waterpower proposition and he has always had a straight course ahead and a wide open way for retreat from the position if perchance he found himself exposed to chance of defeat—just as all good generals have under like circumstances.

His fair blonde person is set off by a fine physique, a boyish yet intellectual face, with alert eyes and a ready and patient smile. The impression is culture, breeding and kindliness. He loves animals. An elderly dog, a dear old dog who looks like a Llewellen setter, follows him about in the executive chamber and watches him with eyes of love. Fine![5]

When Percy announced that he would not run for a third term, his followers were naturally disappointed and a number of them refused to take him at his word. Foremost among these was Mrs. Lucia H. Connor of Fairfield, who actually started circulating nomination papers for him until Percy, stung by newspaper inferences that he was going back on his pledge, specifically asked her to desist.

But the question raised was legitimate and it cropped up constantly. What were his future political plans? He, himself, had teasingly said four weeks before the end: "They say, 'The King is dead. Long live the King.' But I expect to be a lively corpse."

At one point, Percy even had to issue a statement positively denying that he intended to run against either of the state's two incumbent Republican U.S. senators, Frederick

Hale and Bert Fernald, when their present terms ended.

The manner in which he left the governorship created a few suspicions—assuredly in Owen Brewster's mind. Percy ended his stay in office with several headline-grabbing innovations that, intended or not, did seem to deflect attention away from the incoming chief executive. The first of them, ironically, was billed as an attempt to defer to the man who was succeeding him. All previous governors had escorted their successors into the inaugural chamber and remained throughout the ceremonies. Percy broke with tradition by only taking Brewster as far as the door and then leaving him because, as he said, "it should be his day." Yet by doing so, Percy also garnered headlines.

There was no precedent, either, for an outgoing governor to give a farewell address. Percy gave one and it was long and newsworthy. His most important initiative was to throw out a challenge to future legislatures vis-à-vis Katahdin. À la Arthur Gould's gesture to construct a building at the Boy's Training School, Percy offered $10,000 of his own money to match any state contributions for acquiring the land that contained the mountain.

At the farewell party put on for him by his staff and friends, a comic song was sung to the tune of "Ach, der lieber Augustine" and it sounded innocent enough.

> *These are the facts, sir, the facts, sir, the*
> *facts, sir; that we are losing Baxter*
> *For he must leave us.*
> *I feel bad; you feel bad; he feels bad—*
> *We feel bad.*
> *We are losing Baxter.*
> *But Baxter must go.*
>
> *What is the news, sir, the news sir, the news,*

sir; that soon we will have Brewster
when New Years comes in.
I feel glad; you feel glad; he feels glad—
Soon we will have Brewster,
He's fixing to come.

And Percy, himself, had said, "There are many men in Maine eminently qualified to be Governor and I know of no one with whom I would prefer to leave the State's affairs than our Governor-elect [Brewster]."

But it wasn't long before the two men were publicly feuding. From one perspective, Brewster fired the first shot. In a special message to the legislature, he declared that Percy had left the state in a financial mess, with a shortfall in revenues that would lead to a deficit. Nothing could have angered Percy Baxter more. Before leaving office, he had issued a final financial report to the people of Maine, detailing a balance of $1.4 million even after building a new state prison in Thomaston to replace one that had burned. Moreover, Brewster's figures were specious because they did not take a full fiscal year into account—a point Percy was quick to make. As reported in the *Bangor Daily News* on August 12, 1925, Percy's reply was stinging: "MESSAGE NOT BASED ON FACT AND UNWORTHY OF A GOVERNOR OF MAINE" said the headline over a subhead in which Baxter pictures Brewster as a poorly informed fault-finder and jealous politician willing for his own ends to represent a prosperous state as bankrupt.

The harshness of Percy's response had to be all the more painful for Brewster when the end of the fiscal year proved Baxter right and Maine showed a $2.5 million surplus.

It is understandable that the next fight Brewster picked with Percy would be on a more trivial scale. He rejected the design of a plaque commissioned by Percy to be placed on the Memorial Bridge linking Kittery with Portsmouth, New

Hampshire. Designed by the sculptress Bashka Paeff, it was to illustrate the horrors of war and seemed too vividly pacifist for Brewster's taste. But in the end, he made only some minor changes.

Despite their mounting enmity, Percy announced in April 1926 that he had no intention of running for governor. That same month, he also reiterated that he would work to re-elect Fred Hale and Bert Fernald to the U.S. Senate.

Then, on August 27, death once more played a part in his political plans. Senator Bert Fernald died unexpectedly

Today, in the case of a vacancy in the U.S. Senate, a governor would make an interim appointment. At that time, the procedure was to call for a special election.

And first there had to be a special primary election. Lots of names were mentioned as potential seekers of the Republican nod, which would be tantamount to election. Percy was considered the front-runner, ahead of Congressman Wallace H. White and ex-Congressman Frank E. Guernsey.

But the final shakeout saw a different lineup: Percy did announce and so did the current president of the senate, Hodgdon C. Buzzell of Belfast, who was also the Klan candidate, and Louis A. Jack of Lisbon, who'd done poorly in a previous gubernatorial race. Then, a last-minute candidate entered: State Senator Arthur R. Gould of Aroostook County.

The Klan hated Percy and, although beset by internal problems, was still a force in Maine politics. Typical of their attitude toward the ex-governor was a statement by one of their leaders that "the report that Governor Baxter has been asked to join the Klan is a lie. The Klan is fussy about the sort of men it takes into its ranks." Louis A. Jack had nothing personal against Percy; in fact, he had publicly supported his waterpower views, but he was a marginal candidate at best. Gould, it was reported, hadn't wanted to run and only had done so at the last minute when ex-Congressman Guernsey had withdrawn. The business community that Percy had so badly offended, led by Norman Towle, publisher of the *Bangor Daily News,* had strongly urged Gould to run. Gould's motto was, not surprisingly: MORE BUSINESS.

However, it was not ideology that won the primary election for Gould. It was geography. The northern and easternmost parts of the state had not had a U.S. senator from their area since Eugene Hale of Ellsworth retired in 1911. If Percival Baxter were to be elected, there would be two U.S. senators from Portland (the other being Fred Hale). By banding together, these excluded regions could assure themselves a victory—considering that the western and southern vote would be split three ways.

This strategy, plus a certain complacency and over-confidence on Percy's part, led to his defeat. He was swamped in Aroostook and Penobscot Counties, losing by margins of 6-1 and 3-1 respectively. Even in his own Cumberland County, he merely edged out Gould by a 4-3 tally. Many of his supporters admitted afterward that they hadn't gone to the polls, considering him a shoo-in.

The effect of this defeat on Percy was portentous in various aspects. For one thing, he made a vow to himself then and there (although he didn't speak about it publicly until much later) that he would never run for office again. He had lost before and bounced back, always going on to higher heights, but in 1906 and 1910, the political forces against him had seemed impersonal. This loss was qualitatively different. He had been personally tested—he and his entire record—and, despite the obviously geographical bias to the voting, his rejection by his fellow Republicans had to be seen as a rejection of Baxterism, a philosophy that he had actually once boldly spelled out in "fifteen points," à la Woodrow Wilson.

More like a laundry list of political positions, his "set of principles" included such specifics as "non-transmission of power beyond Maine's borders" and "support for women's rights," as well as more general directions like "protection of the people's rights in natural resources" and "tolerance for all religious and political views," and outright motherhood-and-apple-pie generalities like "frankness and openness" and "opposition to special interests."

Such presumption was an open invitation to caricature, and "Patt" Pattangall was happy to oblige. He issued his own fifteen points debunking what he thought of Baxterism, such as "inability to make an accurate statement," "childish cheese-paring" (of state expenses), "demagoguery in the power issue," "interference with all plans of industrial development," "egotism amounting to delusions," etc.

But since Pattangall was such a consistent loser himself in electoral politics, his sardonic chiding could be easily ignored as sour grapes. To be defeated by one's own party was a crueler blow and had to remind Percy of James Phinney's dictum that anyone who stayed in the political arena long enough was bound to end up a disappointed man.

The most important aspect of Percy's decision was that it also had a positive side. He had already shown in his farewell address that he was willing to commit some of his own money to acquire Katahdin. From there, it was but a short step to the idea that he would buy it all.

At this juncture did he contemplate the extraordinary extent of his eventual purchase? Most likely not.

His thoughts about Katahdin seemed to be continually developing. Back in 1921, he gave a speech that in today's Maine, with its furious public debate over clear-cutting and the future of the timber supply, would sound perfectly up-to-date. On that occasion, he said:

A year ago, it was my privilege to climb Mount Katahdin and I shall never forget the pleasurable sensation with which I viewed the tremendous expanse of lakes and forests which are the property of the Maine woods...but when I was told that timber experts had estimated that Maine's supply would last but 20 or 30 years and that from 150,000 to 200,000 acres were stripped and denuded each year, I realized that the days of Maine's forests were numbered unless something was done to check the destruction and to replenish the supply.... Someday I want the State of Maine to own Mount Katahdin. It is one of nature's wonder spots.[6]

Then, three years later, he was offering to donate the value of his 1923 and 1924 gubernatorial salaries, or $10,000 (in a gesture reminiscent of James Phinney's donation of his first year mayor's salary to the Walker Manual Training School) to acquire the corner of the township in Piscataquis County where Katahdin was located, and he was also voicing a slightly different theme. Noting that the legislature had agreed to establish a game preserve in the area, he went on to complain that landholders in the region had plans to restrict its use to hunters with licensed guides. Such preserves were then (and still are) anathema to Maine people, and Percy articulated this populist mantra as a prelude to his Katahdin offer.

The time must never come when the forest areas of Maine are made great hunting preserves to be enjoyed only by the friends and sycophants of powerful interests. Such things savor of feudal times when the lords and barons of England claimed the sole right to the fish and game on their estates....[7]

Percy could afford to give up two years worth of salary to pursue his dream. Yet what exactly were his finances and how did he find the money to pay for the many purchases that in the end were to produce a park of more than 200,000 acres? There has been a lot of speculation and the full truth will probably forever remain a mystery. That the money came from James Phinney has even been questioned, some descendants claiming that it was an inheritance from his mother's Proctor family. Other relatives have claimed that Percy's half-brothers challenged his inheritance from his father in a court battle, while others say no such thing happened.

The probate records appear to tell only part of the story. James Phinney's will is dated October 8, 1919, with a codicil added a year later. Specifically left to Percy was $5,000 "with whatever sum of money I have on deposit in the Portland Savings Bank," the principal to be used to erect a "Baxter Fountain" in Portland. Percy was also given a lot of land on the corner of Park Avenue and Deering Avenue, but this was to be held in trust for James and Edward Tomlinson and to be sold when they were twenty-one. His father's "pictures, books, household goods, furniture, including musical instruments, works of Art, automobiles and personal effects not already disposed of" went to Percy, as well. Percy was to be executor and he and James Phinney, Jr. and Rupert were to act as trustees for all of the property, but only unimproved land was to be sold.

The codicil changed this last stipulation and allowed buildings to be marketed. It also made reference to the fact that Clinton had not been given any money in the first will, as all James Phinney's other children had been. The reason stated was that Clinton had already received his father's share of the Portland Packing Company. However, the codicil now added Clinton's grandchildren and put them on an equal footing with James Phinney's other great-grandchildren.

The total value of the estate, as probated in 1921, was

$267,833 (one of the assessors was Ralph Owen Brewster). Later, it would rise to $341,000 by 1980.

This was hardly a sum that would allow Percy, upon his own death in 1969, to leave $5 million specifically for the care of his Park. So was it true that his money had come from his mother?

As far as the probate records are concerned, it seems unlikely. Hetty's will was probated on November 8, 1914, while James Phinney was still alive. The estate was valued at $162,650, mostly in real estate, since James Phinney had put most of his properties in his wife's name. Percy was the executor and Emily and Madeleine advisory trustees. Each of them received about $32,000 from their mother.

If there is an answer to the puzzle of where Percy acquired the funds he needed for Katahdin and other charities, it has to be sought beyond probate. At his death, his own probated estate was worth no more than $495,000, but reference is made to a 1927 "Trust Agreement" with the Boston Safe Deposit and Trust Company. According to Percy's will, which is dated September 9, 1966 and has that same Boston bank as executor, "its present value is $10 million."

By 1927, as he was beginning his quest to acquire Katahdin, he had already been able to witness the satisfactory conclusion to James Phinney's vision. Baxter Boulevard had been formally dedicated in Portland in 1925. Like everything else connected with the Baxters, it had not been smooth sailing even after the city council had voted unanimously in 1921 to name the thoroughfare after its creator. A year later, one of the councilmen presented an order to change the projected name to Victory Memorial Drive and only two of the city fathers dared to vote against such a patriotic gesture. Supposedly this was the work of the park commission, which had never officially adopted the Baxter designation and resented having the council dictate to it. Then someone—and who else but Governor Baxter could it have been?—prevailed on the mayor to veto the council's latest suggestion. Baxter Boulevard, it remained.

Admittedly, as a vision, the Boulevard was somewhat different in kind from a park at Katahdin. It was nature tamed and adapted for human use, rather than wilderness preserved for posterity. In America's relationship to the outdoors, these are sometimes conflicting, sometimes complementary, trends. James Phinney had been of his time and place, when a conservation ethic was merely struggling to be born in public policy. Now, in the mid-1920s, he had his monument. Percy's odds were equally great, if not greater, as he set out to create his.

For did not the *Portland Press-Herald* pontificate on October 8, 1927:

> The silliest proposal ever made to a Legislature was that of Governor Baxter who advocated the State's buying Mount Katahdin and creating a State Park.[8]

---

[1] Baxter Scrapbooks, Volume 12; page 85.
[2] *Our American Kings* by Frederick L. Collins, The Century Company, New York and London, 1924.
[3] Second Inaugural Address, January 4, 1923.
[4] Legislative Record, 1923; page 33.
[5] All excerpts from "The Inner Man," a column by Arthur G. Staples, *Lewiston Evening Journal*, 1923—"On Percy."
[6] Speech on reforestation, August 6, 1921.
[7] Farewell Address, 1924.
[8] *Portland Press Herald*

12

Katahdin, and Conservation Consciousness

ONE WOULD THINK THAT A mountain, unlike a human, could stay out of the headlines. But just as Percy Baxter and, on occasion, James Phinney continue to make news in the 1990s, so, too, in this same decade, did the inert mass of rock of Maine's highest mountain find its way into the newspaper columns. On June 25, 1992, the *Portland Press Herald* ran a story that Katahdin had grown by four feet. "Like a child and the national debt, the mountain gets bigger each time it's measured," ran the whimsical caption accompanying the article.

After scientists from the University of Maine had finished analyzing satellite data in their computer, Katahdin measured exactly 5,271.13 feet, give or take 3 inches. That was 4 feet higher than the previous measurement of 5,267 feet done by the U.S. Geologic Survey in 1941. The very first measurement done in 1874 by Merritt Caldwell Fernald was a whopping 55 feet lower than the new measurement. Fernald

A PAINTING OF KATAHDIN BY THE RENOWNED NINETEENTH-
CENTURY ARTIST, FREDERICK E. CHURCH, A MEMBER OF THE
"HUDSON RIVER SCHOOL," WHO VISITED THE MOUNTAIN IN
1856 AND 1877.

used mercury barometers while the 1941 survey used triangulation.

The addition of 4 feet in 50 years or even 55 in 118 in no way belies the most famous statement Percival Baxter made about his beloved mountain's permanence. Said Baxter:

Man is Born to Die, His Works are Short-lived,
Buildings Crumble, Monuments Decay, Wealth
Vanishes. But Katahdin In All its Glory
Forever Shall Remain the Mountain of the
People of Maine.

Percy was hardly alone in his expression of reverence for Maine's incomparable landmark, whatever its exact measured height. The Abnaki Indians, whose ancestors entered Maine more than 10,000 years ago, accorded Katahdin (variously translated as "large mountain" or "large thing" or "highest land") a prominent place in their lore. As the abode of gods and spirits (some malevolent), it has always been for them an awesome, even forbidden, place.

Glooskap is the great deity-cultural folk hero of these Algonquian-speaking tribes known as the Abnaki or People of the Dawn. He is not worshipped, but his deeds (which involve a good deal of cunning if not outright lying) are the subject of endless stories. He created humans; he reduced once-giant animals to their current size; he created whole landscapes; and he battled murderous evil spirits such as Pukjinkwest, the she-panther who ate children and had her scissor-bill bird companions snip mermaids in half, or Wuchowsen, a monster bird, who, whenever he snapped his beak or scratched his talons, created devastatingly destructive storms. In one of the tales, Glooskap tires "of saving people from nasty creatures and listening to their woes."[1] He leaves alone with a pack of wolves and no one since has been able to find his abode, although some have said it's a cave on Katahdin. A surprisingly modern story about Glooskap finds him traveling on a ship made out of a wooded island and sailed by a crew of squirrels across the ocean to visit the King of France. (By way of footnote, it is well to remember that historically most of the Maine tribes during the seventeenth and eighteenth centuries sided with the French in their battles with the English during more than a hundred years of "French and Indian" warfare.) Yet once in France, Glooskap was not well received. The French monarch ordered him shot out of a cannon, but instead the artillery piece exploded and killed most of the king's men. Disgusted, Glooskap went back to America and supposedly holed up in a secret cave on Katahdin where he remains to this day, manufacturing arrows for the moment when the Indians will arise and drive the white men out.

However, Glooskap's presence on Katahdin is an iffy proposition. With Pamola (pronounced Bumole), we have a sure bet. This mythic bird-like and moose-like creature is indisputably Katahdin's tutelary god.

When Charles Turner, Jr., a Maine surveyor, made the first recorded ascent of Katahdin on August 13, 1804, he had to plead with his two Indian companions to accompany him. They were literally afraid of Pamola.

An Indian who later braved Pamola's wrath all alone was the famous Penobscot tribal chief or governor, John Neptune, about whom as many tales are told as about Pamola—some equally fantastic, although Neptune was a real person. He was also a shaman (a medicine man) and, as immortalized by Maine writer Fannie Hardy Eckstorm, he performed numerous inexplicable feats of magic. His profession of fur trapper took him far and wide through the northern Maine woods. In the most famous Katahdin story about him, the "Old Governor" climbed the mountain alone in winter despite all warnings, and spent the night in a tiny cabin. From darkness until dawn, Pamola raged outside against the cabin door, tugging and pounding and trying to get at Neptune. But the door was stuck shut since the crafty shaman inside had poured water under it, which had frozen.

This particular yarn came not from Mrs. Eckstorm but from Leroy Dudley, perhaps the one person even more connected to Katahdin than Percival Baxter. In tribute to Dudley's lifelong relationship with Katahdin as guide, ranger, and game warden, Percy always insisted that it was "Roy's mountain."[2] And Pamola, although not Roy Dudley's invention, was perfected by him in the tales he told to his visitors at Chimney Pond; he became a living, breathing legend so visible that the illustrations of this winged, moose-antlered, bearded flying creature by Maurice "Jake" Day, a popular Maine caricaturist, have etched themselves into an unforgettable, Indian-inspired symbol to add to the state's storehouse of folk art.

In Dudley's *Chimney Pond Tales*, Pamola and Roy co-exist side by side on Katahdin. They smoke their pipes together (Pamola's is an empty tar barrel with a ten-foot length of three-inch pipe for a stem and his tobacco is balsam boughs and birch bark). They become friends after a fearful night in which Pamola uses every trick he has of rain and wind and thunder and rock slides, with boulders "as big as houses... bouncing around the basin like basketballs"[3] to chase Roy away from Chimney Pond. After Roy stands his ground, Pamola eventually accepts him and even lets Roy find him a wife named Sukey Guildersleeves, with whom he has a son. That Sukey turns out to be "a female dreadnought," a shrew who leaves him following a short and stormy marriage, is never held against Roy.

Such enlightened nonsense, as Roy Dudley fabricated it,

is but a part of the charm of the Katahdin mystique. This latter is a sense of a place in which human personalities like Roy Dudley, mythic personalities like Pamola or Glooskap, and geographic highlights, whether Chimney Pond or Abol Slide or the Knife Edge, are all rolled up into one entity that engenders a fierce loyalty in those who expose themselves to this small corner of America. Katahdin, in other words, has a haunting effect on people, a presence of its own, a richness even beyond its imposing natural grandeur.

Among the most famous of the visitors who felt this was Henry David Thoreau. He was there in 1846 and he wrote about the mountain in a chapter of his book *The Maine Woods*. Mountain climbing had not yet become fashionable. Thoreau's first reaction to Katahdin went beyond awe to a reverential fear. He considered himself in the presence of gods, too, not Indian gods, but figures of classical mythology.

> It reminded me of the creations of the old epic and dramatic poets, of Atlas, Vulcan, Cyclops and Prometheus. Such was Caucasus and the rock where Prometheus was bound. Aeschylus had no doubt visited such scenery as this. It was vast, Titanic, and such as man never inhabits....
>
> The tops of mountains are among the unfinished parts of the globe, whither it is a slight insult to the gods to climb and pry into their secrets, and try their effect on our humanity. Only daring and insolent men, perchance, go there. Simple races, as savages, do not climb mountains,—their tops are sacred and mysterious tracts never visited by them. Pomola is always angry with those who climb to the summit of Ktaadn.[4]

Thoreau, who did climb the mountain, then cites another of those "daring and insolent men," Dr. Charles T.

Jackson, Maine's state geologist, who had ascended Katahdin seven years earlier and measured it—the tallest of all the calculations, 5,300 feet. By himself, Thoreau stood and marveled at the "countless lakes" he could see—Moosehead, Chesuncook, Millinocket, "and a hundred others without a name; and mountains, also, whose names, for the most part, are known only to the Indians." Descending, rejoining his companions, descending again, through lands burnt long ago by lightning, he waxed almost religiously poetic over not only the appearance but the very idea of wilderness.

> It is difficult to conceive of a region uninhabited by man. We habitually presume his presence and influence everywhere. And yet we have not seen pure Nature, unless we have seen her thus vast and drear and inhuman, though in the midst of cities. Nature was here something savage and awful, though beautiful. I looked with awe at the ground I trod on, to see what the Powers had made there, the form and fashion and material of their work. This was that Earth of which we have heard, made out of Chaos and Old Night. Here was no man's garden, but the unhandseled globe. It was not lawn, nor pasture, nor mead, nor woodland, nor lea, nor arable, nor waste land.
>
> It was the fresh and natural surface of the planet Earth, and it was made forever and ever—to be the dwelling of man, we say—so Nature made it, and man may use it if he can. Man was not to be associated with it. It was Matter, vast, terrific—not his Mother Earth that we have heard of, not for him to tread on, or be buried in—no, it were being too familiar even to let his bones lie there—the home, this, of Necessity and Fate. There was clearly felt the presence of a force not bound to be kind to man. It was a place for heathenism and superstitious rites—to

be inhabited by men nearer of kin to the rocks and to wild animals than we.[5]

Percy Baxter, we are told,[6] read Thoreau's book and was inspired by him. The above passages, with their somewhat pagan enthusiasm and religiosity, seem more aptly tuned to our own times of "deep ecology" and "green politics" than to Baxter's young manhood still in the Victorian era. What portion of *The Maine Woods* touched him most, he has never let us learn. Perhaps he had no idea, himself, how the Concord iconoclast's words were woven into his being: except, there is another passage from *The Maine Woods*, not specifically about Katahdin, crammed into an appendix that Thoreau added after a trip back to Maine in 1853, which an impressionable Percy might have been riveted enough by to mull over for the rest of his life.

> The Kings of England formerly had their forests "to hold the king's game," for sport or food, sometimes destroying villages to create or extend them.... Why should not we, who have renounced the king's authority, have our national preserves, where no villages need be destroyed, in which the bear and panther, and some even of the hunter race, may still exist, and not be "civilized off the face of the earth,"—our forests, not to hold the king's game merely, but to hold and preserve the king himself also, the lord of creation—not for idle sport or food, but for inspiration and our own true recreation? Or shall we, like the villains, grub them all up, poaching on our own national domains?[7]

Such thoughts, so beautifully expressed—before John Muir, before Teddy Roosevelt, before Gifford Pinchot—had to have stuck. We have seen that Percy resisted the idea of private game preserves. An American plan, as expostulated by Thoreau, was a *preserve for everyone* and yet still somehow within the context of Percy's anglophile tradition.

Katahdin kept enticing admirers. The painter, Frederick E. Church, came on two occasions. He was one of the Hudson River School of landscape artists who introduced Americans to the full romantic beauty of the country's scenery. Somewhat of a maverick, Church had often deserted the U.S. for foreign and exotic scenes. But Katahdin drew him. And on his second trip in 1877 (the first was in 1856), he took three other landscapists with him and they spent a month around the mountain, sketching and painting it.

Two years later, a Harvard student entering his senior year climbed Katahdin. He was spending August and September in Maine, living outdoors as part of a regime of building himself up to compensate for a sickly childhood. His name was Theodore Roosevelt. The two Maine guides who accompanied him, William W. Sewall and Wilmot Dow, became his lifelong friends and eventually ran the ranch he bought in South Dakota as a place to recuperate his spirits after the tragic shock of having his young first wife and beloved mother die on the same day. Roosevelt reached the summit of Katahdin and spoke about his experience ever afterward. Here, in truth, was implanted the seed of a conservation ethic that bore fruit in the future on a national scale. As Katahdin inspired Teddy Roosevelt and Roosevelt pointed the way for Percy Baxter, the circle of Katahdin's spell completed itself.

Unfortunately, the area did not long remain as wildly pristine as it had been during Thoreau's visits. Lumbering nearby had been occurring since at least the 1830s, and for a while Bangor was the lumber capital of the world. By the 1870s, the loggers were on the lower reaches of Sourdnahunk Stream, one of the waterways that drain the region, and also on Wassataquoik Stream. Around the turn of the century, civilization of a sort was transported almost whole to a spot not far away from Katahdin along Millinocket Stream in Indian Township 3, which had been sold to a group of high-powered investors from away. At this particular site in 1846, Henry David Thoreau had spied a bald eagle's nest. In 1901, it became Maine's 467th town—named Millinocket—built for the Great Northern Paper Company.

GNP bought thousands of acres of woodland to feed pulp into its voracious machines. It owned some of this land in common with the lumbermen working in the area. One of these early entrepreneurs who managed to amass a sizable acreage was John Ross of Bangor. In 1902, he was cutting in the Sandy Stream area and near Roaring Brook and Basin Ponds, close to Katahdin. It was Ross's son Harry who ended up owning large portions of T3R9, the township containing Katahdin, in conjunction with the Great Northern Paper Company.

Lumbering, papermaking—practical use of the forest resource—predominated during this period. The few parties of vacationers that came, and even the budding tourist industry that had begun in Maine following the Civil War, were secondary to the important business of commercializing wood. It had its own romance about it, too—the Bangor "Tigers," those rugged woodsmen who swept into the bustling river port city for its booze and brothels; the dangers of the picturesque river drives; the manly image of the logging camps; and that fundamental American sense of the wilderness pushed back and tamed.

To this day, the warring of the exploitive ethos and the conservation ethos continues throughout the country and no less in Maine, where the people pungently express it in their saying: "payrolls or pickerel."

It is now difficult to comprehend that a time existed when no one much cared about "pickerel" because, figuratively, the streams and lakes were so full of them.

Percy Baxter never met John Muir. He may not have read any of Muir's writings. And he was a friend of Gifford Pinchot, whose own ideas about conservation clashed with those of the Scotch immigrant whom many historians seem to credit as the "father" of conservation consciousness in the U.S. But Percy had to have been influenced by the career and activities of this gaunt, bearded lover of the wilderness, who fought so tenaciously to preserve such jewels of the American landscape as Yosemite Valley, California and Glacier Bay, Alaska.

Possessed of a magnificent gift of brogue-accented gab, writing talent par excellence, and a mystical, religious attitude toward the natural world, tinged with Celtic poesy, Muir fascinated everyone who did meet him, from Ralph Waldo Emerson to Theodore Roosevelt.

Even those, like Gifford Pinchot, who opposed him were taken with John Muir. Students of environmentalism divide the trends within the movement, almost from its outset, into two warring camps, whose opposing views still clash today. Pinchot versus Muir is one way to describe them. Here it's not *payrolls versus pickerel* but *catching pickerel versus not fishing for them*, or renewable use versus preservation. But Pinchot, the founder of the U.S. Forest Service, whose national forests allowed lumbering and drew Muir's scorn and rage, found the Scotsman absolutely enchanting. His talk, said Pinchot, after their meeting at Belton, Montana, in 1896 "was worth crossing the continent to hear."[8] Pinchot was on a trip with the U.S. government National Forest Commission, and he stole away to spend an evening camping with the great naturalist. "It was such an evening as I have never had before or since,"[9] he declared, even though the ultimate quarrel between the two men over preservation was presaged when Muir refused to let Pinchot kill a tarantula. Muir said it had as much right to be where it was as he and Pinchot.

Setting land aside to save it had begun as early as 1872 with the establishment of Yellowstone National Park. It can't be said that the impetus to do so arose out of a Muir-like respect for an irreplaceable natural treasure. Rather, the site was an oddity, a Barnum attraction, and Jay Cooke, the financier of the Northern Pacific Railroad, promoted its designation by Congress in the hope that hordes of people would ride his railroad to see it. *Scribner's Magazine* predicted that "Yankee enterprise will dot the new Park with hostelries and furrow it with lines of travel."[10] President Ulysses S. Grant was persuaded to sign the bill; two years later, he proved himself no pioneering environmentalist by vetoing legislation to protect the remaining buffalo from slaughter on the plains.

It was nearly twenty years later, in 1891, that the first substantive measure for saving land was slipped into a law and passed in D.C. This amendment authorized the President to create "forest reserves" by withdrawing federal land from the public domain. The idea was the brainchild of William Hallett Phillips, a Washington lawyer and member of the Boone and Crockett Club, an organization of hunters, fishermen, and outdoor lovers created in part by Teddy Roosevelt. Within two years, President Benjamin Harrison had agreed to set aside 13 million acres in 15 reserves.

One of the "reserves" created by Harrison was a 4-million-acre tract known originally as the Sierra Forest Reserve. John Muir's beloved Yosemite Valley and the Mariposa giant redwoods, which were to be included in this "reserve," had actually been under the tenuous protective jurisdiction of California since 1864. But Yosemite did not legally become a national park until June 11, 1906, when Teddy Roosevelt signed the legislation. In order to win California's acquiescence, John Muir, who distrusted the state's ability to preserve the land intact, teamed up with an unlikely ally, Edward Harriman, the owner of the Southern Pacific Railroad, whose lobbyists helped swing the California senate. Harriman, like Jay Cooke, hoped that tourists would flock to the new attraction and ride his railroad to get there, although he was also a personal friend of Muir's and went on camping trips with him to Alaska.

Thus, as the new century opened and Percival Baxter was beginning his legislative career in Maine, the broad forms of the conservation movement in the U.S. had taken shape. Forest lands were being sequestered but under the Gifford Pinchot dictum of renewable use, partly as a strategy to win local support but also because Pinchot and Roosevelt and others believed in it. However, the preservationist idea had surfaced, too, as embodied in saving unique natural and scenic wonders like Yellowstone or Yosemite.

Both approaches faced precarious futures. Benjamin Harrison's action had caused no real controversy. Yet when President Grover Cleveland set aside more than 21 million acres for forest reserves in 1897, Congress rose up against him. The battle ended in a compromise and Cleveland's thirteen new reserves plus Harrison's initial fifteen were, by statute, opened to logging and other use.

The champion early conservationist, of course, was President Theodore Roosevelt. Before his terms ended, he had created 53 wildlife reserves, 16 national monuments, 5 new national parks, 149 national forests, and an expansion of Yosemite. He made "conservation" a household word. Gifford Pinchot prophesied, after Teddy Roosevelt's Governors' Conference on Conservation, "the first of its kind not only in America but in the world...may well be regarded by future historians as a turning point in human history."[11]

Teddy Roosevelt's influence on Baxter came in different guises. The national monuments, which predated the idea of national parks, had helped establish the principle of donating privately bought lands to a governmental entity for public preservation. Baxter's idea of buying Katahdin and its surroundings with his own money and donating it for a public purpose was hardly original.

The first celebrated instance of private land being given to the government to preserve it occurred in California in 1908. William Kent, a native of Marin County (just north of San Francisco), made his mark in Chicago as a businessman and political reformer. Returning home, he learned that some beautifully forested land he owned was about to be seized by a water company through eminent domain, primarily for its timber value. Instead, Kent gave it to the government for a national monument, 47 acres of gorgeous giant redwoods, which he named Muir Woods (today expanded to 485 acres).

An obviously delighted John Muir responded with dry Scot's humor, saying, no doubt with the most exaggerated of highland burrs: "That so fine divine a thing should-a come out o' money-mad Chicago! Wha wad a 'thocht it."[12]

Another well-known example, which had to be familiar to Baxter, occurred in Maine. George Bucknam Dorr was a wealthy Boston Brahmin who summered in Bar Harbor, and on an August day in 1901, he received an invitation from Charles W. Eliot, a fellow summer resident and the president of Harvard, to attend a meeting in Seal Harbor. The purpose was to explore the idea of establishing in and around Mount Desert "reservations" of land for perpetual public use.

Eliot and his friends were transplanting to Maine a mechanism already in place in Massachusetts, where the Trustees of Public Reservations formed one of the earliest land trusts in the U.S. Dorr's ties to the formative conservation movement were through his cousin Charles Sprague Sargent, who ran Harvard's Arnold Arboretum and collaborated with John Muir and Gifford Pinchot.

Out of the gathering in the Music Room in Seal Harbor eventually came Acadia National Park. Dorr, like Baxter, was a lifelong bachelor and devoted his entire life to the creation of a magnificent public park. Like Baxter, he spent his own money to acquire land, but unlike Baxter, he had help along the way. The first gift of property came from Mrs. Charles D. Homans of Boston, and critical support was offered by Dorr's friend, multimillionaire John S. Kennedy, on whose yacht he had sailed aboard to the momentous meeting in Seal Harbor. A verbal bequest from Kennedy on his deathbed was honored by his reluctant executors after pressure from Dorr, who was as tireless as Baxter in his efforts.

That Acadia became a national park rather than a state entity was due to the action of the Maine Legislature. In the 1913 session (Baxter was not a member of it), local realtors and other opponents of any park in their area had a bill introduced to annul the charter of the Maine Trustees of Public Reservations, a group set up through Dorr's influence. Enlisting the help of the speaker of the house, John Peters of Ellsworth, Dorr defeated the attempt. But he then decided he needed federal protection. Three years of lobbying in Washington, D.C., finally brought him to the first stage of his goal—national monument status—and it took another year of lobbying to eke out an appropriation, and finally a bill submitted by Maine's Senator Frederick Hale obtained the coveted title of national park. Called Lafayette National Park at the outset, it became Acadia ten years later with a donation of nearly the entire Schoodic Peninsula from a lady married to an English lord who objected to the name of a Frenchman who had aided American revolutionaries. She would give her land if Dorr changed the name. Acadia, the ancient French name for the region, seemed an ideal compromise.

Therefore, models were not lacking as Baxter developed his own feelings about conservation.

Were there even ethnic and class undertones to what was happening? Stephen Fox, in *John Muir and His Legacy*, discusses George Bucknam Dorr's magnificent obsession as very nearly the swan song of a dominant social group whose power was slipping away. Referring to Dorr, Fox writes:

> In particular, this witness of the decline of his family, class, and region liked nature for inspiring his historical imagination, implying an unbroken tradition that held him to a fading, chimerical past.[13]

But a quote of Dorr's put his motivation more in the context of an American version of Old World institutions, where aristocrats in a country in which aristocrats could not legally exist, had to tailor their notions of "noblesse oblige." Said Dorr:

> Our national parks alone can supply the imaginative appeal that is made in older lands by ancient works of art, by ruins, and old historic associations.[14]

Baxter, in a sense, was cut from the same cloth as people like Dorr and Charles W. Eliot—Anglo-Saxon, rich, well-educated, Harvard Law School, and Yankee. Being from Maine instead of Boston made a difference, to be sure, but only of degree. While governor, he even publicly expressed his support for Lafayette National Park, despite his dislike of federal programs in Maine.

The tie-in between conservation of waterpower resources and conservation of scenic areas was brought vividly to the fore during Percy's freshman term in the Maine Legislature by an issue that erupted in California but attracted national attention. Teddy Roosevelt was president when the oddly named Hetch Hetchy controversy hit the headlines—a furor ignited by John Muir when a part of Yosemite, the magnificent Hetch Hetchy Valley, was threatened with flooding by a reservoir dam built to provide water to the growing city of San Francisco. This battle did not end until the administration of Woodrow Wilson, almost a decade later, and Muir lost. The integrity of Yosemite was violated, and Percy learned that a governmental designation of a piece of land as a "reserve" or "monument" or "park" did not guarantee its preservation—a valuable lesson to keep in mind when he was creating his own park.

The issue of conservation remained hot in presidential politics throughout Percy's formative years in politics. The split between Roosevelt and Taft that helped lead to Percy's defeat in 1910 concerned acreage that Roosevelt and Gifford Pinchot wanted to conserve—primarily waterpower sites—and that Taft's interior secretary, Richard Ballinger, wanted not only to develop but to give away. When Taft fired Pinchot as head of the Forest Service, the clash burst into the open, helped lead to a three-way race for president in 1912 and Democrat Woodrow Wilson's election.

The reaction of both Baxters to the conservation history of this era was not totally consistent. James Phinney greatly admired Teddy Roosevelt, but not necessarily for his conservation ethic. In a tribute that he penned to the former Rough Rider, he was more concerned with Roosevelt's efforts to curb "the rapidly increasing horde of monopolists who were absorbing the wealth of the nation." His fears were that displays of extravagance by the idle rich and by the managers of great industries, if left unchecked, would lead to the "increasing unrest of the proletariat stirred to envy...." Percy's own progressive actions followed from his father's line of self-interested logic, which both of them suspended in 1912 when they supported the Republican Party's candidate Taft instead of Bull Mooser Roosevelt. And although Percy's goal of quitting politics and of buying Katahdin had been formulated by 1926, his public behavior certainly gave the media cause to think otherwise—that, indeed, his ambitions were still political. Possibly the most notable occurrence of this sort was in 1928. Loyal Republican Percy was in Kansas City in June of that year as vice-chairman of the Maine delegation to the G.O.P. National Convention. For reasons best known to himself, he used the occasion to issue a blockbuster of a declaration that drew eight-column headlines back in Maine.

It was nothing less than a brutal frontal attack on Governor Owen Brewster. Percy called his successor a Klansman and a traitor to the Republican Party. This sensational revelation was buttressed by his claim that Brewster had come to him in January 1928 and proposed a diabolical bargain by which he, Baxter, was to run for governor and Brewster for U.S. senator. In return, Brewster, who allegedly joined the Klan in Washington, D.C., would guarantee Percy 20,000 KKK votes and also get rid of any potential Klan candidates. Concluding, Percy declared that "His (Brewster's) nomination to the U.S. Senate, in my opinion, would be a calamity."

Conventional wisdom would deem that such an outburst

was Percy's opening shot to seek the nomination, himself. Yet, perhaps in a subtler fashion, its very outrageousness was a mode for burning all bridges.

In any event, 1928 was also a year that saw the way clearing for Percy to harbor realistic hopes of initiating his Katahdin dream. Death again was a catalyst. Garrett Schenck, the CEO of the Great Northern Paper Company, passed away, removing a principal obstacle to possible negotiations.

---

[1] *How Glooskap Outwits The Ice Giants, And Other Tales of the Maritime Indians* retold by Howard Norman, Little, Brown and Company, Boston, 1989; page 53.

[2] *Chimney Pond Tales.* Yarns told by Leroy Dudley. Assembled by Clayton Hall and Jane Thomas with Elizabeth Harmon, The Pamola Press, Cumberland, Maine, 1991; page xvi.

[3] Ibid; page 9.

[4] *The Maine Woods* by Henry David Thoreau, Bramhall House, New York, 1950; pages 271-72.

[5] Ibid.; pages 277-78.

[6] *Greatest Mountain* by Connie Baxter, Scrimshaw Press.

[7] Ibid.; page 321.

[8] *Breaking New Ground* by Gifford Pinchot, Harcourt Brace and Company, New York, 1947; page 101.

[9] Ibid.

[10] Quoted in *Man's Dominion, The Story of Conservation In America* by Frank Graham, Jr. M. Evans and Company Inc., New York, 1971.

[11] *Breaking New Ground*; page 352.

[12] *John Muir And His Legacy, The American Conservation Movement* by Stephen Fox, Little, Brown and Company, 1981; pages 135-36.

[13] Ibid.; pages 137-38.

KATAHDIN SEEN FROM STACYVILLE. ALLEGEDLY, IT WAS
THIS VIEW, IN 1903, THAT INSPIRED PERCY TO WANT TO
SAVE THE MOUNTAIN FOR THE PEOPLE OF MAINE.

*

CHAPTER 13

Creating A Park

GARRETT SCHENCK, A TOUGH-MINDED
New Jerseyan of Dutch ancestry, moved to Maine and made
his fortune in the paper industry. While managing the Rum-
ford Falls Paper Company in the late 1890s, Schenck was
approached by a Bangor businessman, Charles Mullen, who
had bought a number of lots near Millinocket Stream and envi-
sioned the creation of a great paper company. Schenck had the
appropriate connections, including Joseph Pulitzer, owner of
the newspaper *The New York World*, and by 1897, $1 million in
capital had been raised. Two years later, the Maine Legislature
created the Great Northern Paper Company; its original backers were wealthy Democrats aligned with Grover Cleveland,
which turned out to be ironic given the company's later domination of Republican politics.

By 1900, Great Northern was the largest single landowner in Maine and hip-deep in Maine politics. A successful
1903 legislative battle gave it control of the West Branch

Driving and Reservoir Dam Company, and soon it was adding other entities to its string of dependents. GNP built dams, moved logs, bushwhacked lumbering roads through the wilderness, and cut thousands of acres of timber. Most of Township 3, Range 9, the Katahdin area, including the mountain, became its property in conjunction with John Ross and his son Harry.

Neither Schenck nor his sidekick Fred A. Gilbert, a lumberman who had helped him build the company, had much use for Percival Baxter. Schenck considered him an ambitious politician who was demagoguing the issues of waterpower and Katahdin to attract attention to himself. In 1919, when Baxter was trying to push through one of his Katahdin bills, he wrote to Schenck urging him to reconsider the company's opposition. The response was not encouraging. An earlier letter of Baxter's to Fred Gilbert had not even been answered. The paper company's resistance to Baxter's efforts regarding Katahdin remained implacable, and the lack of warmth between the parties could hardly have been helped by Baxter's public attacks on GNP while he was governor. In 1925 Schenck and Gilbert urged Arthur Gould to run for the U.S. Senate against Baxter and strongly backed him when he did.

Garrett Schenck's death in January 1928 helped set the stage for Percy to begin on a new footing with Great Northern, and Fred Gilbert's forced retirement the next year completed the process. The change of management at the top level proved extremely helpful. The incoming president, William A. Whitcomb, actually admired Percy, as he said, "for having the courage of his convictions and for the battle he put up for what he believed in."[1] The general manager, William O. McKay, also thought highly of the ex-governor, whom he termed "a gentleman," and an official in the Boston office, John McLeod, rendered valuable assistance to Baxter as he sought to buy GNP land.

The first piece to be acquired was obviously the most important—the keystone—since it contained the mountain. On a "well-worn map"[2] that he lugged into GNP's Boston office, Percy had red-penciled an area of 10,000 acres—four miles square—that he wanted to purchase. But he also told Whitcomb he would settle for the top of the mountain.

An important quirk of Maine history enters the picture at this point. Much of the state, after it broke off from Massachusetts, was laid out in townships of 23,000 acres, with the expectation that these parcels would eventually be settled; indeed, within every township, two 1,000-acre "public lots" were set aside to provide income for a schoolteacher and a minister—all the other land was to be in private hands. Sometimes, there would be more than one owner of a township and they would hold the land as *undivided*; in other words, they would not bother to survey out their separate properties. On a map of northern and eastern Maine, the townships in the "Unorganized Territories" are laid out side by side and divided into vertical ranges. A traveler in the region will see roadside markers indicating where he or she is; for example, if it's the township containing Katahdin, the sign will read: T3R9; then it's on to T4R9, T5R9, etc.

Although Percy had the blessings of Great Northern's president and general manager, there was still resistance within the company to selling to him, most notably from William Hilton, manager of the Spruce Woods Department. Nevertheless, on November 12, 1930, the company's board of directors voted to allow Whitcomb to sell 5,760 acres to Baxter. This was GNP's three-eighths undivided interest in the northern two-thirds of T3R9, and it covered most of Katahdin. Six days later, the legal documents were signed and Baxter paid the agreed-upon price of $25,000.

Then, his next problem was to try to convince Harry F.

Ross to sell his five-eighths interest in the top two-thirds of the township. The agreement with GNP was that if he obtained all of that land, he would turn it over to the state with restrictions that it be kept forever wild as a public park and a wildlife sanctuary and that no roads be constructed on it. If he didn't turn the property over to the state, he could sell it back to Great Northern for the same price; if he died and his heirs didn't give it to the state, the company could buy it back for $25,000.

Shortly afterward, this agreement was canceled. Or, rather, a new one was drawn up, applying only to the land in T3R9 that GNP controlled.

That Baxter could even contemplate giving any land to the state was the result of a law the legislature had passed in 1919. It was the substitute for his original bill to create a Mount Katahdin State Park, which had received an unfavorable committee report. Reworded as "An Act to Provide for the Acceptance by the State of Gifts of Land and for the Establishment of a State Park and Forest within the State of Maine," it was permissive legislation that allowed such donations to be made—and undoubtedly some solons silently added, "if anyone is crazy enough to do so."

Even before Percy left the governor's office, his commissioner of Inland Fisheries and Game, Willis E. Parsons, used the legislative authority in the bill to make a game preserve out of 85,000 acres in T3R9, T4R9, T3R10, and T4R10. The legislature later confirmed his action and Great Northern welcomed the move.

Yet, naturally, Percy still wanted his park. Attempts to induce Harry Ross to sell, however, proved fruitless. This crusty Bangor tycoon was as hostile to Percy as Garrett Schenck had been. The newspaper in which he had an ownership interest, the *Bangor Commercial*, regularly poured invective on the Portlander's positions. And in 1919, Ross not only had hired a lobbyist to oppose Percy's park bill but he, himself, journeyed to Augusta to attack the measure in person. When Ross wouldn't budge, Percy had to decide whether he would wait before turning over his deed of only part of the township to the state or gamble on doing it and hope that his action was legal.

The attorney-general, Clement F. Robinson, at first advised Baxter to wait. There were dangers for the state in accepting a three-eighths interest in a large piece of land where the rest was held privately and where the state's portion could not be verified until the property was actually divided. Threats of criticism that might be leveled against him hardly fazed Percy who was inured to political attacks. His priority was to push ahead and force the issue. This he did on March 3, 1931, in a letter to Governor Tudor Gardiner and the Eighty-Fifth Legislature, offering his "undivided three-eighths interest in the western two-thirds of the northern two-thirds of T3R9." A day later, the legislature suspended its rules and rushed through a vote to accept his gift.

The news was reported on March 5, 1931, and perhaps only an historian could have appreciated the irony of the juxtaposition of stories that made headlines that day. A more prominent piece appeared in the *Portland Press Herald* on page three and concerned U.S. Senator Arthur Gould, who had suddenly announced that he was giving up his seat in Washington ahead of time. Here was the man who had knocked Percy Baxter out of politics and set him on the road to fulfilling his magnificent obsession by acquiring Katahdin, stating publicly that he hated the experience. He was quoted as complaining:

No sane businessman should go into the U.S. Senate as long as that confounded clack is going on. I'm going back to my business where I should have been four years ago instead of wasting my time here.

On page five of the same edition, another story bore the modest headline: "MT. KATAHDIN TRACT GIVEN TO THE STATE BY EX-GOV. BAXTER."

It was the first that Maine knew of Percy's intentions.

And once again, the Baxter boldness lent drama and suspense to the ultimate conclusion. What would happen if Harry Ross continued his obstinate refusal to sell?

In his letter of transmittal to the legislature, Percy said that his action was an expression of his appreciation to the people of Maine for the honors they had bestowed upon him. He admitted he was negotiating for the remaining five-eighths interest and hoped to also present that tract to the state. He even wrote of his uncertainty as to whether he should have waited to present the whole package.

Were these public confessions part of a thought-out effort to put additional pressure on Harry Ross? If so, they were unsuccessful. Baxter spoke to Attorney-General Robinson about the possibility of the state taking the land by eminent domain; he would personally foot the bill, paying the assessed value of $6 an acre, which he felt was far more than the land was worth. Such an eventual dire step wasn't needed, although Ross's stubbornness, in Robinson's words,[3] made "Baxter almost sick over it for days." On June 23, 1931, GNP's Board of Directors agreed to allow a court to divide the township, and Harry Ross gave his permission. In September, the settlement was accomplished; GNP had its 5,760 acres free and clear and immediately deeded them to Baxter.

The newspapers, unaware of the legal maneuverings still

necessary, had pointed out at the time of the original announcement that all of the most notable features of Katahdin were included in Baxter's gift. To wit:

Monument Peak, 5,267 feet
Pamola, 4,902 feet
Knife Edge
The Chimney
Chimney Pond and the Tablelands, 4,800 feet
Basin Pond
Whidden Pond
North Peak, 4,000 feet
South Peak, 4,000 feet

KATAHDIN'S PAMOLA AND THE KNIFE EDGE, WITH CHIMNEY PEAK AND SOUTH PEAK.

Within a month of the original offer, Monument Peak, by legislative action, had been renamed Baxter Peak.

Following the successful division of T3R9, Baxter was able to transfer the full title of his parcel to Forest Commissioner Neil Violette, who could accept it for the state since the legislature wasn't in session. When the lawmakers returned early in 1933, they formally accepted the nearly 6,000 acres. They also named the area Baxter State Park.

Having bought the mountain, why did Percy continue his purchases? What was the master plan in his mind? Was there any? Or did circumstances drive him?

Final legal confirmation of his gift to the state had come in 1933, an inauspicious year for a Republican. The governor, Louis Brann, was the first Democratic chief executive elected in almost twenty years. Percy's distrust of Franklin Delano Roosevelt and the New Deal was heightened by Brann's expressed desires to bring more federal money into Maine. That he might do so via grandiose national parks or national forests was a genuine threat to Katahdin. Part of Percy's energized activity in buying more land and adding it to the park may have been to show that he could compete, that his vision could be as large as Washington's.

Events were moving quickly. By the end of 1933, a proposal was afoot for a 1 million acre national forest in Maine. The idea had William Whitcomb at Great Northern extremely disturbed and he pressed his chief lobbyist, a Boston lawyer named Sheldon E. Wardwell, to do what he could with his Democratic friends in D.C. to see that large chunks of the company's acreage in Maine weren't "sterilized" (the term was used to describe land where logging wouldn't be allowed). At the same time, a bill passed in the Maine Legislature, notwithstanding GNP's opposition, to authorize the federal government to purchase land in Maine for forestry purposes. Some land in the vicinity of Katahdin was included and also a provision to establish a Baxter State Park Commission to manage Percy's purchase. This was originally a five-member body made up of the governor, the forest commissioner, the Inland Fisheries and Game commissioner, and two public members, one of whom had to be from Greenville or Millinocket. One reason Great Northern's vaunted political muscle wasn't successful was that many of the local timber owners, hurt by the Depression, were only too happy to sell to the Feds. Even arch-conservative Harry Ross was talking to them. Sheldon Wardwell expressed his disgust with people like a Colonel Shumway of the Merrill Trust in Maine who was pushing for a federal buy-out of lands his bank held as collateral: "...Colonel Shumway seemed to think we ought to join the New Deal and let everyone who wanted get their hands into the dough dish."

Percy Baxter, no friend of the New Deal, may have muted any opposition to the bill that gave a green light to the Feds because of its creation of a Baxter Park Commission. At the same time, smart politician that he was, he achieved a good relationship with the federal authorities setting up a Civilian Conservation Corps camp in the Millinocket area. He even let them name it Baxter Camp, had a fine time visiting the boys there, and requested they put a work site in Baxter Park.

Secretary of the Interior Harold Ickes, whose domain included the National Park Service, had already shown an interest in Katahdin and the possibility of adding it to an extensive national park in Maine. Governor Brann wanted both a national park and a national forest. Since Brann, as governor, was on the Baxter Park Commission, this was a worrisome situation and caused Percy to work for a change in the enabling legislation and the creation of a Park *Authority* that would not include the governor.

The new law, still in existence today, set up the attorney-general, the forest commissioner, and the Inland Fisheries and Game commissioner to run the park as a triumvirate.

None of these early threats to Baxter Park materialized. Since the authorizing bill the Maine Legislature passed had no eminent domain provisions, federal officials soon lost interest in trying to acquire land Downeast. It might have seemed that Percy could relax. But an ostensibly insignificant act of his was to come back to haunt him in 1937. That was the year Ralph Owen Brewster, now a U.S. congressman, revived the idea of a national park in Maine; worse, it was to be a KATAHDIN NATIONAL PARK.

Brewster had a lot to hold against Percy Baxter: the bitter Klansman/Traitor blast, the recount, the budget brouhaha. But in politics, little things often hurt the most. In 1933, after the park was created, Percy (who under the terms of his donation had the right to suggest name changes) asked that "Governor's Spring" on the Geological Survey of Katahdin be changed to "Thoreau Spring." It is unlikely that he didn't know the governor of "Governor's Spring" was Owen Brewster and that the title had been conferred to commemorate Brewster's climb to the peak, the first for a Maine governor while in office. This bit of pettiness was being repaid now that Brewster was in Washington.

Percy felt it immediately. He wrote to his nephew John Baxter, saying that Brewster's motive was "first to injure me and second to get some political advantage by being instrumental in having a National Park in Maine."[4]

Rubbing salt in the wound, Brewster introduced the measure while Percy was out of the country on one of his winter cruises. When called on this lack of common courtesy, Brewster alibied that he'd tried in vain to reach Percy but felt he could wait no longer.

There was a story told in later years by Percy's chauffeur,

Joseph Lee, that has become a legend, illustrative of the relations between Percy Baxter and Owen Brewster and the intensity of their feelings toward each other. On one of his regular trips home from the park to Portland, Percy asked Lee to detour through the town of Dexter. This had been Brewster's hometown and after his demise, which had occurred some years before, his burial place. Percy directed Lee to drive to the cemetery and park while he visited Brewster's grave. The chauffeur thought this was a particularly nice gesture to accord a former enemy, and he said as much to Percy after he returned from his thoughtful vigil. "No," Percy said, smiling and shaking his head, "I just wanted to be sure the sonofabitch was really dead."

Yet there was more than Brewster's enmity behind the move to suck Katahdin into a national park. The mastermind was a man named Myron Avery. A Mainer, a native of Lubec, he was chairman of the Appalachian Trail Conference and according to John Hakola, author of the definitive book on Baxter Park, he "probably knew more about the (Katahdin) region than any man then living."[5] Avery had once written to Percy about what he considered substandard conditions in the park, particularly at Chimney Pond, and this was a theme he harped on, even though a request had gone to Governor Lewis Barrows for money to alleviate the problem.

With his usual tenacity, energy, and outspoken frankness, Percy fought Brewster and Avery. A flurry of letters went to influential individuals, among them Maine's congressional delegation. One letter even went to a Mr. and Mrs. David Gray of Portland, who were related to President Franklin Delano Roosevelt, asking them to intercede with FDR. This particular Baxter missive was passed on to the Interior Department, which gave a report to the president, although he took no action on it, one way or another.

Baxter also rounded up organizations to oppose Brewster's bill.

Since the Appalachian Mountain Club and the Appalachian Trail Conference seemed to be feuding, they came down on opposite sides of the issue. In late April, a Portland newspaper carried a major article by Ronald I. Gower, editor of the AMC's *Katahdin Guide*, expressing the group's adamant opposition to the national park concept. Articles by Myron Avery, including one that Brewster placed in the "Congressional Record," hammered away at the need for protective resources from Washington.

Other opponents Baxter was able to corral, some admittedly far removed from the scene, included the Green Mountain Club, the Brooklyn Institute of Arts and Sciences, the Cosmopolitan Club, the Explorers Club, the Massachusetts Forest and Park Association, as well as the Maine Garden Clubs. Significantly, Baxter was able to enlist two towering figures of the American wilderness conservation movement: Robert Sterling Yard, who headed up the recently formed Wilderness Society, and Robert Marshall, then with the Forest Service, a wealthy pioneer of the "forever wild" concept and for whom the famous Bob Marshall Wilderness is named.

In his promotion of the national park idea, Avery even resorted to personal attacks on Percy. He charged that the ex-governor regarded the park as a personal memorial, pooh-poohed Percy's promise to add unspecified acreage to the original gift, and criticized the one additional purchase already consummated, that of 18,000 acres in T5R9 around Traveller's Mountain, which was miles from Katahdin with an entire intervening township that needed to be bought.

Baxter's retorts were phrased with his usual fervor and measured hyperbole. Picking up on Brewster's promotion of the area for tourism, including "great log cabin hotels, like those at Yellowstone and Yosemite," Percy unloaded with both barrels—indignation and a touch of reverse snobbery.

> To commercialize this magnificent area, to desecrate it with great hotels with their noisy social life, their flaming signs, the roar of motor cars and airplanes coming and going, to break the peace of that great solitude, would be nothing less than sacrilege.

What defeated Avery and Brewster, finally, was not only Baxter's resistance and pledge that a quadrupling of his land purchases was part of his future plans, but the natural aversion of many Maine people to the New Deal in particular and federal programs in general. After all, in 1936, only Maine and Vermont had opposed FDR's re-election, thus prompting one wag to change the old saw about "So goes Maine, so goes the nation" to "So goes Maine, so goes Vermont." When Congress adjourned in late June 1938 without taking action on Brewster's bill, any momentum it had gained was lost. After a little private talk between Percy and Brewster, the congressman decided not to re-introduce the bill. Years later, when one of Brewster's primary rivals sought Percy's support, the latter demurred on the grounds that Brewster had kept his word never to interfere again with Baxter Park.

This near close call was followed by the 1939 change in the administration of the park. Maine government was once more safely Republican and Percy could achieve his goal of replacing the governor. Also dropped were the two public members. While the new Park Authority was given the power to adopt its own rules and procedures, the financial resources the state gave it were consistently meager—mostly in the $3,000-$4,000 range throughout the 1940s. Myron Avery kept up his sniping at state control, even after the demise of

Brewster's bill. And Percy kept on buying land and adding it to the park.

In 1939, two more gifts, including Traveller's Mountain, were accepted. By 1940, Percy had bought into T3Rl0, the township adjacent to the Katahdin purchase in T3R9. During 1941 and 1942, he was able to buy all of T4R9 and secure a contiguous link to Traveller's Mountain. In 1943, he bought the rest of T5R9, where Traveller's was located. The next year, he bought the adjacent township, T5Rl0. The complexities of his land dealings were mind-boggling. Yet nothing seemed to deter him, neither the shocking death of William Whitcomb, who was shot to death by a disgruntled employee in his Boston office fifteen minutes prior to an appointment he had with Percy, nor Harry Ross's ill temper as portrayed in these cutting paragraphs from a letter sent to Baxter on December 19, 1939:

> Soon after I came out of college, my father and I bought an interest in the Katahdin Township and I have taken care of the land since then as best I could and hope to continue.
>
> If you will permit me to say so, my dear sir, you forget that other people as well as yourself indulge in sentiment. Sentiment is not confined to any few.

Ross, by the way, was said to be a very charming man when he wanted to be who used his temper (he was a redhead) as a tactic to try to obtain more money for his land.

In 1949, there came the first indication of any public opposition to what Baxter was doing. The sportsmen of the region were beginning to resent the closing off of some of their hunting grounds and over on the Patten side, they made their feelings known to their legislators. State Senator George

Barnes of Houlton picked up the ball for them. He was the son of Charles Barnes, Percy's old colleague, who had been against him on waterpower but an ally on Katahdin.

With almost clockwork regularity at the beginning of each session in the late 1940s, the legislature received notice of another gift of land from Percival Baxter and a bill to establish the same in law. The rules would be suspended and without reference to a committee, the bill would receive its various readings and be enacted in lightning-quick fashion. This happened early in 1949 when a measure to add 14,286 acres to the 127,426 the ex-governor had already donated gained its usual swift approval. That was on January 12, 1949. At the end of April, however, another bill, "An Act Relating to Katahdin Wildlife Sanctuary" was wending its path through the legislative process when, suddenly, Senator Barnes of Aroostook tabled it. His purpose, it seemed, was to add Senate Amendment A. Sometimes an amendment appears to be totally innocuous, as this one did. It merely contained a description of Baxter State Park that would have, if adopted, constituted a legal description of the entity—in total, 133,443 acres. The trouble was that with Baxter's latest addition in January, the Park had actually reached 141,71 acres. Barnes had lopped off 8,269 acres!

Senator John Ward of Millinocket, the sponsor of the original acceptance legislation, immediately saw Barnes's ploy and moved to kill the amendment. The debate that followed was extraordinary because, replacing the gratitude invariably expressed for Baxter's largesse, it was now questioned, with even a call for it to end. Barnes described how he had been visited in his office in Houlton by "some very prominent men from my locality"[6] who were concerned that a road from Shin Pond into the new acquisition would be closed to hunting:

These men felt that perhaps and not with any disappreciation of the fine service that our former Governor has rendered to the State of Maine, Baxter State Park, including some six townships, had been extended far enough. [7]

Barnes then attacked the method by which the Baxter Park bills were handled and suggested they be referred to committee and public hearings be held on them. He went on to say that he had written to Baxter to inform him that his newest purchase

> would exclude all of this road in that area from open hunting and suggested that perhaps I had better enter an amendment into this Legislature to withdraw or remove the hunting restriction on that area. I received a letter back from Governor Baxter in which he suggested that I was guilty of a breach of faith for even suggesting such a thing.... I am at a loss to see how any one of us could be deemed guilty of a breach of faith in taking a pig in a poke, not knowing what we were accepting in this fashion.

This harsh language was accentuated with the further statement that:

> I feel quite strongly that this particular park has extended far enough.[8]

Then, dramatically, before Jack Ward had his say, George Barnes acknowledged that his amendment had no chance and he would go along with the senator from Millinocket's motion to kill it, but he hoped the next legislature would send any future Baxter Park addition bills to committee.

Those bills kept coming as Percy made further gifts. But more opposition erupted in 1954 when he offered lands north of Trout Brook; among the protesters was his great friend from Patten, the game warden Caleb Scribner. Eventually, despite his own feelings about animals and hunting, Percy Baxter bent like the politician he was and allowed hunting in several sections of the park, areas that remain unposted to this day.

Even after his death in 1969, Percy's park has grown. Using an $80,000 acquisition fund he left in his will, since ballooned to $500,000, the Baxter Park Authority bought an area of 1,046 acres (including two lakes) in December 1992 from the Georgia-Pacific Company, which had bought out Great Northern. It was the first purchase since Baxter had seemingly completed the park in 1962. Almost five years later in the spring of 1997, another parcel was bought with the replenished acquisition fund, an area of 2,669 acres between the West Branch of the Penobscot and the park boundary. The Authority paid yet another owner, the Bowater-Great Northern company $495,000 for the land. It is no doubt possible, given the Baxter-inspired propensity for the park to continue to increase, that additional future purchases will be made.

---

[1] As quoted in *Legacy of a Lifetime, The Story of Baxter State Park* by Dr. John W. Hakola, TBW Books, Woolwich, Maine, 1981; page 68.

[2] Ibid.

[3] Ibid.; page 71.

[4] Percival Baxter to John Baxter, April 14, 1937.

[5] *Legacy of a Lifetime*; page 144.

[6] Legislative Record, April 26, 1949; page 1,606.

[7] Ibid.; page 1,607.

[8] Ibid.; page 1,608.

CHAPTER 14

Travels

NOTWITHSTANDING HIS MANY disclaimers, Percival Baxter often saw his name offered in the media for various government posts, even as late as 1952, when he was seventy-six years old. On that occasion, the *Portland Press* was editorially suggesting to the newly elected Eisenhower Administration that Percy be named ambassador to the Soviet Union. One of Percy's principal qualifications, they stated, was his stature as a world traveler—that in the 1920s and 1930s, he had made four trips to the USSR. Said the editorial's author: "He travels as a student, never as a time-killing tourist."[1] That previous summer, Percy had been in Finland, learning about the small northern country's relationship with its giant neighbor, visiting the Finnish Parliament, meeting high officials, and gaining insight into the Finns' domestic and international problems.

Percy was never offered the job nor was it likely he would have accepted it. In 1952, he was still filling out the park (six

PERCY ON BOARD SHIP, WEARING ONE OF HIS CAPS, WHICH
HE ALWAYS SEEMED TO LOSE.

more additions were offered and accepted in 1955) and, fascinated as he had been by the budding Communist empire in
his younger days, he undoubtedly had no great interest, at his
age, in being in the middle of the rigors of U.S.-Soviet relations a year before Stalin's death.

Although Percy did not travel strictly as a "time-killing
tourist," he did travel well, usually on luxury liners, and he
invariably had a good time, enjoying the interesting people
he met (frequently at the ship captain's table) and seeing the
sights when ashore, as well as indulging his politician's curiosity about what was going on in public life. Occasionally, he
wrote articles for the local press, detailing his impressions

and, in a number of instances, broadcasting extremely strong views.

A case in point was his splenetic attack on Mexico in a *Portland Sunday Telegram* piece, April 21, 1935. It was headlined: "MEXICO GOING RED." Having just returned from south of the border, he felt he had to warn Americans that our neighbor below the Rio Grande had adopted "a Socialist-Communist program...rapidly following the example of Soviet Russia." The "Revolutionary" Mexican ruling party, he added, was also trying to stamp out Roman Catholicism and establish atheism in its place.

His strongest indignation, however, was reserved for the propagandistic artwork of such noted mural painters as Diego Rivera and Jose Clemente Orozco.

> I never saw anything in Russia as inflammatory as these pictures, or as ugly and uncouth.... Colossal figures of golden-haired prostitutes heavy with jewelry and nearly nude are stretched out on the ground, while leaders in business and industry...and members of the Roman Catholic clergy, holding champagne glasses in their hands, look down upon the reclining figures....

Which parts of him—his Victorian sense of moral propriety or his political instincts—were more offended, it is difficult to say. But a few years earlier, he was not nearly as harsh, at least openly, in his judgments on the Soviet experiment in government.

Early in 1929, reporting on one of his trips to the Soviet Union, he argued that it was necessary to study and understand the Communist doctrine. "Bolshevism must be met by argument, not by invective,"[2] he insisted.

"The Russian people are kind and hospitable," he went on, "and they welcome Americans above all foreigners." He also declared that he felt completely safe from crimes of violence while traveling in the Soviet Union.

That same year, he was in touch with U.S. Senator William Borah of Idaho, chairman of the Senate Foreign Relations Committee, who was interested in having the United States establish diplomatic relations with the Stalin regime. He asked Baxter to "study the situation with that problem in mind and let me talk with you after your return."[3]

The trip was made with a bilingual Russian named Serebriakoff as guide. A year later, Baxter was writing to Peter A. Bogdanov, head of AMTORG, the Soviet trading organization in the U.S., trying to arrange another trip. He wished to have Serebriakoff back but if that were not possible, "I should feel entirely safe if I had one of the men connected with the G.P.U. for I understand these men are thoroughly informed and reliable...." Whether Percy fully understood the implication of asking for a secret police agent (the G.P.U. was a predecessor of the K.G.B.) is not readily clear. It *is* clear that he was being very politic in his language with the Soviet officials. No *invective* nor even any hint of negativism here. Indeed, he even intimated that the U.S. was receiving too much anti-Soviet propaganda in its press, and he stated baldly that he would be looking to see the improvements made in social and economic conditions. "I would be interested to go to Archangel and look over the wood industry with its alleged 'forced' labor." The Dnieper Dam, state farms, the Stalingrad tractor factory plant, and a railroad trip to Tashkent in Central Asia were among his other interests. His desire was to go in April 1931, to take a small motion picture camera with him, and to leave the USSR with his films undeveloped.

It was this latter intention, for which he received official approval, that perhaps inspired his extremely jaundiced view of the Soviets later. At the Polish-Russian border on his way out, there was a problem about the film with the customs officials. Although he thought it had been straightened out by a representative of the G.P.U. who ascertained that Baxter had the right to remove his films sight unseen by the authorities, back home Percy found that the film had somehow been ruined. His angry letters were met by polite denials from Soviet officials that anyone had tampered with his photography. All in all, it was a souring experience for Percy.

Still, he may have simply been disguising his feelings all along. He wrote an extensive (sixty-eight-page) paper on his impressions of the USSR, a work he never published and which, in his own annotations, he couldn't remember when he'd written it: "1932?, more probably 1929"—wherein he was brutally blunt. "Russia is 'red' from rim to hub," he wrote. "Communist rule is ruthless and intolerant in the far-away places as in Moscow...if anyone objects, he is effectively eliminated in ways best known to the Communist clique." Illustrating his political analysis were personal experiences: a celebration of the Russian Revolution's anniversary that he shared with Soviet seamen on a ship taking him across the Black Sea from Batum to Constantinople, where the toasts were to Red Russia and world revolution and the sailors sang the "Internationale," which Baxter called "the Revolutionary Hymn of Hate." Or his visit to a chocolate factory, where he had to endure criticism about the execution in Massachusetts of Sacco and Vanzetti, which he countered by asking how Russians would react to American protests over Stalin's summary execution of 500 White Russians. On the final page of his treatise, Percy Baxter, with Senator Borah no doubt in mind, cautioned against the U.S. rushing to recognize the Soviet Union. Later, he was to become a vehement opponent of recognition.

An incident in April 1932 added to his discomfort vis-à-vis the Soviet Union. *The Daily Worker*, the U.S. Communist newspaper, quoted him as praising a "moral and material rebirth in the Soviet Union." The source was none other than a dispatch to the *New York Times* from its Moscow correspondent who had interviewed Baxter in the course of a 7,000-mile trip he was taking with a friend. From the Soviet point of view, the statements of the ex-governor of Maine made great propaganda. For example:

> The enthusiasm of the people we met and their confidence in their ability to accomplish their plans were most striking and indubitably genuine.[4]

Back home, stung by adverse reactions, Baxter wrote to Walter Duranty, the famed *New York Times* correspondent who had interviewed him. "I regret to say you have seriously embarrassed me," he began.[5] Duranty had ignored his request

THE RUSSIAN SHIP, SS *LENIN*, THAT TOOK PERCY ACROSS THE BLACK SEA. THE CREW SANG THE "INTERNATIONALE," WHICH HE CALLED "THE REVOLUTIONARY HYMN OF HATE."

not to be quoted, he claimed, and furthermore had failed to report his premise that "I am as opposed as ever to the Bolshevik program." The letter remained a private communication, however, since Baxter did not want to give the issue any further publicity.

In 1933, when Franklin Roosevelt was contemplating recognizing the Soviet Union, Baxter wrote him in opposition. An interesting sidelight is that he did so at the prompting of William A. Whitcomb, the president of the Great Northern Paper Company, with whom he was negotiating at the time to buy land for the park. Baxter's style as a consummate politician also stands out in this missive to a member of the opposite party whose New Deal policies he hated and who had defeated his close friend, Herbert Hoover. On a chatty personal note, he refers to Franklin Roosevelt's aunt, Mrs. David Gray, a neighbor of his in Portland, at whose home he recently had the pleasure of meeting the president's mother. His statement against recognition, he says, was prepared at the request of "the President of a large and well-managed New England industry," and he ends as if he were one of the Democratic chief executive's strong supporters: "...but I earnestly hope that you will be spared to us and all your plans for the nation's welfare will be successful."[6]

In his reply, Roosevelt said: "I am deeply grateful for your generous word of good will."[7]

Baxter's attitudes toward the other totalitarian powers in the world—the German Nazis, the Italian Fascists, and the Japanese militarists—were not as publicly pronounced at an early stage as were his feelings about communism. In 1928, six years after Benito Mussolini took power, Baxter had occasion to write a review of the Duce's autobiography. Finding the dictator's memoirs "enlightening" and Fascism made "understandable," he drew a contrast between Italy's form of

PERCY LIFTS HIS GLASS IN A TOAST ABOARD THE JAPANESE
SHIP, *ASAMA MARU*, ONE YEAR BEFORE PEARL HARBOR. HE
HAD PREDICTED THAT JAPAN WOULD NEVER GO TO WAR
WITH THE UNITED STATES.

authoritarianism vis-à-vis the Soviet model. "In Russia, Private
Capitalism is in exile," he wrote, "...in Italy, Private Capital is
put to work along with Labor and is respected and fostered."

Planning to visit Germany, he communicated in January
1939 with Hans Thomsen, the German charge d'affaires in
Washington, D.C., and among his requests was to have a
meeting arranged with Adolf Hitler. Thomsen suggested he
try to set it up through the American Embassy in Berlin but
cautioned: "Out of personal experience, I know how much
Mr. Hitler enjoys talking to visitors from abroad. Nevertheless, his very heavily burdened schedule often interferes with
his wishes in this regard."[8] Baxter did visit Nazi Germany, sailing on the Hamburg-America Line about a month before

Hitler invaded Czechoslovakia. He never did meet with the Fuhrer. Among his mementos were postcards of the Brown House in Munich, the cradle of Naziism, and of the *Landhaus das Reichkanzlers*, Hitler's mountaintop retreat at Berchtesgaden.

As for Japan, Baxter made several visits, starting in 1913. A public pronouncement he made about the Japanese in the 1920s was highly sincere albeit eventually inaccurate. "The Japanese are peace-loving and industrious and court no trouble with their neighbors," he declared, "I have not the remotest idea that Japan will ever desire to enter into war with the United States." Years later, in 1939, he was seeking not only to visit Japan again (for the third time) but to travel in their occupied sectors of China, specifically Manchuria and major cities such as Peking and Shanghai. In 1940, the year before Pearl Harbor, he was treated as an important dignitary in Tokyo, the recipient of a VIP lunch presented in his honor by the minister of foreign affairs, Hachiro Arita.

By this time, Baxter had already spoken out publicly against at least one member of the Axis—Germany. A possible motive was the Nazi-Soviet Pact of August 1939, for in his condemnation, Naziism and Communism are linked. "The Nazis and the Bolshevists are blood brothers and the world will suffer terribly before this unholy alliance is broken...," a Portland newspaper reported him saying.[9] His prediction here was all too accurate.

Privately, Percy Baxter had already completed his judgment of Nazi Germany. Although a number of his trip "reports" were published, his twenty-four-page typewritten "Report on Nazi Germany," written sometime in 1939, appears never to have seen the light of day.

March 1939 was a critical time to be traveling in Germany. Munich had already taken place, with the major

European powers—Britain, France and Italy—giving Hitler essentially a free hand in Czechoslovakia. During the middle of Percy's visit, Hitler invaded that now helpless country. Indeed, the Germans marched in only thirty-six hours after Percy had made a quick trip to Prague, a city he found as resignedly quiet as a tomb. His hoped-for chance to have a personal meeting with Hitler, actually scheduled to occur in Vienna, was aborted when the Fuhrer, as he put it, "rushed to Prague to take over his new province."

Concerning this outrage and the howls of protest that arose from the democracies, Percy was ambiguous albeit brutally pragmatic. "It is not for me to defend the Czechs or abuse the Germans," he wrote, "...stern reality remains and force rules in Europe today."

But his long section on Nazi mistreatment of the Jews did reflect a Yankee store of indignation. Descriptions of the sufferings inflicted on the Jewish population drew the statement: "Such brutality and injustice is unspeakable; it is based on hate and envy." Sardonically, he noted that German-Jewish war veterans were not exempted from persecution and remarked: "Wouldn't it be ironic if the Unknown Soldier of Germany were a Jew."

On a train, he met a non-Jewish scientist and his Jewish wife. The Aryan husband had lost his job. As people passed in the corridor, the poor woman looked like a hunted creature, Percy thought. He mentioned, too, that if he ever publicly revealed this scientist's name and the authorities found out, the man would be put in a concentration camp.

Germans he met tried to justify their actions to him. Some complained that the Jews were in control of America and pointed to a "Stop Hitler" parade held in New York City. When Percy referred to an anti-Semitic poster (and he saw signs everywhere: "Jews Not Wanted"), a German replied,

A SCENE FROM PERCY'S 1939 TRIP TO NAZI GERMANY,
TAKEN AT THE SAME TIME THAT HITLER INVADED
CZECHOSLOVAKIA.

"Good, take it back to America and show the States how to treat them." Their paranoid arguments about the Jews taking over Germany were met by Percy's Yankee logic: how could 1 percent of the population dominate the other 99 percent? "Where is your Nordic-Aryan superiority?" he would mischievously ask them, and their evasive answer would be: "You Americans cannot understand."

The "Heil Hitler" phenomenon was at first amusing, then annoying. At a hotel, seven chambermaids welcomed him with the greeting and a stiff-armed salute while an eighth did the same at the door of his room. He calculated that if 90 million Germans gave 50 "Heil Hitlers" a day, that would be 4.5 billion every 24 hours.

Percy also wrote of the "bitter conflict between the swastika and the cross," affecting 30 million German Catholics. But he freely admitted that the Germans seemed united behind Hitler and that the Fuhrer was extremely popular. The crushing unemployment problem had been solved. "He (Hitler) has remade Germany materially and spiritually and the German people I feel sure are happy and proud to have him as their master...," Percy wrote. "I believe the vast majority of all Germans are back of him because he has rescued them from the depths and given them hope for the future."

Nevertheless, Percy presciently recorded his opinion that Hitler needed "a long peace" in order to consolidate his economic gains and that war could be his undoing.

And even before the signing of the Nazi-Soviet Pact in August 1939, Percy was emphasizing in his report the similarities between the two totalitarianisms.

> Except for one principle the Nazis are but copying the doctrines and methods of Lenin the great Bolshevist, that exception being the nationalization or confiscation of private property.... Naziism and Fascism are Communism with a thin veneer of Capitalism....
>
> He did allow, however, that Lenin never fostered racial hatred.

"Give Hitler and his Nazis the chance and even the broad Atlantic may not stop them," Percy continued his foresight, arguing for the democracies to build up their military strength. "If Britain and France do not stop Hitler, the time will come when America will be obliged to do so."

All in all, his trip to the Third Reich provided a cautionary comparison, for he ended his report with a ringing reaffirmation of the system of government he had found so frustrating and unrewarding while in office. Glowingly, he opined: "the representative democracy of the United States is the Eighth and greatest wonder of the world." Never before, he added, had he been so happy to be home in America.

As important to him—or possibly more so—than such interesting fact-finding was the sociability of his trips. Quite often he went with an agreeable companion and even when alone, his gregarious nature allowed him to mingle easily with his fellow passengers and create friendships that he at least continued through postcards and letters. He has left behind a large collection of the printed passenger lists from his many sea voyages. They are marked with checks beside certain names and sometimes comments about the individuals noted in his own handwriting. There is a dizzying variety to the steamship lines he sailed on and the places he visited.

The earliest of the passenger lists he kept was from "A Yachting Cruise in the West Indies" aboard the American Line's twin-screw SS *New York*, sailing from that same city on March 4, 1911. The thirty-five-year-old Percy was traveling with James Phinney, but as a young bachelor he may have been keeping an eye on the female passengers. At any rate, there are check marks beside the names of Miss Clarina Hanks of Santa Barbara, California; Miss Elizabeth Harrington of West Medford, Massachusetts; Misses Eleanor and Sylvia Benson of Salem, Massachusetts; and Miss Margaret Richardson, also of Santa Barbara. This particular voyage went to Cuba, Haiti, Jamaica, Panama, Curacao, Venezuela, Trinidad, Barbados, Martinique, Guadeloupe, St. Thomas, Puerto Rico, and the Bahamas. He was to travel in the Caribbean many times.

All parts of the globe were traversed. A 1927 trip on an Italian vessel, the *Conte Rosso*, took him to Gibraltar, Naples,

and Genoa; a Canadian ship, the *Duchess*, took him in 1937 to
Nova Scotia, then to Glasgow, Belfast, and Liverpool, where
he caught the British MV *Abosso* to Madeira, the Canary
Islands, and a host of ports in West Africa; the Norwegian
Line took him to look at fjords; the SS *Santa Rosa* took him
back to Curacao and to Colombia; a French luxury liner, the
SS *Flandre*, carried him half-way around the world. He went
to Argentina and Rio de Janeiro by ship. He sailed to Alaska,
to Sweden, to Egypt, to Lebanon, to Turkey and Greece. In
March 1940, he was aboard the *Asama Maru*, of Japanese reg-
istry, traveling from San Francisco to Honolulu, Yokohama,
Kobe, and—as he had hoped—Shanghai in Japanese-occupied
China. Thus, there was great truth in the couplet of a poem
dedicated to him by his fellow passengers on the SS *Santa
Sofia*, while traveling from New York to Venezuela and
Colombia in March 1950.

> *Here's to Governor Baxter*
> *of Portland, Maine*
> *The most traveled hombre*
> *from China to Spain.*

The authors of this chummy doggerel were a Mr. and
Mrs. James P. Rohan of Riverdale, New York. Percy's letters
contain numerous other communications from people he be-
friended on his journeys. J. Carroll Stow of Baltimore wrote
of the good time he and a Dr. Palmer had had with Percy as a
trio of bachelors: "We three had many things in common, one
of which is our freedom from the complications that so often
involve some of our fellow men." There was considerable kid-
ding about a woman on board they dubbed "the Countess"
and Percy allowed that if he weren't in his middle seventies,
he might have found her more interesting. Several of these
missives, both to him and from him, seemed to allude to the

fact that the stern temperance ideology of his younger days had vanished, at least on the high seas. The Reverend Carl A. Bergstrom, a Methodist minister who had served as chaplain on a cruise to Brazil, noted that he hadn't had a Planter's Punch, a well-known rum drink, since Trinidad. "I could take some this evening," he wrote to Percy from his home in Amityville, Long Island, "but only if you were around." Percy's own letter to a Mrs. Louise H. Gribbel with whom he'd traveled on the *Stella Polaris* across the Arctic Circle is even more explicit. "I wish we might sit around the table this evening and have some nice conversation together with a few incidental cocktails," he wrote her.

His travel friendships also extended to crew members. He remained in extended correspondence with L. Rolland, the chief library steward aboard the French Line SS *Flandre*. As he did with many of the acquaintances he made, he sent a postcard of Baxter Park and added for Rolland's benefit that "Maine is not like New York. Our people are quiet and simple, there is no great wealth and nobody tries to be a 'big shot.' We all get along nicely together and in our own quiet way get much out of life." He jokingly reminded the Frenchman of the many times he had lost his cap during the voyage and how Rolland had always found it for him.

The steward, who was about to retire to his native Normandy, graciously wrote back that if Monsieur Baxter lost his cap again, just send the measurements to Normandy and he would have one made for him. Added was the observation that if all passengers were such gentlemen as Monsieur Baxter, the work of a ship's steward would be an unmitigated pleasure.

His generosity to worthy causes was sometimes stimulated by those he met. The passenger list of the SS *Brazil* is marked by the startling annotation "Leper" next to the name of a Mrs. Eunice Weaver whose address was Rio de Janeiro. It seems this American woman was president of the Brazilian federation that dealt with the dread disease. By the end of the voyage, she had received a $100 contribution from Percy Baxter. On September 5, 1950, she wrote him: "Soon I may be able to send you a picture of your little Brazilian grandson, your protégé in the prevention home." A cathedral in Alexandria, Egypt, and a hospital in Shiraz, Iran, were also recipients of his largesse.

In planning his trips, Percy was never shy about using whatever influence he could. Letters of introduction from VIP's were especially sought, such as from Charles Evans Hughes, secretary of state, to his diplomatic and consular offices asking them to assist the former governor of Maine, or from Herbert Hoover or Senator Borah or Henry Stimson and Cordell Hull when they were members of FDR's cabinet. On one occasion, Percy requested a letter of introduction from William Cardinal O'Connell of Boston, not for himself but for Madeleine and her two sons who were visiting Rome and wished to have an audience with Pope Pius XI. The Cardinal not only agreed to make the arrangement but added in a warm personal note: "I frequently remember yourself, your good father, and your saintly sister Emily as precious souvenirs of my Portland days."

Another Portland connection Percy used years later was with Ruth B. Shipley, head of the passport division of the U.S. State Department. They had a mutual friend in Miss Philena C. Winslow who lived "almost just across the street" from the Baxters and who had been a close friend of both Percy's and Mrs. Shipley's. This exchange occurred in the late 1940s, right after World War II, when it took a good deal of time to obtain a passport. Percy was trying to hurry the process. "My days of travel are numbered," he wrote her, "but I shall keep on as long as I am able and prefer to die in harness rather than to sit by the fire and wait."[10] He also thought to praise Mrs. Shipley's new boss as secretary of state, General George C. Marshall, calling him "the finest man in this country of ours." His sentiment was no doubt genuine but had to be abetted by his immense pride that he was often told he looked so much like General Marshall.

Special requests went from Percy to his old friend James Newell, president of the Bath Iron Works shipbuilders to help him have his cabin shifted aboard one of the Grace Line vessels, to M. J. Rathbone, president of Standard Oil of New Jersey, of which he was a stockholder (1,036 shares), asking for a guest card to use the Creole Oil Company club while in Maracaibo, and to Horace Albright, former director of the National Park Service and a Bowdoin alumnus, to arrange for VIP treatment when he visited the Grand Canyon, Bryce and Zion National Parks, Lake Mead, and Death Valley. Later, in thanking Albright, he urged him to come to Maine "so I may show you our modest attempts to preserve the wilderness."

Percy may have told Ruth Shipley in 1947 that his traveling days were numbered but in 1952, at age seventy-six, he was still undertaking arduous journeys. Accompanying him to Algeria for a trip into the Sahara was Father John G. Clancy, secretary to the pope in Vatican City, and together with a recent Yale graduate and Fulbright scholar, Tom Dawson, they visited such remote locations as Touggourt, Biskra, and Bou-Saada. Two years later, Percy was planning another trip to North Africa, starting in Tunis, with a number of remote oases such as El Oued, Ouargia, and Laghouat included. His only concession to his age was to give up the idea of a trans-Saharan bus trip to Kano, Nigeria.

Several lists of books he read while traveling have been left among his mementos. In one two-week period, March 24–April 8, 1950, he finished *Mary* by Sholem Asch, *The*

Egyptian by Mika Waltari, and a book titled *Black Ivory*, presumably about slavery. Also three guide books were consulted. Another list included *Tortilla Flat* by John Steinbeck, biographies of Andrew Jackson and Tom Paine, *Mark Twain's Mississippi*, and *Sea Stories and Ships*. A list he kept of people to whom he should send postcards included Governor Frederick Payne of Maine, George J. Stobie, the Maine commissioner of Inland Fisheries and Game and a member of the Park Authority, the game warden Caleb Scribner, and Rupert.

It had to have been this latter person to whom Percy addressed the two most extraordinary letters found in the Baxter collection. The salutation on each was simply "Dear Brother" and they were sent within two days of each other, February 3 and 5, 1930, one from Bulawayo, Rhodesia (now Zimbabwe), and the other from Johannesburg, South Africa, while Percy was on a trip to East and South Africa with his former private secretary, Gilbert Chadbourne.

Chad, as he was universally called, had served Percy throughout his two terms. The two men were presumably close friends as well as associates. Here they were, traveling together on the other side of the world when, suddenly, at least in Percy's view, Chad threw an inexplicable temper tantrum.

The first letter, written from the Grand Hotel in Bulawayo, began:

> Dear Brother—A most extraordinary thing occurred today.... Chad has been very touchy ever since we landed.... Today while driving out to Cecil Rhodes' grave I was telling the driver that motor drives cost too much in Africa, such as $25 for a 60 mile drive; $12.50 for an hour and a half, etc.... Without warning Chad interrupted and said he had heard enough of it; "Cut it out,"

he said. "I am tired of all this." He was all stirred up and could not control himself. I remained calm and said it was not a serious discussion. "Chad, that is not the way to speak between friends; I was not saying anything to offend you; please be reasonable," said I. "You can't be reasonable," was his reply. "You never consider anyone but yourself; you are, and always have been wholly selfish." I was dumbfounded...!

The first explosion past, the tensions between them only grew. Chad complained he had given up a good job to come on the trip, "was getting nothing out of it, and was sorry he had come." Baxter appealed to him on the basis of their years together. "From the day I walked into the office after Parkhurst's death, through our four years together and five years since Augusta, I always was your true and loyal friend," the ex-governor said and pointed out that he had always had Chad to his home and on motor trips and fishing trips and was always happy to be his host.

"You did it for charity, then, did you?" Chad snapped.
"Chad, that is unworthy of you," Baxter gasped.
"I want to go home," Chad insisted.
"I will give you the money," Baxter said.

But then Percy had second thoughts and felt that "for appearances if nothing else," they should finish their trip together.

"All right," Chad agreed.

Trying through his shock and hurt to imagine what had gone wrong, Baxter indulged in a spate of introspection but from his vantage point, could find no answer. His generosity to Chad was stressed again and again.

...he has been given everything. On this trip he has spent exactly 26 cents for me (two postage stamps and a parcel mailed), (I repaid him later) not a penny more. I even paid $22 for the visas on his passports.

Why, I have given Chad $1,000 in American Express checks in his sole name and also a Letter of Credit for $5,000 in our names on which either can draw; $6,000 in all just to protect him should I die or be sick; doesn't that show my confidence in him. How can a man accept a position as a man's secretary and know his intimate life, accept two long expensive trips, his home and family life, his motor trips and still hate him? He spoke with hatred in his voice; whatever he may say later.

...I can hardly keep the tears away. Maybe I am fooling myself all the time. Am I so thoughtless, selfish; so despised, truly am I?

Contributing to Percy's anguish over this quarrel was Chad's hammering on the sore point that Percy's *selfishness* extended to his own nearest relatives. Charging that Percy always tried to put other persons in the wrong, to embarrass them, Chad said: "Even in your own family, you do so with your sister and her boys. You never see the other man's point of view." Worse still, he claimed that Rupert had complained even more about Percy's selfishness.

In riposte, Percy still emphasized his magnanimity. His final paragraph stated:

...In London I dragged myself around to places I had seen several times, just so he could see them.... He used up all my magnesia medicine, I was glad for him to have it. I spare no expense and we drink only bottled water and stay at the best hotels. I am spending $25 per day on him alone; such is gratitude....

PERCY AND GUY GANNETT, NEWSPAPER PUBLISHER AND
POLITICIAN, ABOUT TO LEAVE FOR PUERTO RICO.

These letters open a window, but just a crack, into a private *persona* that Percival Baxter had been at some pains to conceal in his collection of memorabilia, which is heavy on official documents and newspaper clippings. Not that he was always seeking to vaunt himself—highly unflattering articles are liberally included. But here is a peek at his relationship with another person as it really was.

How intimate was that relationship? Were they homosexuals indulging in a lovers' spat? The question has been raised by some who have read these letters, and Percy's failure to marry has lent credence to the suspicion. Yet, all in all, such a thesis seems unlikely. Chad was married and had children and an exemplary family life, and Percy had many traveling companions, plus frequent rumors of affairs with females. The most likely explanation of Chad's blowup was that he had finally reached the limit of his patience with Percy's punctilious penny-pinching habits. That, and what must have been the overwhelming, ever-present consciousness of his dependence on the charity of his former boss. Percy's own lack of sensitivity to this trait of his is shown in his constant references to how much he is spending on Chad. No doubt through the years this *master-slave* juxtaposition, so to speak, despite its outward graciousness, was made abundantly clear to Chad, who finally let all his pent-up resentment show. Percy could be difficult. A possibly apocryphal story has been told about Percy's nephews, the Tomlinson boys, whom he also took on trips and treated royally. Supposedly, when they were angry with him, which happened on occasion, they would go out into the driveway where his car was parked and urinate in the gas tank.

Travel, for Percy, had a few other dangers, as well. On a return trip from Norway aboard the SS *Stavangerfjord* in 1951, a sudden ocean storm was encountered and the seventy-five-year-old gentleman, tossed about in his cabin, was dashed against a wall and broke his arm and shoulder. Yet this was merely physical pain, not the torment of a fractured human relationship. Despite orders to the contrary from the ship's doctor, he was out of bed the next morning and attending breakfast. He seemed quite proud of his ability to mend as quickly as he did.

Misunderstandings are frequent in foreign travel. One that must have tickled Percy occurred during a visit in 1947 to Trinidad, an island where he'd often stopped. As a VIP, he was greeted by the mayor of Port of Spain, the capital, and he made a speech that was covered by the local media. Some of his remarks were about women's rights, and he included the fact that he had been the first U.S. governor to appoint females to public positions. He also spoke about his park.

Trinidad was then under British rule and English thinking prevailed. Thus, a newspaper reported: "Mr. Baxter, who owns an estate of 225 square miles in Maine, said there was a lot of game there but shooting was prohibited."

Percy must have smiled, reading this, remembering his days at Eton House School when some of his classmates may indeed have come from families whose estates could be as large as 225 square miles. While Percy always said that the park belonged to the people of Maine, which he made sure it did, there might just have been a lingering sense of satisfaction, given also his pride in his English ancestry, that he was the *squire* of such a demesne, albeit in American style.

The same article also referred to him as a "naturalist," which must have pleased him, as well.

---

1 *Portland Press*, November 10, 1952.
2 *Portland Sunday Telegram*, March 2, 1929.
3 Borah to Baxter, January 14, 1929.
4 *New York Times*, April 8, 1932.
5 Baxter to Duranty, April 25, 1932.
6 Baxter to FDR, September 28, 1933.
7 FDR to Baxter, October 5, 1933.
8 Thomsen to Baxter, January 25, 1939.
9 *Portland Sunday Telegram*, December 3, 1939.
10 Baxter to Shipley, January 22, 1947.

CHAPTER ✳ **15**

The Later Years

IN ONE OF PERCIVAL BAXTER'S scrapbooks, there is a news photo dated April 5, 1952, showing him with other Maine Republicans at a dinner held in the prestigious Portland Club. To the casual eye, there would be nothing unusual about such a scene. But the guest of honor was Robert L. Jones, a name that means nothing today and meant precious little then. Yet Robert L. Jones was a candidate for the U.S. Senate—that is, for the Republican nomination for that office—and his brief moment in the public sun was due less to his own accomplishments, which seemed non-existent, than to the fact that he was the hand-picked choice of Senator Joseph R. McCarthy to run against Maine's incumbent Republican senator, Margaret Chase Smith.

With her famous "Declaration of Conscience" speech on the floor of the senate, denouncing McCarthy and his tactics, Senator Smith had infuriated the Wisconsin "Red-baiter," who was then riding high politically. Adhering to the old dic-

PERCY, IN HIS LATER YEARS, STANDING BY A MEMORIAL TO HIS IRISH SETTERS.

tum in politics that "you don't get mad, you get even," McCarthy had found someone to run against her. The result was a debacle for McCarthy and Robert L. Jones. Senator Smith demolished her opponent by a 5-1 margin.

So what was Percy Baxter doing at a rally for Joe McCarthy's hand-picked stooge?

Certainly, since the 1930s if not earlier, he had shown himself resolutely anti-Communist in his public pronouncements, although they were tempered by the realism of his trips to the Soviet Union.

In Republican intra-party struggles, he had exhibited maverick traits on occasion, beginning in 1908 when he had bucked the party machine to support Bert Fernald against incumbent Governor William Cobb, only to reverse position a few years later and be one of a handful of President William Howard Taft's supporters against Theodore Roosevelt, the overwhelming favorite of the rest of Maine's National Convention delegation. In 1920, when the Maine G.O.P. delegation was backing favorite son New Englander Calvin Coolidge for president, Percy was the only Maine Republican to vote for Herbert Hoover. In 1956, he caused a commotion by stating publicly that he wouldn't mind seeing Democratic Governor Edmund S. Muskie continue in office, despite the fact that he had been honorary chair of the campaign of Governor Burton Cross, whom Muskie had upset in 1954.

Nowhere in Baxter's papers is there an explanation of why he lent his name to Robert L. Jones's quixotic and revengeful quest. Nor does there seem to be any mention of Margaret Chase Smith, herself, or what Baxter's feelings might have been toward her. Given his strong support for women in politics and Smith's strongly independent positions vis-à-vis the party regulars (following the lead of her late husband Clyde Smith, whose place she took in Congress), one might have expected to find an admiring comment.

Had he become an old moss-back in his seventies, a political reactionary, breathing anti-Communist fire in an era of witch-hunting?

As always, with Percival Baxter, there is plenty of ambiguity.

Almost exactly three years after the dinner with Robert L. Jones (and about a year after McCarthy's political downfall) he was writing to a Miss Lois Langdon, whose hospital in Shiraz, Iran, he helped to support, that "there is altogether too much talk about hydrogen bombs and war.... Russia seems to be working toward better understanding and I am sure the wise ones in Washington will do their utmost to meet the Soviets at least halfway."[1]

That same year, 1955, groundbreaking ceremonies were held for perhaps his most important charity—and contribution to Maine—aside from the park. On November 6, 1955, construction of the Baxter School for the Deaf was inaugurated.

The genesis of the effort was Percy's gift to the state in 1943 of the family's summer home on Mackworth Island. The entire island, which the Baxters owned, was included, as well as the bridge to it, and also Mackworth Rock. His proposed use for the donation was made no clearer than "a State public purpose."

James Phinney had bought Mackworth (also known as Mackey's Island) in 1888. Previously, the family had summered in a cottage on another Casco Bay island, Great Diamond. But because he could control all of his surroundings, Mackworth was more to James Phinney's liking and the Baxters never summered anywhere else. They even wintered there, too, or spent time out-of-season at the retreat they all loved. In pre-colonial times, Cocawesco, the Indian sagamore of the Casco Bay region, also had spent time with his people there, yet very early—in 1631—it had devolved to a friend of Sir Ferdinando Gorges, Arthur Mackworth, who died in 1657 and was buried on the site. So, too, were the Baxter dogs, as well as old fire horses from the Portland Fire Department, who had been put out to pasture and given the run of the place for the rest of their days. The wooden bridge was one of the longest in the state and connected the island to the mainland at Falmouth.

In the deed of trust, Percy reserved the right to his own use of the island and its buildings as long as he paid all expenses, and he included $10,000 as a trust fund to be handled by the state.

During the next six years, Percy spent his summers on the island and maintained the property. When he moved out in 1949, the state took over. One suggestion he made was that it be used as "a home for sick and underprivileged children." It was evident he particularly wanted the place used for kids.

In a communication to Governor Burton Cross in 1953,

PERCY CELEBRATED LATER BIRTHDAYS WITH THE CHILDREN AT THE BAXTER SCHOOL FOR THE DEAF.

he became more specific. He would provide $500,000 for a school project and $125,000 for a new bridge. Rather unrealistically, he outlined a school project actually comprised of two not necessarily compatible institutions: a school for the deaf and a home and school for state wards.

Governor Cross apparently talked him into dropping the idea of dealing with state wards and instead concentrating on helping the deaf. The then existing state school for these kids was located on Spring Street in downtown Portland and was entirely inadequate.

One of Percy's original stipulations was that the construction would have to be begun by January 1, 1955. He later was willing to stretch the deadline by nine months and also upped his commitment by another $100,000. In all, aided by Percy's gift of three-quarters of a million dollars, the state expended $1.4 million, including the erection of a modern causeway to replace the antiquated wooden bridge. The Baxter home on the property was converted to administrative offices and a residence for the superintendent and teachers.

Shown in a photograph with ex-Governor Baxter at the opening ceremonies was five-year-old Curtis Gibbert who shoveled the first load of dirt. The deaf children, unused to the country after their experiences of life in urban Portland, released their pent-up energy by racing all over the grounds and it took some time to round them up.

Percy Baxter showed as much interest in the School for the Deaf as he did in the park. It was officially named for him by the legislature in 1957. Whenever he could, he attended holiday parties with the students and even celebrated his birthdays with them. He assiduously followed everything that pertained to the institution. At age eighty-seven, he actually became locked in a public controversy with the school's new superintendent, Joseph Youngs.

The bone of contention was a $451,000 capital improvement budget that its ambitious new leader had proposed for the institution. Requested of the legislature was a vocational and science building ($238,000), staff quarters ($56,100), alterations to the superintendent's quarters ($20,700), an athletic field ($18,500), and outdoor play courts ($17,500). Governor John Reed quickly got the message that the school's benefactor was upset by so much spending. He cut the whole proposal down to $35,000, most of it for refurbishing the superintendent's residence.

Beyond his usual frugality, Baxter's argument for fiscal restraint was that the school had a capacity for 175 students but only 135 were currently enrolled. In a letter to Youngs opposing the plans of the new superintendent who had just come from California, he was characteristically blunt and definite: "I do not want any major changes made at Mackworth Island." Then he added, rather significantly: "You have been at the Deaf School now but a few months, and I regret you do not enjoy your position."[2]

Youngs, protesting that he did, indeed, enjoy "the wonderful facilities we have on Mackworth Island," beat a hasty retreat.

While Percy continued to make gifts to the school—$5,500 worth of farm machinery, including a diesel tractor and $10,000 to repair the sea wall—he also requested that $82,000 of his money in a Deaf School Trust Fund be transferred to the Baxter State Park Fund. State Comptroller Henry Cranshaw accordingly did so.

Still, emotionally, Percy was always drawn to the deaf children he had helped. During his eighty-ninth and ninetieth birthday parties at the school, he told them how he was eight years old when he first spent a summer on the island. "I had horses, cows, geese, some rabbits, even a peacock." They all knew, too, that his beloved Irish setters were all buried in a little dog cemetery there.

A story told about the gravestone marking this plot concerns an Italian immigrant named Giovanni who had done odd jobs for the Baxters on Mackworth Island before World War I. When Italy joined the fighting, he went home to enlist. Nothing more was heard of him until 1927 when he suddenly showed up at the Baxters' summer home. In the meantime, he had become a stone cutter and with him he carried a white marble memorial on which he had chiseled: "To Governor Baxter's dogs, faithful companions, 1887 to 1927."

The most renowned of Percy Baxter's dogs, of course, was the Garry Owen of half-mast flag fame. So pampered was this pooch that he had his own pass to ride in a coach on the Maine Central Railroad rather than in the baggage car.

Here, too, as with his waterpower fight, Percy's actions later inspired fiction—a novel by a well-known writer of dog books, Arthur C. Bartlett. The book, called *Pal*, appeared in 1932 and began with the flag incident. Bartlett had Maine connections, having gone to Bowdoin and served as a cub reporter on the *Portland Press-Herald*. (Incidentally, the flag-lowering business did not prevent Baxter from being honored in 1940 and 1953 by the American Legion.)

Garry Owen was also featured in one of Percy's lesser-known acts of charity—his donation of kennels to house the sled dogs used by Sir Wilfred Grenfell in his charitable work in Labrador. Built in 1931, these shelters were collectively called the "Garry Baxter Memorial." In 1953, a letter from Charles S. Curtis, superintendent of the New England Grenfell Association tactfully informed Percy that they had found it impractical to continue using dog teams for their transportation and were resorting to snowmobiles. An understanding reply carried the message from Percy that his visit to the mission "stands in my memory as one of the most satis-factory I have ever taken."[3] This was typical Baxterian hyper-bole, but no doubt sincere at the moment it was written.

Sir Wilfred Grenfell had developed a special breed of dog called Grenfell's huskies, black and white in color, that Percy had admired. But years later in 1957, finding himself in an argument over which breed of dog should be named the Maine "State Dog," he vehemently rejected the idea pro-moted by a Senator Dow of Waldo County that it should be a sled dog type, the chinook. Said Percy: "The Arctic breed is not well-known in Maine and as we are a hunting state, it may well be that a hunting dog would be more appropriate...." What type? An Irish Setter, naturally, and he argued that it was the only breed that had ever been officially recognized by the legislature, since in the act accepting Mackworth Island it was written in law that the government of Maine was required to maintain the Irish Setter cemetery and Giovanni's memor-ial stone.

There is no indication in the statute books that the law-makers ever officially created a "State Dog."

Baxter Park and the School for the Deaf were the major donations. Baxter's Woods and Baxter's Pines are also impor-tant. The former was a tract of thirty-two acres well within the Portland city limits, off Forest Avenue, given in 1946 to be preserved from the commercial development springing up all around it. This land had once belonged to an interesting nine-teenth-century Maine politico, a one-time congressman, F. O. J. Smith, nicknamed "Fog." On this wooded site, Smith had built a spacious, three-story brick mansion and it was here, according to local legend, that Samuel Morse, with whom Smith was associated, conducted his first experiments with the telegraph. It was also Smith whom Daniel Webster chose to distribute a "slush fund" in Maine among newspaper editors

PERCY INSPECTING THE PLAQUE COMMEMORATING HIS
GIFT OF BAXTER WOODS TO PORTLAND TO HONOR
JAMES PHINNEY.

and other influential citizens, promoting acceptance of the
Webster-Ashburton Treaty in 1842 that fixed Maine's northern border with Canada. Smith died in 1876, the year Percy
was born, and James Phinney Baxter acquired the property.
Percy also gave to the City of Portland Baxter's Pines, a
smaller, five-acre site in the Deering section, to be kept forever wild.

    Another major gift to Portland by Percy did not involve

land. In January 1947, he offered to install a lighting system on Baxter Boulevard at his own expense. He said that he had been impressed by such municipal lighting on a trip to Rio de Janeiro where "at night the lights on their boulevards form a picture like fairyland." A previous council had turned down his offer but now he was renewing it—125 lamps of 600 candle power to be erected by the Central Maine Power Company using equipment from General Electric and Westinghouse. This time, the city fathers accepted his largesse.

Percy also gave the city money to repair the Baxter Boulevard Memorial and kept an ever watchful eye on his father's heritage. He fought off plans to locate a "rum shop," i.e., a state liquor store, on the Boulevard and in 1930, vigorously complained to the Portland Zoning Committee about an encroachment on the Boulevard to connect with a fire station and a garage. "Other locations can always be found for garages, tire companies, and service stations," he wrote to the chairman, "but there is only one Boulevard and that forever should be left intact and unspoiled."

Although his active career came to an end in 1926, Percy Baxter always kept involved in politics, whether it was allowing his name to be used as honorary chair of the Eisenhower for President campaign in Maine or as the head of Governor Burton Cross's failed re-election effort. For the Republican National Convention in 1928, he was again a delegate, as he had been in 1920 and 1924, and he almost always attended state G.O.P conventions. His friendship with Herbert Hoover, dating from his support for Hoover at the 1920 conclave, almost led him to a diplomatic career once Hoover became president. When Hoover was secretary of commerce and Percy governor, they were frequently in touch. "My whole family, including the dog, would be tremendously pleased if you could come to Washington and stop with us,"

Hoover wrote to the governor in 1923.[4] A year later, Percy was wiring Hoover to accept the vice-presidency. "DON'T WANT THE JOB," Hoover wired back. Percy riposted by letter: "I am looking ahead four years for I have a deep-seated conviction that you are destined to be President of this nation."

After Hoover was in the White House, there was another invitation to Percy, this time to stay overnight in the executive mansion and discuss matters with the president. This visit took place in August 1929. Six months previously, an impressive array of Maine Republicans, including the entire Congressional Delegation, the two National Committee persons, and the officers of the State Committee had endorsed Percival Baxter for an ambassadorship.

The details of the discussion between Baxter and Hoover in the White House were never revealed in any of the Baxter papers. However, a letter to the president does reveal that an offer was made.

> The country you referred to in a way might be interesting but the service I could render in that particular position would seem limited and hardly commensurate with the sacrifice of my personal affairs and life here at home...it seems best that I should not accept your offer.[5]

There was also a cryptic reference to his belief that as a private person, he thought he could acquire information on *"the country adjoining the one you had in mind."* This tantalizing clue could lead to speculation that the ambassadorship he'd been offered was to Finland and that the country next door about which Hoover desired information was its neighbor, the Soviet Union. A further exchange that occurred between the two friends during the same month of August 1929 lent credence to the supposition. Hoover asked Baxter: "Is there some public activity you would like to enter, where it is in my power to assist?"[6] Baxter revealingly replied: "The position for which I seem best qualified is the Senate."[7] And then he stated that the three countries he found most interesting (and presumably where he wished to be ambassador) were Russia, Italy, and Germany.

When a few months later, he was invited to be a member of a Federal Commission on Conservation and Management of the Public Domain, he declined.

It was perhaps after this, and while Hoover was still president, that Percy issued a public statement on December 20, 1929.

> Many people have thought I was an aspirant for diplomatic honors, but such is not the case. My entire interest in politics and in life in general is right here in Maine, where I intend to remain and play my part. Of course it is pleasant to have been offered positions, foreign and domestic, but my ambitions do not run in those channels. So they were appreciatively declined. I prefer my home life here and also have business responsibilities that make it very difficult to leave Maine for a long period.

Also, retroactively, he once articulated how he had reacted to his loss in the G.O.P. senate primary in 1925 by vowing to spend his time working for his native state instead of for himself. "That was the turning point," he stated. "I woke up that morning and decided in that moment to get out of politics and devote my life to the State of Maine."

Yet there is evidence that in the summer of 1931 Percy seriously considered running for governor again. Writing to Rupert, "It is a temptation; vindication is sweet: moreover I believe I could win." He then laid out his objections. Perhaps the most important was that he would not have the support of two of the most important Republican powers in Maine: Owen Brewster and Fred Hale. "Both are my enemies," he wrote. "Certainly it is not for me to become a candidate relying on KKK support or depending on Brewster's good will." He also opined: "I will never get any honors from Coolidge or Hoover and looking ahead I see nothing for me." In closing, he says that he will decline to run for governor because he "must be free to come and go as I please. I go to parts unknown just to get away from these hostile influences." In another letter to Rupert about the same time, he makes the startling revelation: "I am getting to dislike Portland and if I could sell out here, I would never come back."

Then, on August 24, he wrote Rupert that he definitely wouldn't run and enclosed a public statement to this effect for his brother's approval. The $50,000 he might have spent on the campaign, he concluded, "will come in handy for some more mountain."

The same sort of ambiguity, if not contradiction, seemed at work in his relation to Franklin Roosevelt.

FDR's defeat of his friend left Baxter feeling probably even more antagonistic toward the New Deal than his own personal political beliefs would have naturally made him. In 1937, during Roosevelt's attempt to pack the U.S. Supreme Court, Percy responded to a request from Herbert Hoover and successfully lobbied the Maine Legislature to pass a memorial to Congress opposing the move. He did so notwithstanding a plea from the state's G.O.P. congressional delegation to cease his efforts.

He was far more discreet, however, about an earlier attack on FDR—from his own pen—that never actually saw the light of day. The manuscript of "The Secession of Maine, A Satirical Observation by Percival Baxter, former Governor" was marked CONFIDENTIAL, NOT FOR PUBLICATION. But it must have done him some cathartic good to write it after the 1936 FDR landslide.

"Leaving the U.S., Entering Maine," was the sign at the Kittery bridge in his fantasy. Maine had become a part of Canada and resultant benefits were that:

> "Canadian Maine would rise from its lethargy and spring to new life."
>
> "Portland would become a maritime metropolis."
>
> "Quoddy would be completed." [The Quoddy dam project in the Eastport area, first backed but then abandoned by FDR.]
>
> "Bath would turn out ships for the British Navy."
>
> "An American Queen may soon reign in Buckingham Palace." [A reference to Edward VII's romance with Mrs. Wallis Simpson, an American citizen. Percy had once been on shipboard with the King when he was the Prince of Wales.]

Percy suggested that if Maine were attacked by the U.S., it should appeal to the League of Nations and open the Kittery drawbridge. "Here the tax-oppressed would find refuge from their heavy burdens and from the threat of the American GPU," was his next rather ham-handed stab at humor—nor did he seem any more deft in his caricature by stating that the people of New Brunswick and Nova Scotia were closer in stock to Maine than "are most of the mixed breeds of Boston, Florida, and California."

Finishing, he commented tartly on what he described as a suggestion the president had made saying that those who didn't like his administration should leave the country. "This writer always intends to remain a U.S. citizen," Percy concluded.

Yet, as we have seen, when he did write personally to

FDR, no venom was evident. Indeed, he sounded almost obsequious. The same was true in his communication to John F. Kennedy, who had sent him greetings on his eighty-seventh birthday.

> Although I now cannot officially speak for the people of my State, I know that you have their confidence and affection. I speak for myself from my heart and thank you for the good care you are taking of us.[8]

A year earlier, Secretary of the Interior Stewart Udall had sent a congratulatory telegram to "one of America's truly great conservation leaders," to whom his department had awarded a prestigious medal. On Percy's ninety-first birthday, President Lyndon Johnson praised him for his "unmatched decades of selfless public service...and achievements for the beauty of America."

That Democrats honored him never seemed to be a problem, whatever his private thoughts might have been. He once sent a letter to Harry Truman in August 1945, praising a radio address the newly installed president had made and saying, with his customary exaggeration, that "it ranks with that of Lincoln at Gettysburg."

One area where he was diffident about accepting honors was in the matter of honorary degrees from universities. In June 1940, he was offered two Doctor of Laws degrees, one from the University of Maine and one from his old alma mater, Bowdoin. He turned them both down.

His motivation seemed tortured in these instances. Part of it was that the University of Maine authorities had been angry with him for twenty years after he had vetoed their appropriation, were just now getting over it, and he would offend them if he refused to go to Orono but did accept Bowdoin's offer. Then there was the matter of his veto that had killed Bowdoin's medical school. His ex-roommate, Kenneth Sills, still president of the college in 1940, in urging him to accept wrote: "if you are troubled with your con- science, you might appease it by the thought that you are doing this...simply to please your old roommate."[9] Replying at the start of the Battle of Britain, Percy explained: "With the terrible events in Europe, I have no heart for anything. My people, like yours, all are English, both sides, and I see only agony and grief for England."[10]

PERCY LEADING THE PROCESSION AT A BOWDOIN COLLEGE COMMENCEMENT. WITH HIM IS KENNETH SILLS, PRESIDENT OF THE COLLEGE, HIS ROOMMATE FOR ONE YEAR DURING THEIR UNDERGRADUATE DAYS. DESPITE SILLS'S PLEADING, PERCY REFUSED TO ACCEPT AN HONORARY DEGREE FROM HIS ALMA MATER.

PERCY POSES FOR HIS BUST. HE TRAVELED TO ROME, ITALY, WHERE SCULPTOR WALKER HANCOCK CREATED HIS LIKENESS.

Fourteen years later, he was again offered a Doctor of Laws by the University of Maine and again he declined. On this occasion, he revealed an extraordinary occurence that may well have influenced his entire attitude toward honorary degrees. It had happened in the spring of 1923 when he was governor. Colby College had invited him to receive an honorary LL.D. He went to the ceremony, dutifully sat through it on the stage, but was never given the degree. He was told later that one of the trustees had convinced the others to rescind it. That the trustee in question turned out to be Chief Justice Cornish, the man who had sworn him in as governor, made this unbelievable and humiliating situation even more intolerable.

There were echoes of his bitterness in his response to President Arthur Hauck of the University of Maine in declining their second request. "When Governor," he said, "a Degree would have been a recognition of my service, would have meant something to me."

In 1955, he again refused Bowdoin. But other awards were graciously accepted. The Baxter School in Portland was named in his honor, and he visited the school frequently.

In 1956, a special committee authorized by the legislature and chaired by State Senator Benjamin Butler, a Farmington Republican, reported its recommendation that a bust of Governor Baxter be commissioned and placed in the statehouse. It was to be a suitable memorial in appreciation of his "service and altruistic generosity" to the people of Maine and had the former governor's approval, although he had opposed the idea of a statue of him in Baxter Park.

The sculptor chosen was a native of Gloucester, Massachusetts, Walker Hancock, who at the time was the director of the American Academy of Art in Rome, Italy. Percy actually journeyed to Rome for the sittings. Then Hancock came to Augusta to supervise the placing of the bronze figurine on its five-foot-high Tuscan marble pedestal while eighty-one-year-old Percy sat nearby and observed. In January, 1958, the unveiling officially took place—a bipartisan tribute led by Democrat Governor Edmund S. Muskie and Republican Senate President Robert Haskell and spiced with a telegram from President Dwight D. Eisenhower, stating to Percy that "In every portion of the State, there is a splendid evidence of your work and charity."

His environmental efforts were also specifically recognized. On October 20, 1948, Horace Albright informed him that he would receive the Gold Medal of the American Scenic and Historic Preservation Society—a decoration known as the

Pugsley Medal and considered the highest recognition in the U.S. for park achievements. Not only did Percy travel to New York City to pick up the award in person, but he used the occasion to plan a future trip to various national parks in the West, acquiring the services of Miner Tillotson, a career park official, who was presented with the Silver Medal in the same ceremony.

Apart from his well-known major gifts like Baxter Park, his own individual charitable donations were ubiquitous and seemingly inexhaustible. Sometimes the gift was simply of his time and prestige, such as his willingness to be general chairman of Portland's Community Chest campaign in 1935. Sometimes the recipients were out-of-state, such as the Essex Institute in Salem, Massachusetts, which received from him a bust of his maternal grandfather, Abel Proctor, described as "one of the pioneer tanners of Danvers" and member of a family identified with Danvers, Peabody, and Salem. Other communities in Maine besides Portland were beneficiaries. His father's birthplace, Gorham, was given a parcel of land known as the Baxter Park Lot and it was originally slated to be kept forever wild until Percy allowed the town to divert part of it for the wing of a new high school. He also gave Gorham a portrait of his father for the town hall. A number of paintings were donated to St. Joseph's Convent as a memorial to Emily. They included "Christmas and the Three Marys" by G. Guadabarhi and "Mary at the Cross" by Charles Felix, an artist with no arms who painted with his foot. These pictures, which James Phinney had purchased in 1885, had hung in the family home at 61 Deering Street, Portland, for thirty-six years. From the same home came an organ that he donated to Sacred Heart, Emily's church, where she had been an organist. Percy, too, had studied the organ. A collection of objects that he, himself, had amassed went to the Maine State

Museum. Indeed, in later years, Percy felt he had really helped to create the museum, an operation confined in 1921, when he was governor, to the statehouse basement and today a prize-winning operation housed in a beautiful building adjacent to the capitol. Among the objects he tendered the institution were Indian relics found on Mackworth Island, an Arab gun he had acquired during his travels, a carving done in lava from Mount Vesuvius, and the silver loving cup the legislature of 1923 had given him, despite their quarrels.

One possession he never donated anywhere was a Smith and Wesson .32 caliber revolver; he had a permit that allowed him to carry it as a concealed weapon. Why he wanted the handgun was never explained. The permit, issued in the early 1950s, listed his eyes as gray (they were allegedly blue) and cited his residence in Portland as 92 West Street.

Of the ultimate disposition of the family homestead, 61 Deering Street, where he no longer resided, only a sad tale can be told. In the early 1970s, the vacant and dilapidated structure, which had been converted to apartments, was threatened with demolition. A group in Portland tried to save it, applying to have the building put on the National Register of Historic Places and seeking to raise the $250,000 necessary for renovation. The author, then a gubernatorial assistant, was sent to inspect the premises.

Ironically, it was the only house on Deering Street in disrepair. Its windows were broken and boarded up. Inside was a jumble of wreckage, the stairway torn out, the fireplace badly damaged, charred wood everywhere, old copies of *Yankee* magazine strewn through the debris.

In the application to the National Register, the Baxter home was considered "an excellent example of the typical two-story, brick, mansard-roofed, Victorian house erected throughout Portland's west side following the fire of 1866."

The application went on to state hopefully that "this house is in fair condition and is structurally sound." Yet the funds to save it could not be found. In the ultimate of ironies, the boyhood home of the man who saved Mount Katahdin for the people of Maine and the U.S. and the adult home of the man who beautified Portland was torn down and the site paved over for a parking lot.

Many mysteries remain in the life of Percival Baxter. Why did he want a concealed weapon? Why did he let his family home deteriorate? What of his relationships with women? The latter puzzlement, unlike the others, which practically no one knew about, seemed public property, open to everybody's speculation. Percy, himself, had an answer, epitomized in his response to Frederick L. Collins when Collins interviewed the Maine chief executive for his 1924 book on the nation's governors. Said Percy:

> I've always had a ready-made family. My brothers and sisters, all older than myself, married and had children while I was still too young to do so. Then, as a young man, I moved about a good deal, school here and in Europe, college at Bowdoin, law school at Cambridge, around the world generally. When I did settle down, it was with my father, a busy, active man, absorbed in everything that had to do with the best interests of the State of Maine. I became absorbed, too. I've been in public life ever since. When my father died, my widowed sister and her two young sons came to live with me. They're with me now. You see, I have a family and the responsibilities of family life. You might say that I have been deflected from matrimony.[11]

The story of the actress Alma Tell has already been told.

Was it a threat by James Phinney to disinherit him that ended this affair? Another tale told is that of the daughter of a leading Portland family to whom Percy proposed but was rejected only to have the lady propose to him twenty years later and be turned down. A Portland policeman and legislator, the late John Joyce, once spoke (to this author) about an alleged romantic involvement between Percy and Grace Locke ("real good-looking"), a Bryn Mawr graduate from an old Portland family.

Then, there are the tantalizing photographs of stunning women in his scrapbooks, with little or no explanation of who they were or how he knew them.

A 1913 picture of a lovely Japanese girl has only her name, Mame Chiyo.

Then, in the 1920s, a beautiful Italian princess, Dr. Santa Borghese, an educator, visited Maine, lectured on Italian art, and was the guest of Dr. A. O. Thomas, the state commissioner of education. Percy kept photos of her among his mementos, as well as the notice in 1925 of her marriage to Prince Herculani. In the 1950s, he apparently visited her in Italy.

There are numerous photographs and communications with a woman named Winnifred Sackville Stoner who also called herself "Mother Stoner," and ran a correspondence school and kiddy theater in New York City. Very attractive, herself, she had an extremely good-looking daughter about whose reading skills ("she knew one thousand classics when she was but five years of age") the doting mother boasted. The monthly bulletin that she published had a piece about Governor Percy, "a great lover of children and animals," and how his friends wanted to get him married. In November 1924, Percy attended a party at Mother Stoner's establishment

THE PICTURES OF THREE BEAUTIFUL WOMEN FOUND IN
PERCY'S SCRAPBOOKS, WITH NO EXPLANATIONS OF WHAT
HIS RELATIONSHIPS TO THEM MIGHT BE; TOP LEFT: THE
JAPANESE GIRL, MAME CHIYO; RIGHT: THE ITALIAN
PRINCESS, SANTA BORGHESE; LOWER LEFT: MOTHER
STONER'S DAUGHTER, WINIFRED; RIGHT: MOTHER STONER
SITS IN GOVERNOR BAXTER'S CHAIR.

in New York and a month later, mother and daughter sent him their pictures on a Christmas card. It is also known that they visited him in Augusta while he was in office, and he let Mother Stoner sit in the governor's chair.

A tantalizing hint of a possible romance when he was fifty-two is included in a letter to Rupert. Returning from a trip to Russia, Percy wrote from the Picadilly Hotel in London and included cryptic remarks about his staying in New York to see some friends named Winslow off on a trip to the West Indies. Then, he said: "The other young lady may or may not be with them. I know not. At all events, that complicates the situation...."

A key paragraph follows:

> The article about marrying at fifty was amusing, though true. I guess it is too late; I know it is too late to begin a family; I also have grave doubts of being accepted, even finally, and propose to be very thoughtful before I say any more. Under these circumstances it is difficult to be normal or natural.

If any serious entanglement had been afoot there, it obviously came to nothing.

An interesting, if not obvious, question to ask is whether Percy ever read his father's journals. From almost the very first entry, January 1, 1859, there is a tone of implied pain born of the sorrow and suffering that family loss entails. In James Phinney, here was a man who lived through the deaths of two wives and three children, a son-in-law and daughter-in-law, the near death of a grandson, and the knowledge of the fatal illness of yet another daughter. Constant worry over loved ones fills those journal pages. Indeed, that very first entry begins on a joyous note: the first tooth of his first child, the baby Florence; how he and Sarah exulted over it as brand-new parents—and a few months later, their grief that their baby was dead.

Aside from the possible disapproval of his father over a mate he may have chosen at one time, how much was Percy influenced in maintaining his lifetime bachelorhood by the knowledge that family life had its dark side—particularly the prospect of loss? His tightly controlled Yankee exterior notwithstanding, he was a person of an inner sensitivity at least as deep as his father's. Had not Percy as a boy in Europe cried his eyes out at seeing a sheep mistreated? The loss of each of his dogs also affected him greatly. An attachment through marriage to another human being may well have been beyond his emotional capacity. Perhaps his capacity for love found its sublimation in a project that engaged him completely—the park, a legacy, unlike the children his father had lost, that would never die.

Personal mysteries aside, there was also headshaking over some of his political flip-flops, undertaken for no ostensible gain. Before he left the governor's chair, he let one of his pet projects, the Water Storage Commission, die by inexplicably pocket-vetoing its extension. And several years later, he drew harsh criticism for reversing himself publicly on the export of power from Maine, saying that he was now for it.

One secret that he deliberately carried with him to his grave was how much he had paid for the park. When asked this question by Forest Commissioner Austin Wilkens, Percy tapped his heart and replied cryptically: "Only in here, Austin. Only in here."

If there is an epitaph of sorts for him—his own view of how he would like to be remembered—it lies perhaps in a capsule biography he had prepared, a shorthand listing of what he thought important about himself. It seems instructive to review the list and see what he chose among the many, many activities and accomplishments of his life.

> Delegate to National Republican Conventions, 1920, 1924, 1928;
>
> Advocated and had charge of Women's Suffrage bills in the Maine Legislature and father of the first Anti-Vivisection law;
>
> Donor to the State of Maine of Baxter Park and also Mackworth Island, 100 acres;
>
> Donor to Portland of Mayor Baxter Woods, 32 acres, and modern electrical lighting system for Baxter Boulevard;
>
> Trustee, Portland Public Library and Gorham Public Library, Chairman, Draft Board, World War I;
>
> Republican, Congregationalist, unmarried, address: 562 Congress Street.

---

[1] Baxter to Langdon; April 16, 1955.

[2] Baxter to Youngs; February 15, 1962.

[3] Baxter to Charles S. Curtis; May 19, 1953.

[4] Hoover to Baxter; January 30, 1923.

[5] Baxter to Hoover; August 5, 1929.

[6] Hoover to Baxter; August 7, 1929.

[7] Baxter to Hoover; August 15, 1929.

[8] Baxter to JFK; January 24, 1963. Percy's grandnephew Houghton White and his wife Mary report that in 1960, after they both confessed they had voted for Kennedy in the presidential election, Uncle Percy leaned forward and whispered, "So did I."

[9] Sills to Baxter; June 6, 1940.

[10] Baxter to Sills; January 8, 1940.

[11] Collins: *Our American Kings*; page 61.

PERCY ON VISITS TO THE PARK.

CHAPTER ✳

16

Managing The Heritage

PERCIVAL PROCTOR BAXTER DIED on June 13, 1969 at his home, 92 West Street, Portland. He was ninety-two years old. At his own request, there was no funeral, no flowers, no memorial service. Yet Governor Kenneth M. Curtis quickly ordered all flags in Maine lowered to half mast for a week, and the then-uncontroversial bust in the Hall of Flags of the state capitol was draped in black and ornamented with a wreath.

"MAINE MOURNS BAXTER'S DEATH" blared a headline on June 14, and the newspapers were full of editorial encomiums for what he had done for Maine.

The *Portland Press Herald*, which had so often derided him and called his plan for Katahdin the silliest piece of legislation ever proposed, couldn't seem to praise him enough.

> His action in acquiring the vast unspoiled area has been called an example of conservationist foresight not duplicated anywhere else in this country by one man.[1]

All this was done not to perpetuate a name, to prove a generous nature or to make any other point. It was done because he loved the State of Maine and the wild things that favored its fields and forests. It was his good fortune to be able to preserve great tracts of that State in which those creatures may survive unmolested. It was Maine's good fortune that "The Governor" was one of its people.[2]

Perhaps it was just irony or perhaps it was an indication of the reach of the ideas that Baxter had been championing but on the very day of his death, the conservation movement was progressing both nationally and statewide.

In the United States Senate on June 13, Maine Senator Edmund S. Muskie was calling for the "creation of a new agency at the White House level to coordinate a federal attack on all forms of pollution, clutter, crowding, and destructive waste of the American environment."

It was to be known as the Office of Environmental Quality, and Muskie had lined up thirty-nine co-sponsors on a bipartisan basis. Equally bipartisan was a companion measure, the Marine Resources Preservation Act, which would set aside shorelines, tidewater lands, and parts of the Continental Shelf for protection. Maine's other U.S. senator, Margaret Chase Smith, had signed on to this bill.

Meanwhile, in the Republican-dominated Maine State Senate, an anti-pollution bill requiring zoning for the protection of shorelands and inshore waters and to regulate mining was receiving its first reading. Senator Richard N. Berry of Cape Elizabeth, chairman of the Natural Resources Committee, labeled it " a historic landmark in environmental control."

Such developments showed how far the nation and the State of Maine had traveled since the era when Baxter seemed like a lone voice in the wilderness crying out for wilderness

SECRETARY OF THE INTERIOR STEWART UDALL CONGRATU-
LATES PERCY ON HIS CONSERVATION ACHIEVEMENTS. ED
MUSKIE LOOKS ON.

values—that *some* aspects of nature should be preserved rather than universally exploited. He had finally received official national recognition in 1962 for his solo efforts when he became one of five Americans to receive the Interior Department's Conservation Service Award. That July, Secretary of the Interior Stewart Udall stopped in Portland, en route to look at the Passamaquoddy and Allagash areas, to present the honor personally to Baxter, who was at that time temporarily hospitalized in the Maine Medical Center. While Senator Ed Muskie sat on Baxter's bed and Udall on a windowsill, the presentation was made. It was also an opportunity for Percy to declare that he had reached his goal of 200,000 acres for his park.

On June 18, 1969, Baxter's ashes were flown to the park and scattered over Katahdin. The next day, the contents of his will were revealed and the people of Maine were in for another pleasant surprise from their most generous citizen. The *Portland Press Herald*'s front-page headline on this occasion was:

> "Baxter Wills State $5 Million." Trust property to be used for maintenance of Park and "to acquire and maintain additional lands for recreational and reforestation purposes."

These weren't his only bequests. Grants of $100,000 each went to the Portland City Hospital, the Maine Medical Center, the Baxter School for the Deaf, and the institution his father had constructed a building for, the Portland Public Library. There were lesser amounts to maintain Baxter Woods, to the local Animal Rescue League, to the family's ancestral home town of Gorham, and to the aforementioned St. Agatha School in northern Maine. Money also was earmarked to complete his father's "pantheon" project in Boston.

The great bulk of the estate was left for the park—and, as the headline indicated, for additions as well as for maintenance. There was special emphasis on another of his oft-expressed goals, namely to buy "...areas of unproductive forest lands, burned over, cut and rocky, which are of little or no value" and reforest them in a scientific, experimental manner.

Thus, a large section of the park in the extreme northeast corner has been set aside for special handling as a Scientific Forest Management Area, with its own staff and advisory committee. The SFMA, as it is known, supplies firewood and other wood products for the park's internal use (partly in an effort to keep campers from foraging for firewood on their own) and offers some revenue through sales of logs and pulp. Its primary aim, however, is working toward "developing better forest practices...in the management philosophy developed from Governor Baxter's Trust Deeds for the SFMA."[3]

Management of the park has become a major operation. In a typical year, the Baxter Park rangers, for example, make contact with nearly 80,000 park users, some of them more than once. Supplementing the efforts of the paid staff is the work of more than 200 volunteers who provide approximately 10,000 hours of free work. Not only do these volunteers come from all over the United States (as far away as California), but there have been groups from overseas, such as the Volunteers for Peace, with participants from France, Germany, Italy, Holland, and Scotland. An average season also records arrests and prosecutions of those who violate criminal laws, evictions for willful failure to obey the park's ordinances, automobile accidents, search and rescue incidents, and, on occasion, death in the park. The policy instituted in 1989 of requiring park users to *carry-in, carry-out* whatever they brought with them has resulted in a dramatic reduction of rubbish from previous levels. Budget problems on the state level always impact the park. When the state government, itself, "shut down" over the Fourth of July weekend in 1991, twelve of the staff, working as volunteers, attempted to do work usually done by fifty persons.

Irvin C. Caverly Jr., universally known as "Buzz," has been the director of the park for many years. He began working there in 1960, having started his career as a ranger at Russell Pond. His enthusiastic discussion about the park and its operations is invariably peppered with referrals to the man whose ideals serve as a constant guide for him—The Governor—and he relishes his memories of Percival Baxter, who was already in his eighties when Buzz Caverly first met him.

According to Buzz, on his trips to inspect the park the governor followed a certain undeviating routine. His dark-blue Cadillac bearing the Maine license plate 111-111, chauffeured by Joseph Lee, would arrive in Millinocket via Route 11 or Route 2. He stayed at a boarding house run by a local widow, a Mrs. Chase, and he never failed to buy gas at George DeCorsey's service station where he would chat with DeCorsey, who was a great storyteller. Another stop would be at the First National grocery store, where he bought his food if he was planning to have a picnic.

A picnic in the park is the background of one of Buzz's favorite stories about Percival Baxter. At one of the park's campsites, the Baxter party had started grilling steaks for a cookout when a lapse in everybody's attention allowed several raccoons to sneak up on the grill and snatch the meat away. Percy's chauffeur and others wanted to give chase but the governor, animal lover that he was, restrained them. The upshot was that Joe Lee had to drive the fifty-plus miles back to Millinocket to buy more steaks at the First National.

Buzz Caverly loves to tell these anecdotes. Another deals with a situation that occurred in the early years when a small section of the primitive road through the park was paved. No one knew how "The Governor" would react to this touch of "civilization." And no one cared to find out. When they were approaching the stretch on one of Percy's inspection trips, invariably someone would try to distract him. "See the moose!" they would cry or some other subterfuge to divert his attention until they had driven over the patch. This went on for a number of years until finally, an amused Baxter could contain himself no longer. He told them to stop bothering since he'd known from the start what they were doing, having spotted the hardtop the first time they'd driven by.

Buzz's boss when he'd joined the staff was a man named Helon Taylor, as celebrated a Katahdin character as Roy Dudley. He was the director (the term was then supervisor) of the park for seventeen years, from 1950 to 1967. Buzz tells of an incident when the governor had Taylor drive his car to Togue Pond and then pick him up the next morning; as soon as he got into the front seat he checked the speedometer and said, "Thirty-six miles, that's exactly right." This characteristic penny-pinching mentality of a man who gave away millions was frequently on display. Buzz relates how he once was sending a letter to Baxter and had put four cents worth of stamps on the envelope. The needed postage, however, was three cents. Helon Taylor wouldn't let him send it, claiming Baxter would be upset, and so Buzz had to steam off the pair of two-cent stamps and find a three-cent one. The letter, incidentally, was a thank-you to the governor for an entirely spontaneous $50 he'd sent in responding with regrets that due to ill health, he would not be able to travel to Enfield to attend Buzz's wedding.

Percy's sensitivity to the employees of the park perhaps reached its apogee after a trip Helon Taylor made to see the governor in Portland, when he stayed overnight at the house on West Street. The old gentleman worried aloud that the bed in the guest room was too short for Taylor's rangy frame. He then had a seven-foot-long bed constructed for him in anticipation of his next visit.

On December 4, 1968, Buzz Caverly received a letter signed Percival P. Baxter, which contained an expression of the governor's philosophy vis-à-vis the park workers. "We are partners in this project," he declared. "please tell your associates that I depend on you and them to make the Park successful." And for Baxter, *success* was measured, according to Buzz, by the answer to the question he always asked upon arrival during his spring and fall tours: "Are the people enjoying their Park?"

In that December 1968 letter, Baxter also thanked "Irving" (he hadn't realized it was Irvin) for sending him birthday greetings. "These birthdays come and go and we cannot avoid them," he wrote. No one could know that it was the last he would celebrate.

The complex problems of managing Baxter Park cover a wide gamut. Any human enterprise of large scale brings with it personality clashes, financial stresses, competing interests, etc., and all are present at Baxter, plus a lot more.

Safety is a primary concern when thousands of people are engaged in potentially dangerous activities like mountain climbing and entering a wilderness habitat where it is all too easy to become lost. People do die at Baxter Park. In 1991, a seventy-six-year-old man named Robert Areson from Savannah, Georgia, climbing with his family on the OJI trail, stepped off a ledge, fell 200 feet, and died instantly. The previous year, a group of Boy Scouts from Long Island, New York, were struck by lightning on Katahdin. David Passalaqua, thirteen years old, was killed instantly and another Scout and the Scout leader injured. That same year, there was a dramatic rescue of a Mrs. Helen Ciarcavino, a seventy-five-year-old woman hiking alone in 48-degree weather on the extremely difficult Knife Edge Trail. Back in 1963, a similar situation had led to the death not only of a woman hiker but of Ranger Ralph W. Heath, who had gone to rescue her.

By far the most famous search and rescue operation in Baxter Park occurred in 1939. Ironically, the national notoriety received was an immense publicity boost for the park and heavily contributed to its growing fame outside of Maine. The case was that of a twelve-year-old boy, Donn Fendler of Rye,

New York, who became separated from his father and twin brother while climbing Katahdin. For nine days, Donn Fendler traveled through the wilderness alone, half-naked, shoeless after he lost his sneakers, covering himself with a piece of rotted burlap he had found in a deserted cabin, swollen with insect bites and bloodied from scratches, his only food the wild berries he could find. An army of 400–500 searchers combed the area for him and finally, sadly, concluded that the boy could not possibly be alive. But still, as the *Boston Transcript* of July 27, 1939 put it, "thousands of mothers in America did not give up hope." Then, Donn Fendler came out of the woods on the East Branch of the Penobscot River opposite Lunksoos Camp, some eight miles from Stacyville, and the camp owner, Nelson McMoarn, spotted him and brought him to safety. In all, he had traveled more than thirty miles and lost sixteen pounds during his ordeal. A hero's welcome awaited him in Millinocket and a medal when he left the hospital in Bangor. A year later, the number of visitors to the park, alerted to its existence by the publicity, mounted to 10,000.

The exponential rate of increase of usage over the years is a never-ending concern. Systems are in place to try to make the utilization of limited resources such as campgrounds as fair as possible. Reservations often need to be made half a year in advance. A particular difficulty in the past was the private camp leases that came with the property Percy bought. The policy question became: should those leases be renewed when they expired? Initially, the answer was yes. The Kidney Pond Camps and York's Twin Pine Camps were examples, and their continual existence as sporting camps, making money from fishermen and hunters, drew the antagonism of the redoubtable Millinocket Fin and Feather Club, whose members felt this constituted favoritism. The conflict was between open use and the restrictions of "No Trespassing" signs posted by the leaseholders. In 1967, the Authority began phasing out the leases. One of these leases, actually, was held by the Fin and Feather Club, itself, a lot on Abol Pond, which it had obtained from Great Northern. To terminate their lease, the Authority had to go to court.

A troubling aspect of some of these camps (the most elegant was built for Colt family of Colt Firearms fame and was frequented by, among others, Ethel Barrymore, the famous actress) was their inclusion of flush toilets and showers. Located next to ponds, they presented an environmental hazard since they discharged into the water and were causing pollution. Those same camps, currently part of the park's camping system, now all have outhouses and no running water.

Another dicey decision had to be made concerning pets in the park. Given Percy Baxter's love of animals, it took an inordinate amount of aggravation to lead to the ban on pets that now exists. For a long while, the rangers allowed people in with their pets. But in 1964, a man drove in with a dog and went to Russell Pond. Then, it turned out, he had concealed the cat he'd brought with him. Soon, it was evident he had other beasts with him, as well. A pair of chickens began pecking around the campsite. And the final straw was a rooster, whose crowing disturbed all the other campers. Told the story, Governor Baxter reluctantly assented to the ban.

Wildlife presents perennial difficulties for the park management. Nuisance bear and beaver regularly have had to be moved. At one time, the park had dumps in it and it is well known in Maine that dumps attract bears. In some rural Maine communities, a dump at eventide is like an outdoor movie, crowded with carloads of people watching the bruins scavenge. To the horror of one woman at a remote dumpsite in the park, the bear she was watching was shot before her eyes by an unprincipled hunter. After the incident was reported, all park dumps were closed. Buzz Caverly is worried about the growing practice of baiting bears on the borders of the park. Some hunters will set out food to lure the park's ample bear population and shoot them under conditions equally as unsporting as that infamous dump scene.

Another "critter" causing alarm is the eastern coyote. It is now firmly established in Maine and the target of hunters' ire because it kills deer. Outside of the park, clearcutting has deprived the deer of much of their habitat and pressure is building on the park to allow predator control within its boundaries, since it serves as a haven for all types of animals, including coyotes. When a local game warden snared more than fifty coyotes in the northeast corner of the park (where hunting is allowed), controversy flared. Buzz Caverly took the position that Percival Baxter's philosophy was "an absolute minimum of human influence" and has stated that "until he is presented with enough evidence to suggest otherwise, he will not permit any predator control in the park."[4]

A relationship with animals in a more positive vein is also part of the history of the park. There have been two attempts to re-introduce caribou into the area. Once Maine was criss-crossed by large herds of caribou. Baxter, himself, was supportive of the first reintroduction, started in 1961. A series of letters to his old friend Caleb Scribner spelled out his interest in the matter. "A few years ago the thought came to me that we might introduce caribou into the Katahdin area and I corresponded with certain officials of the Interior Department asking their advice about bringing caribou into Maine," he wrote in 1961 in response to an invitation from Scribner to join a planning group meeting at Shin Pond.[5] Unfortunately, he went on, those officials were extremely negative and he had dropped the idea. But he cheered Scribner on and three years later, he was writing:

I want to congratulate you upon the successful outcome of the Caribou-Mount Katahdin matter. You certainly deserve the credit for this interesting undertaking and I want you to know I am pleased that you accomplished your purpose. This is something well worthwhile for the State of Maine. No doubt some day visitors to the Park will see the Caribou and that certainly will give a great thrill.[6]

However, such euphoria was not to last. The caribou placed on the mountain all either died or disappeared.

Incidentally, Baxter's letters to Scribner always included a nostalgic reference to the wilderness trips they had taken together, and a letter from Helon Taylor to Caleb Scribner put those trips in an appropriate perspective:

I hear from Governor Baxter often and he is well this winter. He often speaks of you and the grand times you had together. Some place you went by canoe one time stands out as one of the highlights of his life.[7]

After Baxter's death, another caribou-planting effort was made in the late 1980s, also with the same disappointing results.

There is a Baxter State Park naturalist, and the fauna and flora of the park are constantly scrutinized. A long-term program involves working on the ecology of pine martens, weasel-like creatures, which are captured and radio-collared and their movements then monitored. Some of these live-trapped beasts have been sent to Vermont to increase populations in the Green Mountain State. Counts of loons for the Maine Audubon Society have been done on various water bodies within the park, and a bird census at Daicey Pond recorded an overall total of forty-five species. Studies of old-growth forests and mushroom regeneration in burned-over sections are other projects undertaken by park personnel or other researchers using this vast and diverse resource. In addition, educational programs in 1991 drew many local school children and adult groups, as well as a Canadian Boy Scout troop from Fredericton, New Brunswick.

Policy decisions on matters unforeseen by Percy Baxter have proved to be an ongoing problem. The question of the use of snowmobiles in the park has been hotly contested. John Hakola calls it "the single most controversial issue in the history of the park up to that point (the 1960s)."[8] By 1965, allowing snowmobiling by local groups and winter campers was beginning to attract criticism. In the late '60s, the Park Authority held that their use must be limited to roads, a policy according to the then-chairman, Forest Commissioner Austin Wilkins, that had been checked with Baxter, himself. In 1971, two years after Baxter's death, it was learned that he had written a letter opposing widespread use of the machines in the park and the controversy started up again; a ban on non-official use was eventually muted into use restricted to the perimeter road—amid strong outcries on both sides of the subject.

The same sort of public argument developed over the disposition of "blow-downs"—trees toppled by natural forces. Should they be removed from areas where no cutting rights were still in effect or left in a totally natural state? The problem with the latter course, especially when a lot of blow-downs occurred such as in areas where the trees had been weakened or killed by spruce budworm infestation, was that the tangled mass became a fire hazard.

While Baxter was alive, the blow-down problem was discussed with him and his deed of trust for the park was revised to include permissive language that the State of Maine:

is authorized to clean, protect and restore areas of forest growth damaged by ACTS OF NATURE such as blow-downs, fire, floods, slides, infestation of insects and disease or other damage caused by ACTS OF NATURE in order that the forest growth of the Park may be protected, encouraged and restored.[9]

Nevertheless, the extent of the salvage operation needed after the spruce budworm outbreak of the 1970s caused a good deal of public dispute.

A real bare-knuckled fight broke out in 1972 over cutting rights in the park. Great Northern, in selling portions of T2R9 and T3R9 to Baxter, had retained cutting rights until December 31, 1973. The company was willing to swap these rights for an option on 110,000 cords of wood in T6R10, to be harvested by April 1975. The Baxter Park Authority initially declared itself in favor of such a deal.

The James Sewall Company of Old Town, a professional timber cruising organization, estimated that there were 160,000 cords in the area GNP was giving up, with a value of $860,000. Others, however, and they included an ex-supervisor of the park, Harry Kearney, claimed that the value was grossly inflated and that it was physically impossible for GNP even to cut in the area it was trading. Governor Ken Curtis, pressured to intervene, said he was unhappy with the deal but that it was apparently the best that could be made.

Then, Baxter's former chauffeur Joseph Lee entered the fray and created a sensation. In a statement quoted in the press, he charged that the Authority "wouldn't be making deals to cut timber in the Park if Governor Baxter was still alive."[10] Even more sensationally, he insisted that the Authority "had pulled a fast one on him (Baxter) six or eight months before he died"[11] by buying property with trust money

324

without his permission. The reference was to $55,000 spent to furnish a sporting camp at Kidney Pond. Lee's contention was that Baxter never had any use for the Authority afterward. "That's when he started to die," was Lee's bitter comment.

Other opponents of the proposed swap included Lyle Chamberlain, a former wood-cutting jobber with Great Northern and a man whom Forest Commissioner Wilkins had once fired, and William Osborne, an attorney for Ralph Nader's Task Force.

On the other side of the battle, Baxter's nephew, John L. Baxter of Topsham, supported the swap and referred to Kearney and Lee's complaints as "sour grapes." He specifically disputed Lee on his uncle's feelings toward the Authority in his last months and also on his alleged reaction to the expenditures at Kidney Pond.

With Governor Curtis maintaining a hands-off position, it seemed inevitable that the deal would proceed. But still more resistance developed.

An official of the Land Use Regulation Commission, the state's zoning mechanism for the entire unorganized territory of Maine, pointed out that his regulatory agency hadn't been consulted. The Natural Resources Council of Maine, an umbrella organization for most of the state's environmental groups, went further. The NRC said it would sue to stop the exchange. The Authority at least agreed to a postponement.

After one Maine newspaper editorialized: "Poor Governor Percival Baxter, they just won't allow him to rest in peace,"[12] a new development as a result of elections that November affected the ultimate outcome. Although the Republicans retained control of the legislature and thus of the constitutional officers, there was a change in the position of attorney-general. Former State Representative Jon Lund replaced James S. Erwin, a supporter of the trade with GNP.

Lund, also a past president of the Natural Resources Council, strongly opposed what the Authority wanted to do and threatened he would join the environmental group's court action. The final upshot was that the cutting never took place. The state bought out GNP's interest for $725,000.

Like Katahdin's weathering millennia upon millennia of storms and other natural elements, the park continues to withstand the human-driven tempests that rage around it. As an institution, it is now as solidly grounded as the mountain it protects.

The entire area has a magic to it, a mystique. A panoply of names of different locales springs to mind—places like Kidney Pond, Trout Brook, Wassataquoik Stream, Nesowadnehunk Field, Abol Slide, Dudley Trail, Matagamon Lake, to name but a fraction—setting off an irresistible urge to explore them all, every nook and cranny—and, no doubt, some people will spend a complete lifetime of their recreation hours in pursuit of the full range of attractions Baxter State Park offers. From gate to gate (now that there are only two gates open), the drive is more than forty miles long—a deliberately slowed drive over a narrow, primitive road, kept that way, past the entrances to enticing trails, signs for campgrounds, roaring whitewater streams, views of wildlife (frequent partridges in the road, maybe a moose), and certain well-known landmarks, some new, some old, that have a flavor all their own. For example: the white cross by the roadside and a marker, commemorating the grave of "The Unknown River Driver." Buzz Caverly said that the cross was Baxter's idea, replacing rocks that had originally delineated the site where a man from Canada, drowned in the course of running logs, had been placed in two pork barrels for a coffin and buried. Another example: Pockwockamus Rock, just before the gatehouse at Togue Pond. Originally covered with unsightly (and scatolog-

PERCY ON ONE OF HIS FREQUENT VISITS TO THE PARK.

ical) graffiti, this immense boulder by the side of the road was transformed by members of the Maine Youth Conservation Corps under the direction of a professor of art from Colby College into a magnificently painted wildlife and nature scene bearing the captioned message: "KEEP MAINE BEAUTIFUL." Buzz Caverly's favorite story about it is of a shaggy-haired, roughly dressed motorcyclist who approached the rock, stopped his bike, studied the mural quizzically and finally pronounced his judgment, "Hey, cool, man," before he rode on.

327

Percival Baxter, in a spate of hyperbole, once voiced aloud the thought that Baxter Park might someday be the only patch of green left in Maine. The recent concern about clearcutting in the northern half of the state, which led to the referendum of November 1996 to ban the practice—a continuing controversy that has not yet been settled—lends credence to the late governor's concern. An environmental activist, Charles Fitzgerald, who has been an advisor to the park's Scientific Forest Management Area, puts it this way: "What you have in Baxter, if you fly over it, is a tiny postage stamp of green, healthy forest stuck on a much larger, much less healthy background."[13] Buzz Caverly's position is that if the park could increase according to provisions of the Land Acquisition Account left by Governor Baxter, the people of Maine would be increasingly blessed.

In this regard, fear about the future of the entire northeastern forest led to an ambitious proposal by the U.S. Forest Service and the states of Maine, New Hampshire, Vermont, and New York to restrict land use on 26 million wooded acres from northern New England to the Adirondacks. However, the backlash from landowners was so severe that even ordinarily environmentally oriented legislators like Maine's U.S. senators at the time, George Mitchell and William S. Cohen, withdrew their support for $13 million in planning money to study ways to implement such restrictions.[14]

These battles in the north woods are always intense. Whether it was the Big A dam that Great Northern wanted to build on the West Branch of the Penobscot but retreated before the massive opposition from environmentalists, fishermen, and whitewater rafting outfits, or the re-licensing of dams in the area or the threat that the paper companies will sell off large blocks of land for subdivisions, the contentious issues continue to flare up.

THE UNVEILING OF THE FAMOUS BUST. NO ONE COULD
PREDICT THE VICISSITUDES IT WOULD SUFFER.

Thus, within Baxter State Park and all around it, nothing
remains utterly serene. The human pressures that Percival
Baxter so presciently foresaw sometimes break like a stormy
sea around the island of relative tranquillity that he singlehandedly created. His wonderful park is as safe as it can rea-
sonably be, and in the hands of those who, like Buzz Caverly,
will continue to adhere to Baxter's precepts or to interpret

them in the light of his intentions, it will no doubt stay the oasis it has been, despite the increase of human activity in the vicinity.

Baxter had no fears for his park as long as he lived. In the more than a quarter of a century since his death, the park has successfully institutionalized itself. It has survived the vicissitudes of political retribution as in the case of the West Gate controversy and, if bruised by the loss of some of its road money, it has nevertheless persevered and even expanded. The bust of Percival Baxter—despite Charles Pray and Timothy Fairfield—still maintains its place of prominence in the Augusta capitol's Hall of Flags. But perhaps more important is the place Percy's magnanimous action occupies in the minds and hearts of most Maine people. No other state, they can proudly boast, ever had anyone like him.

[1] *Portland Press-Herald*, June 13, 1969; page 1.
[2] *Portland Press-Herald*, June 14, 1969; page 6.
[3] Baxter State Park 1990 Annual Report; page 11.
[4] *Maine Sunday Telegram*, March 14, 1993; page 7B.
[5] Baxter to Scribner, September 20, 1961.
[6] Baxter to Scribner, January 2, 1964.
[7] Helon Taylor to Scribner, January 14, 1962.
[8] *Legacy of A Lifetime*; page 240.
[9] Ibid.; page 114.
[10] *Maine Sunday Telegram*, November 19, 1972.
[11] Ibid.
[12] *Kennebec Journal*, January 25, 1972.
[13] *Maine Sunday Telegram*, March 14, 1993; page 7B.
[14] *The New York Times*

※

An Author's Note
And Afterword

IN A PECULIAR SENSE, THIS BOOK is
the fulfillment of an unmet obligation. When I was working as
an assistant to Governor Kenneth M. Curtis in the late 1960s
and early 1970s, one of my duties was to handle the media.
Early in June 1969, the governor's state police aide, the late
Don Nichols, stopped by my desk and mentioned that the
"old gentleman" (his and Ken's term for Governor Percival
Baxter) was having serious health difficulties and, if I had time,
would I draft up in advance an obituary and a statement for
the governor to issue upon his expected demise.

It so happened that the press of immediate activities took
precedence and this act of foresight, like so many others,
never did get accomplished.

Then, during a long weekend, when my wife and I had
traveled to rural Washington County and were ensconced in a
sylvan cabin outside the tiny town of Robbinston that a friend
had arranged for us, there was a knock on our door at the
crack of dawn. It was Albion Goodwin, our friend, and he said
I had gotten a call the night before at his home in Pembroke
and I was to call Don Nichols as soon as I could.

Finding a phone in Robbinston in the early morning
hours is not an adventure that needs relating. Suffice it to say
that I connected with Don and what he wanted was to know
where to look on my cluttered desk for the piece on Governor

Baxter. Sheepishly, I had to admit that I hadn't written it.

Needless to say, this book is not what I would have penned then. Most likely, a string of platitudes, centered on Katahdin, plus a few biographical details, would have been added to the mix of what public people uttered at the time. And maybe a brief mention that his father, James Phinney, had been mayor of Portland six times would have found its way into the copy.

In point of fact, so little has been said about the Baxters, despite the wealth of material each has left behind—James Phinney, with his journals, his other writings, and letters, and Percy, with his scrapbooks and files of documents. An era of Maine history comes to life through them and poses questions of public import still with us today, not only about our state, but about our nation and ourselves.

I am not glad I left that work undone more than a quarter of a century ago. I don't think I needed the goad of guilt to lead me to the work of telling the story of these two extraordinary sons of Maine. It was never my privilege to have met Percival Baxter, except through the materials of history, and James Phinney, of course, died a decade before I was born. Whether I would have liked them, I don't know. But I feel now that, for all their reticences and mysteries, they have become alive to me, showing how much the force of personality can make its mark upon the play of human events, even within a restricted area such as the State of Maine.

It is ironic, indeed, that James Phinney should have chosen as the hero of his *magnum opus* the sixteenth-seventeenth-century English philosopher and politician, Sir Francis Bacon. James Phinney thought he had added a magnificent contribution to world literature by proving once and for all that Bacon had written Shakespeare's plays. In this, he essentially failed. Yet a feature of Sir Francis Bacon's actual intellectual production that James Phinney missed was his role in popularizing the notion that the human species must dominate nature for its own ends. Bacon had added rationalism as a weapon to join a thought unleashed by the Bible in Genesis, and it had been used since in a seemingly permanent effort to banish an ancient awed reverence for the natural environment to the scornful category of primitivism. The industrialists who brought "civilization" and "progress" to Maine were Baconians, although they assuredly didn't know it.

James Phinney Baxter was an industrialist, too. He probably never heard of Jacobus Arminius, the Dutch religious leader whose ideas on free will versus predestination helped free Puritans to be businessmen, despite James Phinney's unconscious following of the creed. At the same time, the spark of an original Puritan mentality that all success was to be spiritual; i.e., that the "City on the Hill" they were building in Massachusetts was to shine its beacon to the world in an unworldly, ethical light—remained tucked unconsciously as well in his subliminal being. It was this same spark that ignited in Emerson and, particularly, in Thoreau, and kept alive the notion that the untouched planet was God's work, too. Cotton Mather might rail against the "howling wilderness" and the "savages" (read satanic devils) that inhabited it, but he was really speaking in metaphorical terms about good and evil; in Boston, Puritan businessmen who did not conduct themselves ethically or made too large a profit could risk ostracism.

Couple these inchoate legacies from his ancestors with James Phinney's attraction to nature during his stays in the White Mountains or his fishing trips to the Rangeley Lakes, and the "greening" of the Baxters can be discerned. James Phinney's battles against commercialism and for a kinder, gentler environment within the growing city of Portland were background for the values formed by the youngest of his sons.

Add Hetty's concerns for the afflicted and for missionary activity, which saw their apotheosis in Emily's social work, and the twin beacons of Percy's gifts to his fellow Mainers—the park and the School for the Deaf—become understandable.

But it is primarily as an environmentalist that we remember and honor Percival Baxter. Gone are the days when not only Thoreau but John Muir and Teddy Roosevelt and Gifford Pinchot were considered simply "kooks" who could be ignored. Their ideas have remained and flourished, albeit they have not yet prevailed. We mainly see Percival Baxter as one of these early pioneers who stuck to his guns more than half a century ago, to our benefit. And that is the mist in which we have wrapped him.

Still, he was a curious mix. An owner of real estate, an investor, a *rentier* living off income from stocks and bonds, he should have been the quintessential capitalist, a Daddy Warbucks—and, in some respects, in his later years, that role of free enterprise guru was a part of him. In 1931, he made his first donation of the land he had bought to the "People of Maine" while simultaneously, following one of his trips to the Soviet Union, denouncing Bolshevism with all of the same fervor of his earlier attacks on the Associated Industries of Maine and the Great Northern Paper Company. During the 1950s, he apparently even briefly flirted with McCarthyism. Yet here was also a man who had taken on the Ku Klux Klan almost singlehandedly at the height of its power in Maine, had fought for Women's Suffrage, preached tolerance toward races and religions, and drew the ire of war hawks after World War I for refusing to allow the state to participate in "Preparedness Day."

In his views on conservation, he did not hew to a single path; there was a bit of Pinchot in him since he was always talking about buying up cut-over land and managing it scientifically for crops of trees; and there was a lot of John Muir in him, the exact opposite tendency, that of the die-hard preservationist—keep at least one part of Maine as it always had been.

He was an aristocrat but only in the American sense of a second generation descended from a father who had made it big. What pride of family there might have been had to bend to the American value, especially strong in Maine's essentially Jeffersonian tradition, that any one person is as good as any other (at least to start with). It is tempting to speculate about Percy as a boy when his father brought him to England, where he found himself in school with the upper crust. Did he visit the vast private estates of the English landed gentry? Quite conceivably he did. Could that have been an inspiration for him—the never-acknowledged concept of leaving behind a landed monument to one's name, only Yankee-style, not British-style, an estate open to all—nature left undominated, untamed and as luxuriant as any manorial demesne or enclosed hunting preserve while available to everyone? "How are the people enjoying their Park?" he was gracious enough to ask. But it was really his park, one that he had given them.

To be sure, he gave a lot more, as his father James Phinney Baxter had before him. It could be argued that the greatest gift of both was foresight. Paradoxically, the contributions of these two remarkable and complex men are so much a part of the Maine scene today that they have almost gone unheralded. Most Maine people know the name Baxter. Few know their full story. It is an utterly human story, full of success and failure, but infused with a certain glow that has made it unforgettable.

And, needless to say, there is always Katahdin, a beacon of beauty in the wilderness, everlasting and pristine, permanently rising against the skyline to remind us forever of two incomparable Downeast visionaries.

*

Index

Page numbers in italics indicate illustrations or photographs.

✳

Illustration Credits

MOST OF THE ILLUSTRATIONS IN THIS BOOK were kindly provided by the Baxter Collection at the Maine State Library in Augusta, Maine. Other generous sources are listed below:

Houghton White, Brunswick, Maine: pages 15, 40, 42, 43, 56, 58, 65 (top), 116, 130, 133, 137, 190

Maine Historic Preservation Commission, Augusta, Maine: pages 29, 36, 73, 92, 108, 142, 158, and the lower photo on page 189.

Maine State Museum, Augusta, Maine: pages xi and 7.

Portland High School, Portland, Maine: page 62.